DECOLONIZING FEMINISMS
Piya Chatterjee, Series Editor

Unruly Figures

Queerness, Sex Work, and the
Politics of Sexuality in Kerala

Navaneetha Mokkil

UNIVERSITY OF WASHINGTON PRESS
Seattle

Unruly Figures was made possible in part by the University of Washington Press Authors Fund.

UNIVERSITY OF WASHINGTON PRESS
www.washington.edu/uwpress

LIBRARY OF CONGRESS CATALOGING-IN-PUBLICATION DATA
Names: Mokkil, Navaneetha, author.
Title: Unruly figures : queerness, sex work, and the politics of sexuality in Kerala / Navaneetha Mokkil.
Description: Seattle : University of Washington Press, [2019] | Series: Decolonizing feminisms | Includes bibliographical references and index. |
Identifiers: LCCN 2018046905 (print) | LCCN 2018049029 (ebook) |
    ISBN 9780295745565 (ebook) | ISBN 9780295745558 (hardcover : alk. paper) |
    ISBN 9780295745572 (pbk. : alk. paper)
Subjects: LCSH: Prostitution—India—Kerala. | Lesbianism—India—Kerala. | Sex in mass media. | Feminist theory.
Classification: LCC HQ239.K47 (ebook) | LCC HQ239.K47 M65\ 2019 (print) | DDC 305.4201—dc23
LC record available at https://lccn.loc.gov/2018046905

COVER: One of many instances of Sally and Nimmi's closeness: frame grab from *Deshadanakkili karayarilla* (1986), from the Surya-Sun TV Network

Contents

Acknowledgments

This book has traveled with me through many spaces and times. It has been an everyday preoccupation for many years—stealing on me at unexpected moments, insisting on getting written. I have procrastinated the penning of the acknowledgments because it is difficult to put a full stop to an obsessive exercise. But here I go.

Unruly Figures materialized because of the support of so many people—too numerous to name. I thank everyone who participated in the making of this book. Multiple conversations I have been part of— late-night phone calls, pitched arguments, stories shared during research trips, and insights from classrooms—have seeped into the textures of this book.

This book initially came into being as I looked back at Kerala while traversing academic, political, and intimate spaces outside it. Thus, my own trajectories over more than a decade are fused into the making of this book. The precursors to this project are my MA days in the University of Hyderabad and the excitement of encountering Audre Lorde and Ismat Chughtai in English literature classrooms. Then came more focused engagement with theorizations on gender and sexuality at Central Institute of English and Foreign Languages, Hyderabad (now EFLU). The politically vibrant atmosphere of both these campuses challenged me to think in new directions. I am immensely grateful to Susie Tharu for her inspiration and guidance during my formative Hyderabad days. I am also indebted to Alladi Uma, Hoshang Merchant, and Rajiv C. Krishnan for opening up new possibilities.

My sincere gratitude to all the faculty, staff, and friends at University of Michigan who helped me navigate the confusing maze of the US academy. I express my deep gratitude to my exceptional mentors, Anne Herrmann and Sarita Echavez See; they anchored this project in more ways than one. Anne's words of advice, often scrawled on the margins of my drafts, have stayed with me because she made me pay attention to the very act of writing. Sarita's spirited and generous ways of inhabiting the world, as both a scholar and a mentor, have shaped me in indelible ways. Her critical acumen, enthusiasm, and unfailing sense of humor continue to be affirming even at a distance.

Manishita Dass has been unstinting in her support and encouragement over the years. I also thank Sumathi Ramaswamy for her valuable contributions in framing this project. Carroll Smith-Rosenberg, John Kucich, Mamadou Diouf, and Maria Sanchez sharpened my ways of thinking about sexuality and narrative forms. The interactions with Adela Pinch, Giorgio Bertellini, Christi A. Merrill, Nadine Naber, and Victor Mendoza enabled me to position this project in differing disciplinary locations.

I thank my colleagues at the Center for Women's Studies (CWS), G. Arunima, Lata Singh, Mallarika Sinha Roy, and Papori Bora, and other faculty at Jawaharlal Nehru University (JNU), Delhi, for creating an energizing environment that allowed me to complete this manuscript—in spite of all the churnings on campus. Special thanks to the office staff in CWS for always being ready to lend a helping hand. My fellow researchers in the faculty room in the JNU library have been a source of companionship. My gratitude to all the students that I have taught and supervised in Central University of Gujarat and JNU; interactions with them have helped me clarify and further develop my ideas.

The material collection for this book has been from different sites. For reconstructing historical events and AIDS programs in Kerala, I relied on the oral narratives of social workers, activists, and media persons; my immense gratitude to everyone who spoke to me, especially senior photographer C. Choyikutty. I am indebted to activist organizations, especially Sahayatrika, for giving me access to their reports. The resourceful staff at the Hatcher Graduate Library and Askwith Media Library, University of Michigan, facilitated smooth access to a wide range of print and visual texts. Sincere thanks to the activists and staff in feminist and sexuality organizations in Kerala: Anweshi Women's Counseling Center (Calicut), Sakhi Resource Center for Women (Trivandrum), Vanitha

Society (Calicut), and Federation for Integrated Research in Mental Health (FIRM) for opening up their print and visual media collections. I also thank the staff at Appan Thampuran Library, Kerala State AIDS Control Society (KSACS), and the *Mathrubhumi* and *Madhyamam* newspaper archive; Saju David at Surya-Sun TV network for helping me retrieve film materials that were difficult to access; and Anitha Thampi for allowing me translate and use her poem in this book.

During the process of material collection in Kerala, I had the active involvement of many friends who accompanied me on research trips and hunted for materials on short notice; many thanks to Abhilash Ayykkarakkudy, Deepa Vasudevan, Reshma Radhakrishnan, and A. V. Sherine. Aryakrishnan Ramakrishnan shared valuable insights and texts about sexuality politics and visual art in Kerala. Many of my family members were also pulled into my research. I thank Murali *maman* and family for facilitating my research trips in Trivandrum and my parents and Sheeja *ammayi* for help with material collection.

This book has benefited immensely from multiple edits by friends. Sharmila Sreekumar, Samhita Sunya, and Ratheesh Radhakrishan had the enthusiasm and patience to read through and comment on full versions of the manuscript; Jessi Jan, Maithreyi M. R., and Veena Hariharan helped me craft the introduction to the book.

I have presented materials from this book at Jadavpur University, University of Hyderabad, Indian Institute of Technology Bombay, Jawaharlal Nehru University, Nehru Memorial Museum and Library, New York University, University of Michigan, Madison South Asia Conference, Cultural Studies Association Conference, and National Women's Studies Association Conference. The productive discussions in these spaces enabled me to flesh out this book and to think about how to address a wide range of readers.

An earlier version of sections of chapter one was published as "Re-Viewing *Her Nights*: Modes of Excess in Indian Cinema" (2011) in *South Asian Popular Culture* 9 (3): 273–85 and "Remembering the Prostitute: Unsettling Imaginations of Sexuality" (2013) in *Tapasam: A Quarterly Journal for Kerala Studies* VIII (1–4): 86–113. Prior versions of sections of chapter three appeared as "Shifting Spaces, Frozen Frames: Trajectories of Queer Politics in Contemporary India" (2009) in *Inter Asia Cultural Studies* 10 (1): 12–30 and "Lives Worth Grieving For: Lesbian Narratives from Kerala" (2011) in *Intimate Others: Marriage and Sexualities in India*, edited by Samita Sen, Ranjita Biswas, and Nandita Dhawan, 391–413, Stree Samya Publishers, Kolkata. A small section of the introduction has appeared as "Visual Practices, Affect, and the Body: The Story of a Night-Vigil in Kerala, India" (2018) in *Women's Studies Quarterly* 46 (3–4): 158–74. I thank these publications for their engagement with my ideas.

My deepest gratitude to Larin McLaughlin at University of Washington Press for her faith in my writing, consistent support and sharp understanding of the stakes of this book. Piya Chatterjee, the series editor of Decolonizing Feminisms, was always willing to reach out, and her timely advice kept me going while completing this book. I am indebted to the two anonymous reviewers at the University of Washington Press whose perceptive comments were crucial in gaining greater clarity on theoretical frames and fashioning the structure of this book. I thank the entire team at UW Press, especially Michael Baccam and Amy Maddox, for their involvement in the production of this book. Many thanks to Ritty Lukose and Tani Barlow for their suggestions during different stages of publication. Thanks to Sreejat Guha for indexing the book.

A web of friendships that cut across different cities provided me with a range of people to think with and develop my arguments. Ann Arbor came alive, in spite of all the sunless days, because of the spirited exchanges with friends. Many thanks to Aniket Joshi, Aswin Punathambekar, Christa Vogelius, Lee Ann Wang, Mandira Bhaduri, Hemanth Kadambi, Orian Zakai, Pavitra Sundar, Renee Echols, Roxana Galusca, Sudipa Topdar, and Ying Zhang. My gratitude to Malavika Chandra and Meghna Gilani for being perfect housemates; Sri Nair, for the comfort of sharing a language; and Manan Desai for being a cotraveler through the ups and downs of graduate student life.

Udaya Kumar has been an oasis of calm and an invaluable intellectual anchor as I revised this manuscript while negotiating my relocation to India. Thank you to Bindu K. C., Jayasree Kalathil, Jenson Joseph, Maithreyi M. R., Nithin Manayath, Nitya Vasudevan, Ratheesh Kumar, Papori Bora, Ramesh Bairy, Surabhi Sharma, Sharmadip Basu, and Varuni Bhatia for the simple and complex pleasures of being in each other's company; Poorva Rajaram, for her incredible energy and faith in the power of women's friendships: Reshma Radhakrishnan for insightful and animated conversations; Jomy Abraham, Madhumita Biswal, Shiju Sam Varughese, and Urmila Bhirdikar for bringing music, wine, and camaraderie to life in Gujarat and after; Paulomi Chakraborty and Vebhuti Duggal for sharing the excitement and anxieties of research and writing; D. Vasanta, Girija K. P., Madhava Prasad, R. Srivatsan, Shalini Moolechalil, Sibi Jose, S. Sanjeev, and T. Muraleedharan for stimulating discussions and relaxed evenings during research days; and Aswathy V. Nair, P. Anima and Rosemary Abraham for the warmth of long-term friendships. Ameet Parameswaran, Arathi P. M., Prachinkumar Rajeshrao, Ratna Appender, Semeena Kader, Sneha Sharma, Sreejith Divakaran, and Veena Hariharan—all our moments together have brightened up Delhi life.

I am grateful to Shefali Jha and Samata Biswas—two constants in my life—for all the banter, debates and laughter; Shital Morjaria for the substance of everything we have shared. Sharmila Sreekumar passionately engaged with the key concerns of this book from its initial stages to its completion. I thank her for sustaining me in innumerable ways.

Ratheesh Radhakrishnan immersed himself so completely in the conceptualization and everyday mechanics of the making of this book. Our never-ending conversations kept me afloat through the exhausting loop of writing and rewriting. My gratitude for the rhythms of our togetherness even when afar; for all our shared love(s).

Warm thanks to everyone in my family who have contributed in ways that are difficult to measure—my sister Vineetha Mokkil, for keeping alive my fascination for stories and opening up the potential of other worlds; for always looking out for me. My father, Ramachandran Nair, for his eagerness to teach and for instilling in me intellectual curiosity. My mother, M. Snehaprabha, for being my first window to the charged landscape of Kerala; for gifting me with an unconventional upbringing. My younger sister, Sumeetha Mokkil, for her unwavering sense of care and concern. My aunt, M. Jayasree, and uncles, M. Gopakumar and M. Ajaykumar, for their affection and support. Special thanks to my niece, Meghna, and nephew, Aman, for bestowing on me the joys of being an aunt.

The many spaces I have inhabited while picturing and writing this book—libraries, theaters, women's hostels, classrooms, activist offices, feminist research centers, and campus tea shops, to name a few—have been pulsating locations that allowed me to think, desire, imagine, explore, and write. The energies in these transitory sites of connection and creativity drive this book. My thanks to everyone who passed through these spaces with me.

Unruly Figures

Introduction

Sexual Figures of Kerala

Burnt
cigarette stubs
grow back
to join the lips
and the fire asks
Fallen strands of hair
entwine together
to form a glimmering oiled plait
and the flower asks
As the night spreads like dirt
coagulating from the veins
dreams lie next to each other
thirsting for water.

In a land where fire has not been discovered
in a desert where a flower has never bloomed
what you think is fire
what I think is a flower
—for that speck of red
we will keep searching till the light of dawn.

—ANITHA THAMPI, "KAZHINJU" (AFTER)

"AFTER," OR "KAZHINJU" IN MALAYALAM, PUSHES THE READER
into a sensational and haunted world where there is no boundary between
before and after—burned-out stubs grow back; scattered strands of hair
slither back and reunite. Dreams become embodied as corporeal urges;

flowers and fire speak. The cadences of the poem capture the nonlinear acts of performing a journey with no set destination. I open this book with the translation of Anitha Thampi's (2010) poem because its movements mirror the choreography of this book, which aims to unravel the trajectories of sexual imaginations in Kerala, a state in South India.[1] In this book, Kerala functions as the geographical and cultural site through which I explore the politics of sexuality in India. Translation as an act that foregrounds the layered workings of language, and the labor of moving constantly between incommensurable worlds, is central to the field of sexuality in nonmetropolitan contexts.[2] By drawing attention to the form of poetry, acts of reading, and translation, I signal to the reader that this book explores how subjectivities are shaped through the shifting networks of cultural practices.

One of the key questions that drives this book is, How does the cultural materialize the horizons of subjectivity? The formative relationship between the sexual subject and the sexual figure anchors this book. I track the cultural practices through which sexual figures are produced in the public imagination and how these figures are accessed and deployed by marginalized sexual subjects, primarily the sex worker and the lesbian, as they stage their own fractured journeys of resistance in the post-1990s context of globalization. I argue that such intermedial and intertextual cultural traffic is the basis of a vernacular politics of sexuality. My desire to assemble an archive of iconic texts and events, drawn from different points of the history of postcolonial Kerala, was motivated by a dissatisfaction with the dominant national and global discourse in which a metropolitan and transnational language of sexual progress tends to erase vernacular formations of sexuality and subjectivity.[3] The interventions of this project will participate in emerging scholarly and activist attempts to reorient the debates on sexuality in India by taking into account fraught trajectories of the political that trouble the framework of identity and rights. Moving away from an emphasis on law and policy making as the site for social transformation, I navigate the pulsating links between subjective negotiations and the world-making capacity of cultural practices. My task is to examine the memory-driven processes of subject formation that challenge set blueprints of agency.

I intend to critically analyze the convergence of discourses of public health and HIV/AIDS awareness and prevention, regional identity construction, liberal feminism, and identity politics around sexuality. Each of these discourses reifies the empowered subject and institutionalizes a linear story about coming into consciousness. I call these stories and developmental frameworks into question. This book disrupts the broad brushstrokes that link globalization to sexual progress and that frame the period after economic liberalization in 1991 in India by showing how different sexual formations coexist in the space of the nation. By assembling and analyzing a Malayalam language archive, the book demonstrates how vernacular formations of the politics of sexuality, marked by mourning and loss, failure and rewriting, cannot be contained within scripts of visibility, rights, and recognition. This book is in conversation with scholarship on the noncohesive registers of sexuality in other linguistic and spatial locations in India.

Kerala: A Portrait/Landscape
Mediated Protests

As a state that has a long history of political protests, especially because of the central role played by leftist parties in this region, in 2014 Kerala garnered national attention owing to the innovative Kiss of Love campaign that moved away from familiar forms of protest such as marches and strikes. The kiss as a form of public protest in the Chumbanasamaram (Kiss of Love campaign) in November 2014 created waves throughout the entire nation. This campaign was organized against increasing surveillance by vigilante groups, especially in newly emerging public spaces of consumption and leisure such as cafes and parks, perceived to be hubs of new youth cultures. The immediate trigger for this protest was an incident in which right-wing groups vandalized Downtown Café in Calicut on grounds of immorality. After a hectic period of mobilization on social media sites, on November 2, 2014, groups of people gathered together and marched toward the Marine Drive in Kochi and kissed and hugged in public. The images that populated the media after the protest in Kochi captured both the state policing against this show of intimacy and the intense curiosity of the onlookers who gathered to watch and record the displays of affection in public. The national media was flooded with multiple images of people passionately kissing even while the police dragged them into vans, right-wing groups attacked them, and onlookers recorded their acts with mobile phone cameras. The protestors were restrained using extreme physical force, and the police detained them. Activists and supporters all over the country criticized the violent police action. In solidarity, Kiss of Love protests were organized in campuses and other public spaces in different parts of India. The Kiss of Love campaign consciously deployed the spectacle of gendered bodies and intimate acts in public to shock and jolt the onlooker. But its capacity to proliferate and produce replications in different parts of the country hinged on the mediated working of contemporary publics. Photographs and recordings of the protests, which circulated profusely on television, newspapers, and digital media, made it a national and international event.

In multiple photographs and recordings of the Kiss of Love protests, there is a lip-lock between two acts: the physicality of the kiss and the mechanics of the camera recording it. There is a recurring pattern in these images—the kissing couple at the center encircled by an array of mobile phones and TV cameras that capture and transmit the kiss, rendering it as a public, political act. The Kiss of Love campaign brings to the fore the multiple registers of sex and publicity in a specific regional context that speaks to national and transnational debates on the challenges of staging political campaigns centered on intimate acts and bodies in public. How do sexual actors in specific contexts assemble themselves as political subjects vis-à-vis shifting technologies of visuality and legibility? What are the stories we can tell about sexuality, politics, and subjectivity when we engage with the mediated landscape of contemporary Kerala?

While many commentators herald the Kiss of Love protests as the belated entry of globalization and the corresponding openness toward sexual intimacy in Kerala, my analysis in this book firmly pushes against this linear history. I point to a history of visual and literary cultural practices in postcolonial Kerala in which formations of gender and sexuality are constantly destabilized. In these cultural circuits, possibilities of disruptive sexual practices coexist simultaneously with discourses on femininity, domesticity, and protectionism. Instead of reading these protests as a sudden eruption, a quick transition from silence to celebration, it is more productive to analyze them in the context of the history of sexuality in different parts of India where the public has been a volatile formation shot through with erotic tensions.

An understanding of the mediated landscape of Kerala becomes essential to engaging with the specificities of this context. Brightly colored film posters on roadside walls, huge billboards that advertise a range of consumables from gold jewelry to mobile phones, banners of political meetings and cultural programs, state-sponsored public interest advertisements on safe-sex practices or self-help schemes—navigating everyday spaces in Kerala involves a constant sensory interaction with visual and verbal stimuli. The ubiquitous presence of film songs in public spaces, the long queues outside film theaters in different towns, the prominent posters of popular film stars, and the huge crowds that attend the annual International Film Festival of Kerala (IFFK) in Trivandrum point toward the pervasive presence of cinema in the public sphere of Kerala. If you travel by train in India, one of the noticeable features that mark railway stations in Kerala is a wide-ranging, exhaustive selection in the bookshops on railway platforms. These small kiosks are packed with different kinds of publications and magazines dangled before you in an enticing fashion. Recent Malayalam fiction, high-culture magazines such as *Mathrubhumi*, sensational Malayalam weeklies such as *Fire*, film magazines such as *Nana* and *Chithrabhumi*, screenplays, popular women's magazines such as *Vanitha* and *Grihalakshmi*, Malayalam translations of Gabríel Garcia Márquez or Milan Kundera, writings by Communist leaders—multiple genres and eye-catching book covers jostle for one's attention. You do not have to go in search of a well-stocked bookshop; it meets you on your way and becomes part of the journey itself. The routine practice of train travel is interwoven with cultural practices of reading, pointing to one of the significant aspects of Kerala as a state and its avid, everyday consumption of print and visual media. Most middle-class households in Kerala subscribe to at least one newspaper, and illustrated magazines coexist with television sets as quotidian forms of entertainment and information in the living rooms. Thus, visual and literary cultural forms circulate widely and provide the fabric for a shifting, contested public imagination.

Scholars have studied the history of print culture, both in terms of language and literature in the nineteenth and early twentieth centuries, and its formative role in the production of the "public sphere" in different regions of colonial India (Naregal 2001; Orsini 2002; Arunima 2006). Historical explorations point to how print culture demonstrates the struggles over the representation of sexuality, staged through the opposing frameworks of obscenity and respectability and centrally linked to the recasting of structures of caste, gender, and community (Gupta 2001; Chandra 2012). J. Devika analyzes print culture in late nineteenth- and twentieth-century Kerala to locate "the discursive conditions and practices under which it became possible to speak of such categories as 'Men' and 'Women'" (2007a: 18). Udaya Kumar observes that the public sphere mediated through print culture that emerges in the second half of the nineteenth century in Kerala "addressed a much larger public with widely varied backgrounds and competences," and therefore literature in its modern form stands "synecdochially, for the idea of an inclusive, contestatory space of public utterances—a status it possesses in Kerala even today" (2016: 21). Analyzing the modes of address in print journalism in the early twentieth century, Kumar argues, "*Janam* or people are transformed into *pothujnam* or public through a process of address and education" (2007: 417). Thus the public in Kerala is a unit bound together by ties created through cultural practices such as reading newspapers, magazines and novels, and, more recently, viewing films and television.

Print and Visual Culture

Robin Jeffrey labels Kerala as "India's most newspaper-hungry state" (2000: 86) and observes, "By 1971, Kerala had entered a mass-media era with daily-newspaper penetration rates exceeding fifty daily newspapers per thousand people" (231). He provides us with ethnographic accounts of community reading practices in teashops, where people read newspapers aloud and discussed the contents (1992: 210). Other scholars have pointed to how the establishment of reading rooms and libraries in multiple locations in the state had happened well before Kerala became a political unit in 1956 (Menon 1994: 145). The public library movement since the nineteenth century, which lead to the establishment of a network of libraries and reading rooms in different territorial units that now belong to the state of Kerala, and the literacy movement, which lead to the declaration in 1991 of Kerala as the first totally literate state in India, played an important role in making print culture central to Kerala's public sphere.[4]

The state has a thriving film culture, and although the Malayalam film industry is smaller than the gigantic film industries in Hindi, Tamil,

Kannada, and Telugu, it has a significant position in the conglomeration of the Indian film industry (see Vijayakrishnan 2004). The vast realm of film production in Malayalam, its reception through multiple modes of public and home-based viewing practices, and the widespread circulation of different constituents such as dialogues, songs, film clips, posters, and still images, makes cinema play a formative role in practices of subject formation. Cinema and print media continue to be highly influential cultural forms in contemporary Kerala along with the expansion of television since the 1980s and digital media technologies in the 2000s (see Sreekumar 2011; Menon 2013).[5]

Film scholars have argued that the specific history of the cinematic form is marked by its ability to draw an audience from all sections of the society, and because of its appeal to the "masses," it has been seen as a lower art form with corrupting influences. Since the early period of the emergence of cinema in India in the 1930s, theaters were often characterized as seedy spaces where unregulated contact between different castes, classes, and sexes were possible,[6] and the sensual and sexual potential of cinema as a form of mass publicity has been the cause of anxiety (Mazzarella 2013: 207). My analysis will show that because of the investment in print culture in Kerala, cinema is often placed in close affinity to literature, and practices of reading and writing are introduced into the cinematic space in order to give it more legitimacy as a cultural form.[7] Anxieties about the corporeal excess of cinema and its embodied modes of consumption run parallel in Kerala with a discourse about the potential of harnessing cinema as a mass entertainment form to address serious social concerns (see Joseph 2012; Menon 2014). Malayalam film culture has been characterized as traversing two extremes. On the one hand, it is seen as synonymous with art house cinema, with a host of auteurs such as John Abraham and Adoor Gopalakrishnan. It has also been marked as a region invested in "world cinema" through the film society movements from the 1960s and the popularity of film festivals today. On the other hand, it is associated with sensational, low-budget films noted for their explicit sexual content, and there are multiple narratives about theater spaces and practices of consumption of sexually explicit films. In print culture also there are hierarchical boundaries between popular forms such as sensational romance novels and "serious" literature. Complicating these binaries, I analyze the continual traffic between different cinematic and literary modes such as realism and melodrama, and the intimate links between literary and cinematic forms.

Film and literature are the two main media that recur in this book because reading print materials and viewing films are social acts that have historically produced the sexually charged public sphere of Kerala. Since the late 1990s, we see a range of authors—such as sex workers, tribal activists, transgender individuals, and rebellious catholic nuns— lay claim to forms such as autobiographies and testimonials, leading to a boom in the publication of life narratives. Many of these books that experiment with form, content, and protocols of authorship garner much attention in the regional and national contexts. I explore both the interactions between recent texts that are openly invested in the production of sexual identities and the longer history of circulation and reception of sexually explicit cinema and literature—from popular commercial cinema to novellas that form part of the Progressive Writer's Movement. I analyze these transactions across differing genres and mediums in order to trace sexual imaginations that spill out of the mold of contained domesticity.

The Choreography of the "Kerala Woman"

The cultural practices of Kerala are linked to its status as an "advanced" state in India. Scholars link the "present-pervasive modernity" (Sreekumar 2009: 3) of Kerala to its history of benign monarchies, the Christian missionaries, the Left movements, and social reform of the late nineteenth and early twentieth centuries. In 1957, Kerala became the first region in Asia to elect a Communist government through parliamentary procedure, and in the years that followed, Left parties have played an important role in shaping its political landscape.[8] The development paradigm is one of the primary ways in which Kerala has been framed since the 1970s. Kerala was celebrated as a model state within the developing world in the 1970s and 1980s because of the high level of quality of life for people in the region even when economic development is low.[9] As one of the most literate states in India, it has been upheld as exemplary primarily because of its achievements in women's education and reproductive health (Dreze and Sen 1995, 1996). In fact, the "Kerala woman" is positioned as the foundation of this model of development.

Since the 1990s the Kerala model of development has come under much criticism, and today we see a Kerala mired in multiple crisis narratives, even as its "utopic" self-construction coexists with the more "dystopic" visions (Sreekumar 2009: 82). The 1990s saw the liberalization of the Indian economy and its opening up to global market forces that marked a shift from the earlier model of state-regulated development. In this changing scenario, there has been an increasing push toward privatization and the positioning of individuals as viable economic agents. Ritty Lukose (2009) observes that the process of India's liberalization is enmeshed with regional trajectories of development and migration to mediate the particular impact of globalization in Kerala. Because of Kerala's long-standing commitment to a state-regulated model of development, the economic and public policy changes brought about by globalization are contested issues. In addition, the expansion of consumption and mass media forms in the last three decades has impacted everyday life (25). This has also resulted in anxious debates about the changing formations of femininity and masculinity and the need to protect the "Kerala woman" from corrupting influences.

The dominant caste middle-class woman is often projected as emblematic of Kerala's progress. This process of the making of the representative woman can be linked to histories of reform since the late nineteenth century in India. There is a large body of scholarship on the formations of femininity and the ideologies of domesticity in South Asia that trouble the construction of the heterosexual, monogamous, reproductive, and patrilineal family as a timeless and unitary institution.[10] The rich body of work that focuses on the legal abolishment of the matrilineal system in the late nineteenth century in Kerala, as a "deviant" kinship structure that had to be recast for the region's entry into modernity, points to the ruptured histories of configuration of the family in Kerala.[11] J. Devika's (2007a) pioneering historical study of early twentieth-century Kerala maps how new ideals of gendered subjectivity are assembled in that time period as the project of individualizing is interlinked to the process of engendering. The fashioning of the modern man and woman is entwined with the spread of ideas regarding modern domesticity and the conjugal family (6). Devika observes, "Whole set of practices, some restrictive and others positive, were recommended as aids . . . to produce 'Womanly women' and 'Manly men.' For instance, in the early twentieth century, the sexuality of teachers and students in colleges were subjected to strict surveillance and anything that seemed to indicate the presence of same-sex affections were carefully weeded out" (27). Thus, she argues that the production of the monogamous, patrifocal family as the desired ideal becomes necessary to Kerala's entry into the sphere of the nation. This process of positioning women as the anchor of the reproductive family, integral to the symbolic and administrative edifice of the nation and region, is an ongoing one. From advertisements to newspaper reports, public health posters to textbooks, there are many sites in which we can locate the projection of the emblematic Kerala woman.

Robin Jeffrey argues that the Kerala woman has a status that is superior to the larger category of the "Indian woman" as one "who has retained a position of autonomy unique in India" (1992: 4). The markedly lower gender gap in terms of education and health facilities in Kerala has been interpreted in scholarly and official state discourses as an indication of greater well-being among women in the state.[12] Countering these celebratory accounts, Praveena Kodoth and Mridula Eapen argue that Kerala's example shows how access to education and health facilities can coexist with a fashioning of women held as primarily responsible for sustaining the structures of the family: "There seems to be a generalized social commitment to female domesticity in Kerala" (2005: 3285). The discourse about domesticity, conjugality, and motherhood as spheres that all women must aspire to inhabit is coterminous in Kerala with narratives about women's capacity to excel in fields such as higher education. Noncoerced acceptance of family planning through active participation by women is hailed as one of the markers of Kerala's "model" status (Devika 2008c: 4). But Devika argues that family planning through voluntary means, from the 1930s to 1970s, is connected to the increasing domestication of Kerala society and the solidification of the role of the modern woman as mother/homemaker (22). Thus Kerala's narrative of progress is achieved through the disciplining of women's bodies and sexual practices, as "patriarchy in Kerala rests upon the agency of the 'Kerala Model Woman'—the better educated, more healthy, less fertile, new elite woman" (Devika and Sukumar 2006: 4472). In the post-1990s context, there is greater public recognition of the "paradoxical" situation of women in the state, who in spite of certain markers of gender equity, face a high rate of physical and sexual violence, both in public and domestic spaces.[13]

This period also witnesses a persistent questioning of the universal category of "woman" and exposition of the elisions in the dominant narrative of Kerala as an emancipated state. Jenny Rowena and Carmel Christy (2006) argue that the notion of Kerala as always already progressive, in comparison to other states of India, is often used to undercut discussions on caste and gender in this region. Rekha Raj (2005: 29) argues that Dalit[14] and tribal women have been excluded from Kerala's history of development as upper caste women's issues are codified in Kerala public discourse as "women's" issues.[15] Carmel Christy (2015) in her analysis of the media coverage of the serial rape of a high school girl in 1996—commonly referred to as the "Suryanelli case"—focuses on the polyvalent nature of gendered sexual identity constituted in the public space. She argues that unlike the dominant caste woman who is projected as the unmarked embodiment of ideal femininity, Dalit women are hypervisible as "excess subjects," even in terms of the sexual violence they undergo (130).

Sharmila Sreekumar (2009) explores the asymmetrical experiences of "dominant women" shaped in relation to the divergent self-descriptions of Kerala. This is a position of relative privilege predominantly occupied by upper caste women, such as Nair women, who belong to communities that have accessed the trappings of modernity since the nineteenth century in the form of education and employment. The iconography of the "dominant woman" is shaped through markers of class capital, even though she may not always have financial capital at her disposal. This is signaled in terms of outward appearance, such as suitably feminine clothing and comportment, grooming of the body, access to English language, appreciation of art and literature, and with an ease in occupying spaces of modernity such as educational institutions and the well-furnished modern home. Sreekumar observes that the lesbian and the sex worker, positioned outside the structure of conjugal domesticity, needs to be placed alongside other categories—"illiterate women, Muslim women, poor women, single women"—who "invariably find themselves being disqualified from being *the* representative female subject of Kerala" (2009: 16).

The shadowy "others" against whom the domestic woman defines herself (Sreekumar 2009: 247) is not the central focus of Sreekumar's analysis, but she observes that the relation between these figures brings into relief how the boundaries of the dominant woman is constantly formed and transformed. In this book I build on her proposition that rather than conceptualizing the domestic woman as a stabilized category, we need to locate the multiple contestations in the composition of this figure. The transactions between femininity and domesticity come into play in a different manner in my analysis because my primary attention is on the figurations of the sex worker and the lesbian. While existing scholarship on Kerala has extensively studied femininity and its constitutive links to domesticity, my focus on the unhomely figurations of the sex worker and the lesbian opens up the links between cultural practices, gender, and domesticity in new directions.

I will analyze how both the sex worker and the lesbian inhabit, disturb, and speak back to the mold of the domestic woman. LGBT politics and sex workers' mobilizations in Kerala, which I will analyze in this book, bring to the fore significant questions about labor, economic resources, mobility, and modes of navigating the public, especially for marginal subjects who are not placed within the state-sanctioned unit of the standardized family.[16] In political activism in Kerala, especially in its early phase from the late 1990s to early 2000s, there have been important alliances between sex workers' collectives[17] and LGBT groups.[18] My project points to the need to engage in greater depth with the points of convergence between the sex worker and the lesbian in regional contexts in India. I do not read the sex worker and lesbian as fixed identity categories. My focus is on their manifestation as figures in the public sphere and how processes of subjectification are inextricably entangled with ways of imagining and addressing sexual figures. I am wary of the risk of celebrating and romanticizing either the sex worker or the lesbian as emblems of pleasure and rebellion. By focusing primarily on the volatile networks of cultural practices and events, I argue that the containment of feminine bodies and sexuality within the bounds of domesticity is constantly destabilized in the public sphere. The policing of sexuality is never a finished project, and in focusing on the instabilities of cultural practices, we can access the vulnerabilities of these regulatory processes.

Running Threads That Do Not Bind

A focused attention on the local or the particular that is an imperative in the Foucauldian framework for the study of sexuality shapes this project in significant ways. Though his investigations are primarily located in the West and have their own limitations,[19] Foucault's call for an examination of the productive, "imaginative" (1978: 86) processes of power that are not embedded solely in regulatory state apparatuses has deeply influenced theorizations of sexuality in India. The introduction to one of the initial anthologies on sexuality in contemporary India points to the need for the study of "specific and historical mutable sites" (John and Nair 1998: 9) through which discourses of sexuality in India can be tracked. John and Nair call for "a historical and political mode of conceptualizing sexual economies that would be true to our experiences of an uneven modernity" (7). Because of the dispersed terrain of the Indian nation and stark differences in the linguistic, political, cultural, and economic profiles of different states, the region is an understudied domain that demands a dense account of the workings of sexuality in contemporary India.

It is important to note here that the region, as a real and imagined entity, is constantly formed through national and transnational circuits. Recent work on the region has attempted to move away from the nation/region dyad that has dominated studies on Kerala. Scholars have attempted to track the cosmopolitan trajectories of Kerala modernity and its intellectual and commercial links with territories that far exceed the current boundaries of the Indian nation (Menon 2010; Devika 2012). Instead of approaching the region as a bounded linguistic and geographical unit paradigmatically connected to the larger formation of the nation, either as an exception or as a "fragment"[20] that disturbs the homogeneity of the nation, these studies conceptualize the region as a rhizomatic assemblage of diverse space-times of "various geographies, both physical/material and mental/ideational" (Bose and Varughese 2015: 10). Ratheesh Radhakrishnan proposes that we need to analyze the regional subject as a "non-integrated performative subject for whom the nation is only one of the many possible horizons of universality" (2016: 694). While my work is not directly taking on the conceptual task of theorizing the region, by exploring the links between figuration, cultural practices, and subjectivity, this book approaches the region as a layered, unstable, and mutable space.

Unruly Figurations

As the title of the book suggests, *Unruly Figures* traces the practices through which the sex worker and the lesbian take shape in the public sphere using visual and verbal mediums. Figuration can be defined as (1) "the act or process of creating or providing a figure" and (2) "an act or instance of representation in figures and shapes."[21] The concept of the figure has been productive for the study of contemporary cultural forms in India such as political theater and popular cinema since it moves away from fixed essences and points to the conjoining of the material and the semiotic (Parameswaran 2017: 188) and remains excessive because of its visual, sensory, and sensual energy (Sen 2013: 3). Thus, the "figure" unravels the expressive and disruptive aspects of cultural production, and I aim to analyze the links between figuration and subject formation. I seek to ask, How do "lesbian" or "sex worker" become recognizable figures in the public imagination of Kerala? What are the modalities through which these figures emerge as autobiographical subjects, fictional protagonists, targets of governmentality, sites of injury, or political icons? What are the excesses triggered by these figurations? Instead of solely relying on forms that have been associated with the fashioning of modern subjects, such as the novel, life narrative, or poetry, my analysis insists that subjectivity is staged in and through modes, forms, and styles that span a range of interlinked domains such as the state, the media, the publishing industry, and art practices. Thus the relation between interiority and exteriority, private and public, and subject and figure are continually explored and realigned in my analysis.

The differing genres that you will engage with in this book—such as popular cinema, news photography, novels, and autobiographies—are sites where the marginalized subject lays claim to recognition, but they are also simultaneously the surfaces through which sexual figures are exposed to public view. The post-1990s is marked by the emergence of the sex worker and lesbian as political actors in Kerala society through collective mobilizations. This has produced texts and events that embody the experiments of self-fashioning by sexually marginalized actors. In these sites of cultural production, such as the dual autobiographical project by Nalini Jameela,[22] which I analyze in the second chapter, the sex worker enters into representation by critiquing the recognizable tropes through which a prostitute is addressed and configured by the state and nongovernmental institutions. There is no original story that Jameela tells, no new picture she paints. I argue that the power of her project of self-production must be read as a form of "stuttering" that exposes the limits of paradigms of voicing.

The very transaction through which a marginalized subject claims the status of "I" is a negotiation with the grammar of the social world that she inhabits. This is an exposure of the self in ways that can be rendered legible to the other, whether it is the public or, in some instances, the witness within the narrative. While self-narratives are often read as an expression of interiority, recent scholarship on first-person narratives in India dislodges this link. Drawing on Judith Butler's observations on the "constitutive exposedness" that impels autobiographical acts, Udaya Kumar argues that self-narration "must be also seen as resolutely public utterances" (2016: 20). In this book I problematize the conception of an occluded sexual subject that the researcher has to discover or uncover, especially when dealing with historically marginalized actors from the global south (see Weston 1993; Arondekar 2009). Instead, I analyze the transactions through which the subject negotiates his or her relation to structures of visibility and legibility. There is a long array of autobiographies, as-told-to narratives, and testimonials by marginalized actors published in Malayalam since the late 1990s, yet the first-person voice and direct address spills over to many other forms, whether they are interviews, oral narratives, reality TV shows, documentary films, or public service advertisements produced by the state, the media, and multinational public health agencies. The formal transactions in these texts and their modes of circulation and address become the ground through which I dismantle the interlocked binaries of passivity/activity and victimhood/empowerment. In bringing together public utterances that hinge on the transactions between figuration and subjectification, I analyze the links between the politics of sexuality, publicity, and subjectivity in regional contexts in India.

The relationship between the subject and the figure is a negotiated one that is always in process. The figure can be seen as a representation that acquires iconic value within a public sphere. For example, the domestic woman is an idealized figure in the public imagination of Kerala, and this foundational figure is constructed through repeated tropes in cultural productions. I analyze public events and cultural circuits that provide a visualization of the process of sedimentation through which such emblematic figures are made. By using the terms "figure" and "figuration," I also underline the interlinkages between language and imagery, visual and verbal, as symbiotic practices in the making of the public sphere of Kerala. As Mieke Bal observes, "Narrative and image need each other as much as cultures need them. For in a culture of figuration, the figural . . . is the privileged site of contestation" (2004: 1291). Rhetorical acts are often at the intersection of the visual and the verbal. The concept of figures of speech, though linguistic in its origin, holds within it practices of perception—since the idea of the figure is also visual. These figures are recognizable because of their reiteration in the public sphere. But I must also caution readers that the reason these figures lend themselves to analysis is because they are never completely solidified and are always in the process and open to contestation. The process of figuring through cultural practices retains a level of instability that disturbs unilateral conceptions of femininity.

The importance of the concept of the figure and why it lends itself to my investigation lies in its formulation through the public imagination. I trace how the vocabulary of desire, pain, despair, and belonging that scripts sexual subjects emanate from and speak back to the public imagination of contemporary Kerala. Disruptions of structures of reproductive heterosexuality are shaped through the ongoing and, at times, torturous movements of sexualized actors inhabiting the cultural domain. Practices of figuration point towards how "culturally variable principles of formativity and intelligibility" (Butler 1993: 33) are crucial to the subject. Butler argues that the subject has to repetitively inhabit existing formations of gender and sexuality in order to be rendered legible: "If matter never appears without its *schema*, that means it only appears under a certain grammatical form and that the principle of its recognizability, its characteristic gesture or usual dress, is indissoluble from what constitutes it as matter" (33). Here she refers to the many meanings of the term "schema"—"form, shape, figure, appearance, dress, gesture, figure of a syllogism, and grammatical form" (33). The constitutive relation between matter and its schema, the body and its dress, suggests that it is through the historical and cultural workings of language, imagery, and form that a subject reaches toward personhood. In this book you will encounter the unruly moves of sexual actors who inhabit and yet disrupt the conventions through which the sex worker or the lesbian becomes a recognizable presence in the public sphere.

The ceaseless movements between subject and figure, "the imperfect inhabitation of narrativizable identities" (Kumar 2016: 42), are what I term as unruly figurations. In order to trace these movements, I will develop a theoretical vocabulary consisting of terms that emerge from the sites that I inhabit, such as stutter, blur, *azhinjattam* (loose dance), and *deshadanam* (wandering). There are terms that point to the rhetorical dimension of figuration and beckon toward the generative possibilities of intense and disruptive gestures that do not cohere to produce a solid entity.[23] This book seeks to investigate the political stakes of these tentative, fragile, and volatile moves. The design of the book signals toward this unruliness; I move back and forth interlinking different forms, texts, genres, and events in order to demonstrate how sexual subjects are neither finished portraits nor silenced bodies eager to claim visibility and recognition. Rather, the stuttered transactions between the subject and the figure point to the breaks in the conception of a cohesive, visible, and agential political actor.[24] Marginalized subjects participate in world-making practices even as struggles for representation are marked by the deadly costs of making the self legible within existing codes. Yet these ceaseless movements, unruly figurations, lead to perverse rewritings of scripts of gender and sexuality.

Circulation and Subjectification

It is in the mediated zone of contact between viewing and reading publics and cultural events that figuration takes place. Thus the process of circulation is central to unruly figurations. I do not approach circulation in terms of practices of reception by specific communities of readers or viewers, which is often how circulation is studied in media studies and reception studies. Rather, circulation, as I analyze it in this book, includes: (1) close attention to the material networks through which literature and cinema travel and the slippery processes of classifying and labeling texts,

(2) the afterlives of texts and events as they reappear in other cultural sites or forms, such as the placement of literary texts and traditions of writing in key moments in films, and (3) the affective and memory-driven interactions between spectators/readers and texts that form the canvas for subject formation. My analysis will show that to engage with the links between figuration and subjectification, it is important to trace the interconnected levels at which circulation works.

The economies of distribution and exhibition impact the material ways in which cultural practices shape the sensorium of viewers or readers. There are obvious differences between the circulation of an Indian film distributed by a global media company, such as The Criterion Collection, Inc., and a film distributed by a regional company. A global production and distribution company often labels a film as an LGBT film and positions it in transnational spaces of consumption, such as film festivals or urban multiplex theaters. A regional distributor targets audiences in theaters in Kerala and also television viewers and might therefore market the film using other generic categories, such as comedy or drama. As media technologies change—for example, with the emergence of online media sites such as YouTube, or of piracy—the material practices of circulation are also transformed. From billboards to pamphlets, documentary films to personal narratives, forms of cultural production have differing modes of circulation that determine their role in the configuration of publics.

The shifting labels and meanings that texts acquire are linked to institutional structures and circuits within which they travel and get embedded. I pay attention to how there are constant slippages in attempts to classify texts within specific genres and how these practices of classification then reinvent the boundaries between realism and pornography, pulp fiction and "serious" literature. The instability of these frames and categories plays a role in the fashioning of sexual subjects. Some of the visual and literary experiments that you will encounter in this book draw on and reinvent existing practices of disjointed circulation within degraded cultural forms in India. S. V. Srinivas (2003: 55–56) discusses the "B-circuit" film distribution in Andhra Pradesh in which low-investment films circulate in low-budget cinema halls and are linked with practices of questionable legality, such as the splicing of sexually explicit sequences in censored films referred to as "bits" or "cut-pieces."

In the last chapter of the book, I look at how the grainy footage of a transgender activist singing a sensual Malayalam film song on female desire becomes a cut-piece in the footage on the queer pride in artist and activist Aryakrishnan's art exhibition. Here the ephemerality of the cut-piece as a cultural form that oscillates between presence and absence—a focal point for public anxieties and fantasies (Hoek 2013: 4)—is deployed to gesture toward the generative linkages between sexuality politics and the unstable circuits of "obscene" cultural forms. I analyze how embodied modes of performing politics often draw on networks of delegitimized cultural institutions and resignify them through performative utterances or gestures. This cross-fertilization between the "perverse," the affective, and the political is a running thread in all the chapters in this book.

Subjectification, the technology through which the "individual constitutes and recognizes himself *qua* subject" (Foucault 1985: 6), is tied to cultural and institutional forms that have specific regional histories. The dense circuits of visual and verbal media forms produce a disjointed and feverish archive of images, words, tropes, emotions, gestures, and expressions that are remembered, reiterated, and interwoven with processes of subjectification. Let me substantiate this dynamic by drawing the reader's attention to a telling instance from a memoir—a modern literary form that fleshes out the fragile links between memory and subjectivity. In "A Rain That Doesn't Make Me Wet," noted short story writer Priya recounts her romantic experience of rain by filtering it through a much-remembered sequence in an iconic Malayalam film: "The rain reminds me of Padmarajan. The rain that comes routinely every time Clara and Jayakrishnan reunite in *Thoovanathumbikal*. It is that rain that fills my mind every time I see rain" (Priya A. S. 2003: 50). In this popular film by Padmarajan about the impossible yet celebrated romance between an upper caste, middle-class hero and a prostitute, the screen flickers with silver threads at every clandestine encounter between Clara and Jayakrishnan. The idiom of romance as transgression that the film offers, without undoing the edifice of dominant caste conjugality, needs to be linked to the popularity of this film. Priya in her memoir stages her desire by transposing a cinematic sequence onto her subjective experience of rain. This extract from Priya's memoir is emblematic of the generative links between subjectification and cultural practices. Watching a film or reading a book is not a one-time activity undertaken by a preformed subject. The interactions between the viewer or reader and the screen or the page leave indelible impressions. I argue that the afterlives of cinematic and literary production provide the compositional tools for subjectification. As the writer dissolves her corporeal experience of "this" rain with the memory of "that" on-screen rain, there is an emotional connection she aims to make with the reader because she assumes that her affective response will resonate with the popular reception of this film.

In sharp contrast to this, when marginalized actors lay claim to cultural practices and redeploy narrative forms and tropes, it exposes the crisis and fragility of technologies of composing the subject. The "failure" to possess the form, which I will discuss in the context of a sex worker's stuttered processes of writing and rewriting her life story, is symptomatic of differing actors and their relative ease and unease with inhabiting available structures of romance, interiority, and selfhood. Whether it is the dramatic persona of a sex worker who becomes empowered through HIV/AIDS programs in state-produced documentaries such as *Thiricharivinte koottaymakkayi* (A collective through realization, 2006) or the coming-of-age 1980s film *Deshadanakkili karayarilla* (The wandering bird does not cry, 1986), which features two young women on the run, modern narrative forms invested in exhibiting the progression of a subject come undone in the archive that I pull together, which follows the tense, frictional, and intimate links between figuration and subjectification.

The afterlives of certain texts and events have the power to question the foundational narratives of Kerala as a region, and not merely because of the representation of desire in these texts. Indeed, some of these texts, such as the Malayalam film *Avalude ravukal* (Her nights, 1978) that I discuss in chapter 1, are not celebrations of transgressive desire per se. But the messy trajectories of the production and circulation of these texts and events give us access to the shifting contours of a regional public sphere shot through by erotic tensions. The practices of accessing cultural texts and events are not captured entirely by the acts of reading or viewing films. These events and texts circulate spatially and temporally and become interwoven into the fabric of vernacular life worlds. There is an intimate, quotidian, and shifting relationship between texts, events, and the regional public. They provide the vocabulary to organize the everyday and shape the gestures that constitute subjects. For example, romantic love as enacted by lesbian women in a marginalized community in Kerala is noted as *painkili*—a reference to a vernacular genre of sentimental, sensual fiction—by a journalist who investigates lesbian suicides. Here the aesthetics of pulp fiction are seen as shaping the performance of romantic love between women. Romantic acts and sentiments in fiction are cited in a "real life" context and acquire different implications. Thus, I examine how cultural practices through which sexuality politics are staged in contemporary Kerala are fashioned through the everyday workings of caste and class. I pay close attention to how public debates about "good" and "bad" representations and the corresponding hierarchies between realism and pornography, romantic poetry and sentimental fiction, hinge on the threat of the unschooled audience who lack the "good taste" to appreciate "art." My analysis focuses on how marginalized sexual actors stage their struggles through the deployment of delegitimized forms of cultural production.

These forms of cultural production, whether written or visual, involve a process of reiteration. There is openness to this process. If they can fail or be used for other purposes than the reconsolidation of norms, then there is a radical instability to the cultural sphere.[25] As Susie Tharu (2007: 12) observes, the "hazard of performance" is central to the alchemy of citation-reiteration. The multiple possibilities and affective responses triggered by cultural production cannot be completely streamlined or controlled. The "dissemination, transformation and proliferation" (13) through which cultural texts come alive and become imbued with multiple meanings is crucial for a vernacular politics of sexuality. It is through the perverse reenactments and transpositions of cultural texts and events that sexual norms are disturbed.

Butler (1993) argues that the aim of radical inclusivity in terms of representation is not to create a singular discourse in which every marginal position is included, for this would also mean that all differences are domesticated to forge a singular discourse that does not meet its limits anywhere. What is more challenging is to locate the "disruptive site of linguistic impropriety" that illuminates the violent and contingent boundaries of the normative regime (53). The post-1990s in Kerala are a time of flux due in part to economic restructuring and new forms of political struggles. As the shadowy others of the domestic woman claim representation, the limits and contingencies of the boundaries of the vernacular public are exposed, "for if the copies speak, or if what is merely material begins to signify, the scenography of reason is rocked by the crisis on which it was always built" (52). The claims for presence and struggles for representation that I analyze in this book render visible the already existing crisis of the rational, contained ordering of the social. The key task of this project is to track the cultural practices that "rock" the neat organization of the public. Recognizing the excesses of the public sphere make possible models of feminist and sexuality politics in which the rational, rights-bearing subject is not taken for granted. This will allow us to locate politics in "mediating and constantly shifting" negotiations of public cultures (Gopinath 2005: 150), instead of working within the regulatory logic of "categorization, visibility and enumeration" (151).

Sexuality Politics and Questions of Marginality

This book pays attention to how the "lives of caste" (Bairy 2010) and related dynamics of privilege and marginality structure the production and circulation of sexual figures in contemporary Kerala. Scholars have argued that idealized imaginations of heterosexual desire and romance are historically produced in late nineteenth century Kerala through the conduit of caste; "Falling in love and the consent of individuals is also a question of consenting to a new nair identity; it is as much about caste as about individual affect" (Menon 2006: 97).[26] Therefore, interiorized expressions of desire that become a significant trope in post-1990s articulations of sexuality politics have to be read alongside the fact that in the contemporary canvas of Kerala, "Desire becomes an ambivalent marker of a modern, nevertheless, caste identity" (97). Thus we need to critically examine how hierarchies, especially on the axis of caste, intrinsically structure imaginations of sexual desire in India.[27] The possibilities of being publically recognized as a desiring and desirable subject and the ease with which an individual can be projected as an icon of romance and agency is coterminous with caste privilege. The structure of caste grants greater autonomy, mobility, and desirability to certain sections of the population. This book pays attention to how the cinematic and literary codes of romance privilege the dominant caste Nair milieu as *the* locus from which a story of transgressive desire can be told. Similarly, I demonstrate that hierarchies of caste structure the production of a political subject who can seamlessly fit into the mold of liberation and autonomy.

Rather than treating castes as "finished, available products/identities that are then deployed by people in various ways and for different purposes" (Bairy 2010: 21), I pay attention to how sexual subjects are assembled in a matrix in which the dynamics of caste are constantly operationalized. Gopal Guru argues that we need to examine how "the culturally specific practice of humiliation produces its different forms across both time and space" (2009: 17) in order to reproduce structures of caste discrimination. Guru's emphasis is on the generative force and counterhegemonic potential of practices through which bodies are stigmatized. For he observes that "since humiliation does not get defined unless it is claimed, it naturally involves the capacity to protest" (18). Thus these critical interventions pay attention to the everyday practices, related to caste, that produce subjects who struggle to navigate the overlapping territories of victimhood and resistance. We need to take into account the persistent mobilization of caste as "horizons of meaning" (Bairy 2010: 14) that determine the valences of public and private acts. In my analysis of a sex worker's self-narratives and oral narratives on lesbian suicides, I argue that these texts can be unpacked only by taking into consideration the positioning of the non-dominant caste woman as dispossessed on multiple levels—materially and culturally denied entry into architectures of self-fashioning that are often a given for the upper caste, middle class Kerala woman. This ranges from the possession of the concrete structure of the home and property that are guarantees of social mobility,[28] and access to institutional structures such as educational and health facilities, to owning a body and modes of sartoriality that cast a person as desirable within a dominant sexual economy, as well as a corresponding access to cultural forms and practices of self-making through which a legible subject is produced. Marginalized subjects who are unanchored and illegible at multiple levels disturb the entrenched ordering of sex, gender, and desire by wrestling against these structures of exclusion. Through tracing this process, I analyze how the very conception of the political subject is reenvisioned.

My analysis is influenced by recent studies on Dalit literature that reflect on the "impossibility" of subject formation and on how it throws into crisis the "the brahmanical modernist formation of the citizen-subject" (Tharu 1999: 195) by focusing on bodies "that shuttle, always deficient, always in excess" (203). Udaya Kumar analyzes how and why "spectral speech" (2010: 185) provides a mode of narrating Dalit identity in contemporary Kerala. Literary forms that push against scripts of linear progression and traverse the haunted space between speech and silence become essential to representing subjectivities that defy consolidation. These studies question the parceling out of vectors of identity and challenge the presumption that forms of exclusion can be measured, quantified, and calculated in order to create manageable scales of social exclusion. In my analysis of the figuration of the lesbian and sex worker in contemporary Kerala, I trace the tenuous negotiations of subjects who are unmoored and yet struggle to "re-notate the world" (Tharu 1999: 202) and rework the very institutions that render them homeless. The challenging task of analyzing political subjectivities at the precarious edges of the social is to find critical tools to keep alive the tensions, incommensurabilities, and hauntings of being dispossessed in a social world. I locate the stuttered formation of the political subject through the key events I analyze, whether it is the police custody murder case of Kunjeebi in 1987, the "lesbian suicide" in central Kerala that Sahayatrika (Co-traveler) documented in 2002–2003,[29] or the memorialization of the murder of transgender activist Sweet Maria in 2012.

Events in the Making

I argue that what the post-1990s makes possible is a vantage point from which to track the trajectories of sexual figures and events—how they travel and become embedded in public memory. Since "event" is a term that has multiple usages and theoretical implications, let me explain in what particular ways I invoke it. The sexual events I examine can be mainly classified into two groups: (1) political events that have at their center the question of sexuality, such as the murder of the prostitute Kunjeebi in 1987, which led to a feminist mobilization in Kerala, and (2) cultural texts that become events because of their tumultuous circulation in the public sphere. The second category includes the publication of the dual autobiographies by Nalini Jameela that grabbed national attention due to their pioneering status as the first published autobiographies by a sex worker. Thus "event," as I use it, does not refer to a spontaneous, mass-scale occurrence that changes the trajectory of a nation or a region, like the partition of India. Nor does it refer to a staged performance for an audience, as the term would be used in performance studies. My use of the term "event" refers to texts and "real" happenings that circulate and are sedimented in the public sphere. They have an illuminating power to show the process of containment and excess at work within discourses of sexuality.

These events are valuable because they provide a node through which I can explore how possibilities of difference and resistance are kept alive in spite of violent, regulatory mechanisms. Subaltern studies historian Shahid Amin has done crucial work on the processes through which one event becomes written in and out of nationalist history: "I write about the riot as an event fixed in time (early 1922) and also as a metaphor gathering significances outside this time-frame" (1995: 3). While the riot, like Kunjeebi's death, is a factual event, my analysis is mainly focused on the process through which such events accrue meaning as they circulate and become part of public memory. Tracking the trajectories of the making of these events and the multiple ways in which they come to acquire significance in the public sphere enables me "to rediscover the ruptural effects of conflict and struggle that the order imposed by functionalist or systematizing thought is destined to mask" (Foucault 1980: 82). Thus it interferes with the "smug, smooth tracing of a familiar line" (Wexler 2000: 56) of history.

My account of both the pre-1990s and post-1990s tracks the excesses of events that are often erased in dominant retelling. By "excess" I refer here to that which has to be excised in order to create a sanitized account of a region. For example, the first chapter of the book examines the popular and critical reception of a cult Malayalam film from the 1970s, *Avalude ravukal*, which has a sustained presence in the public memory of Kerala even today. This film was labeled "soft porn" at the time of its release, but in the last decade there have been critical attempts to reclaim the film as a realist text about the life of a subaltern prostitute. The traveling of this film text, the differing ways in which it is embedded in popular memory, and the debates it triggers about the conventions of representation provides a ruptured map of the anxieties about sexuality in Kerala, especially around the figure of the prostitute. My analysis deploys the *Avalude ravukal* debate to point to the contradictions in the field of sexuality, where the prostitute is both the object of desire and the spectacle of suffering and censure. The shifting networks of circulation of this film are closely linked to the production of unruly publics. This is an affect-laden public that demonstrates that "unruly energies are everywhere. They are not 'in' subjects or objects, and consequently they are not 'in' one group of people rather than in another, or 'in' one or another category of image-objects. Rather, they are triggered as emergent potentials in performative settings, all the way from the most banal ritualized interactions of everyday life through the most elaborately staged performances, whether on screen, on stage, or in the streets" (Mazzarella 2013: 29). As Mazzarella astutely observes, it would be misleading and reductive to locate the corporeal and sensory potential in our engagements with media as "integral sites of freedom" (25). Pointing to the affective workings of the public is not tantamount to valorizing it as a liberatory space. The conception of "pornographic publics" that I put forward in the next section underlines the challenges of political practices and actors embedded within these transactions.

Fashioning Conceptual Frameworks
The Public as Pornographic

My reading practice is centered on the conception of the public sphere as volatile and affective. To illustrate what I mean by this conception of the public sphere, I offer the case of a controversial event. On March 7, 2008, a group of activists organized a night vigil outside the secretariat, the headquarters of government administration in Trivandrum, the capital of Kerala. The night vigil was in support of the ongoing Chengara land struggle, a struggle by landless people, especially Dalits in Kerala, demanding ownership of cultivatable land.[30] The vigil started at six in the evening and ended at six the next morning. The protest was inaugurated by a powerful speech by Dalit activist and intellectual Sunny Kapikkad (2011: 484). After the speeches were over, the participants in the vigil settled down to spend the night in the protest space. A group of men and women laughed and chatted. One woman smoked a cigarette; a man and woman hugged each other. Media cameras recorded this event without the knowledge of the protestors. The Kairali People's Channel, a regional television channel owned by the Communist Party of India (Marxist)—or CPI (M), the ruling party in the state at the time—and *Deshabhimani*, a newspaper that is aligned with the CPI (M), published photographs and showed footage of this event. They criticized the "immoral" and obscene activity going on in the name of protest. The footage was initially shown as a "scoop" or "breaking news" sequence during the daily news hour and later in a Kairali TV popular news program called "Sakshi" (Witness).[31] The *Deshabhimani* front-page report titled "The Masala-Filled Night Protest" describes how "in the night vigil scenes were staged which were more steamy than scenes from masala films" (*Deshabhimani* 2008).[32] There was a second report in the same newspaper about the night vigil that was titled "Avarude ravukal" (Their nights; Shatamanyu 2008), citing the sensational Malayalam film *Avalude ravukal*, and this report was accompanied by a suggestive sketch of a group of people cavorting behind a curtain.

In contrast to the *Avalude ravukal* debate, where soft porn is reappropriated as realism, here the actions in a political protest are derided as "pornographic." A range of responses to this occurrence, in different forms such as poetry, articles, cartoons, and a short fictional piece, circulated in print magazines and on the internet. There have been multiple violent incidents of the disciplining of gendered bodies in public in Kerala, and the night vigil could be categorized as another instance of "moral policing." However, this event demands further critical attention because it raises questions about ways of looking, the structure of modern publics, and formative links to feminist and sexuality politics. How does a careful unraveling of the mechanics of visibility complicate models of agency? If subjects in the public are navigating a precarious visual field, shot through by sexual and affective tensions, how does this understanding push us to reimagine the political?

On March 10, soon after the March 8 International Women's Day celebrations, members of the state unit of AIDWA (All India Democratic Women's Association), the women's wing of the CPI (M), went with brooms and water and enacted a ritual cleansing of the space of the protest.[33] The night vigil was controversial because the perception of suitable gendered behavior in the public was disturbed when women and men intermingled freely in a space of protest. The ritual purification conducted by the AIDWA members further complicates this picture and shows how the historical boundaries between purity and impurity, inside and outside, are constructed through simultaneously operating vectors of caste and gender. The night vigil and its repercussions produced a spur of debates in print, on the internet, and in public forums about how women's bodies function as the site of sexual anxiety within the "progressive" public sphere of Kerala. This episode provides a microcosm of the regional public as it is mediated through visual and print networks and introduces the reader to the struggle between rational containment and pornographic excess.[34] These tensions and indeterminacies reenacted in the political representations by sex workers and lesbians are the central concerns of this book.

One of the influential debates around this episode took place between J. Devika and the association secretary of AIDWA, K. K. Shailaja, in *Mathrubhumi Weekly*. Shailaja uncritically endorsed the AIDWA response to the night vigil, while Devika (2008a, 20008b) used this episode to map the constitutive links between gender, public conduct, and sanctioned forms of protest. Shailaja is critical of the activists who used a public space of protest as a "pleasure camp": "The AIDWA do not think that women and men should fight for the oppressed by smoking cigarettes, drinking in bars, and embracing on public streets. We do not think that our culture will collapse if men and women stand close to each other, or become overcome by passion and kiss each other. But in public stages, protest grounds, public transport, if you are overcome by passion and indulge in such acts it is not suited for a modern society" (2008: 29). She stresses how self-discipline and restrained bodily conduct are essential for any protest to be taken seriously. It is not the acts per se that offend her, but the staging of those acts in a public place. Modern society, she argues, does not encourage shows of affection, pleasure, and companionship in public places—here men and women should behave as rational beings, not be "overcome by passion." The term "overcome by passion" is repeated twice, reiterating how passion is a forceful emotion that subjugates the experiencing subject. It is framed as a powerful impulse that uproots people from a rational framework, and giving in to such irrational emotions in a space of protest is seen as an indulgence. In the case of the night vigil, what is also criticized is how the protestors converted a serious place of protest into a space for the show of affection, companionship, and camaraderie.[35]

Devika defends the participants by using historical events to show how women's bodies can function in the public sphere as a sign of resistance. A "topless" struggle is Shailaja's dystopic imagination of feminism gone wild. But Devika argues that when women knowingly bare their bodies in public, the act can take on dimensions beyond the sexual: "The only topless struggle that has happened in Kerala is a CITU [Centre of Indian Trade Unions] struggle. In the beginning of 1960s in a cashew nut factory in Kollam, the owner unilaterally withdrew all welfare and benefit measures for the workers. Enraged the laborers blockaded the factory. When armed policemen came in and tried to disperse the crowd, a young woman laborer came to the front of the protestors, removed her blouse and told them to shoot her on her bare breast if they were brave enough to do so" (Devika 2008a: 55). This incident is Devika's clinching historical evidence against the criticism by Shailaja about the improper behavior of the night vigil protestors as imitating Western modes of feminism. Devika draws on the historical memory of another woman's body to question conventional assumptions about women's bodies, propriety, and political protest. In her account of the 1960s struggle, it is the bare body of a working-class woman that becomes the symbol of organized labor protest. Thus she shows how women's bodies have become emblems of protest within the Marxist movement itself, which ironically is the tradition of protest that Shailaja struggles to preserve.

The distance between the cashew nut laborer and the women in the night vigil is not merely historical. The female cashew factory employee is a representative of a group that "constituted the largest single group of registered workers in Kerala" (Lindberg 2005: 5). Organized in trade unions since the 1940s, they have often been "the most militant of all workers, as measured by man-days lost due to strikes" (5). Unlike them, the men and women in the night vigil were not organized under a particular political banner. While the participants of the vigil cut across multiple sections of society, the orchestrated media coverage by Kairali TV and *Deshabhimani* captured and highlighted the images of younger, middle-class men and women. One of the concerns voiced in the debates around the night vigil was how the bodies of privileged women who conducted a solidarity protest for a marginalized section of Kerala society became the center of media attention diverting focus from the issue of the land struggle. Devika in her critical response to Shailaja circumvents this question of the difference in women's bodies and attaches significance to modes of protest used by women when a radical coming out makes possible a resignification of the female body as a threat rather than an erotic object. Though there is an erasure of the differences in the women involved, Devika does point to how disrupting regimes of looking can become a political gesture. The question remains as to which woman is called upon to enact such a radical act. This dramatic moment of a woman's topless body, as the spectacle of resistance to state power, draws attention to the process of embodiment. The radical edge of this act is that the common sense meanings of the nude female body as erotic are challenged when it is repeated in a different set of circumstances for a political purpose.

The night vigil and the debates that followed bring to the fore the volatile, mediated public sphere in which events are created and ascribed meaning. For example, the night vigil participants and their supporters criticized the voyeuristic gaze of the camera. Feminist activist C. S. Chandrika (2008) in her support statement for the protest says how deplorable it is that newspapers and television channels will "even secretly peep into the bedrooms" of those who support a struggle for survival. In a short, theatrical collaborative response to the uproar caused by their show of public affection, titled "Love in the Time of Chengara," night vigil participants Gargi and Hasan mourn that "those who viewed our public behavior through perverse eyes have become the moral guardians of society" (2008). Describing this gaze as "perverse eyes" marks it as a hidden, nonsanctioned way of viewing. The space occupied by the protestors is a public one, but it acquires a closed quality here because the camera peeps into it. It is not a bedroom, nor are the acts staged here sexual per se, but the peeping camera has the power to saturate the space with the sexual. The footage circulates when it is played on TV, and at that level it becomes available for public viewing. Thus there are two levels of mediation through which this event is seen. The first level is the recording stage and the second, the stage of transmission. At the second level, there are codes of looking that are characterized in the debate as "pornographic." "Look when we walk on the street I feel people recognize us, it seems like we have walked out of the blue films they saw last night" (Gargi and Hasan 2008). The remark suggests how the TV news clip was viewed by the public as if it were a pornographic film. Here, there is a conflation of the "peeping" gaze of the camera and the ways of viewing it calls for, and both are characterized by their erotic overtones.

The use of hidden cameras and the blurred and shadowy quality of the footage lends it an aura of illegitimacy. Namita Malhotra argues that since amateur videography plays a significant role in the proliferation of sexually explicit materials in India, the markers of the unfinished product such as "the pixilated quality of a mobile phone video, the static far away shots from a CCTV camera, the absence of an audio track or popular songs attached post facto to the video, the video on loop or otherwise edited by anonymous people" become the markers of pornography itself.[36] The blurred and unfinished quality of the footage of the night vigil can be linked to how it calls for ways of viewing associated with watching pornography. This is accentuated by the fact that it was a hidden camera recording the event, and this made the recording unclear and dimly lit. In an informal conversation I had with one of the participants of the vigil, my conversant observed that the grainy, shaky footage made even the act of walking look "pornographic."[37] Her comment draws attention to how a covert camera operation and its codes of looking get tied to assumed codes of looking that operate when watching pornography.

I would like to pause here and attempt to unravel what is meant by a "pornographic look." Is it marked by voyeurism? Viewing pleasure? Eroticization of bodies and acts? I would argue that what emerges in this debate is a conception of the pornographic as marked by excess—that which is not rational or controlled. What happens when the pornographic ceases to be the particular instance of the hidden camera recording the night vigil and becomes the everyday mode through which the public watches images—television, in this specific instance? In that case, the eroticized look becomes ubiquitous. It is not a marker of the "perversity" of the peeping camera; rather, it signals a modern way of regulating bodies in space through constant, nonclinical surveillance. By pushing this argument, we can question the assumption that looking is a rational, controlled activity. The look that controls is not necessarily a controlled one; it can be an anxiety-ridden, emotional gaze, and that is why there are always instabilities in it.[38]

The significance of the night vigil is that it draws attention to an all-pervasive yet unstable regime of looking that configures bodies in public. This way of looking is not a momentary aberration or a fall from the rational gaze through which the social should be organized. Rather, this is the visual regime that orders modern spaces. The distaste of the pornographic, as a mode of looking, is founded on its purported emotional excess, but I point to how the gaze that structures the public is affective to begin with. By acknowledging the affective charge that nestles within all acts of seeing, the event of the night vigil makes it possible to question dominant assumptions about visibility and women's agency. If coming out into the public entails negotiating gazes whose meanings cannot be fixed in advance, then visibility is a risky enterprise. This is one example of my larger claim in the book that "coming out" as a political strategy is complicated because of visibility's contradictions. Echoing Laura Hyun Yi Kang's pertinent query in the context of the category of Asian American women, I also ask in the context of regional politics of sexuality in India, "Is emergence into a field of vision (optical and/or political) so natural and beneficial, and if so, for whom?" (2002: 12).

Recent writings on women in public spaces introduce the category of "risk" and push for women's right to take risks as against established rhetoric of safety and protectionism (Phadke, Khan, and Ranade 2011). The woman who claims the right to court risk seeks a "reciprocal relationship with the city" (62) in which "the very presence of women in public is seen as transgressive" (33). In this analysis the concept of the "public" functions primarily as a spatial grid, a solid geography out there that one day all kinds of people may hope to "freely occupy" (40). When we conceptualize the public as a dense network that is formed through a play of affective looks, it becomes a more contingent force field of fears, desires, and anxieties. Within this intersubjective field, the fantasy of open expanses "where everyone can just be themselves" (71) becomes untenable since what we can or cannot be is not prior to our embedding in this network. Affect, argue Puar and Pellegrini (2009: 37), allows us to "imagine the body as an open system" constantly shaped through intersubjective transactions. It is within the contingent formation of the public that one can locate the possibility of ruptures. Thus, we cannot simply read the responses to the night vigil as signaling toward a policing gaze without a possibility of escape. The reference to the pornographic brings in unsanitized elements of fantasy and pleasure through the sensory circulation and reception of visual images. The incessant watching of men and women in public spaces can also be read as a sign of crisis, gesturing toward the anxieties caused by bodies out of control. Thus it signals the unruliness and unpredictability of the public sphere, which is not organized through a rational gaze. These conceptions of the public sphere as a volatile space of frictional looks frame my reading of cultural texts and events.

Arguing that the "pornographic" gaze is one that operates ubiquitously and orders the public sphere can have important implications in understanding how different women's bodies are framed. Nitya Vasudevan observes that claims to publicness within new political campaigns such as SlutWalk and Pink Chaddi Campaign have to tackle the long-standing interventions by Dalit feminists about the "histories of Dalit women's bodies being made available publicly in ways that they do not necessarily always control" (2015: 53). Jenny Rowena argues that uncritical celebration of the sensuality of women's bodies often erases the contrasting positions of the upper caste and subaltern women where sexual energies are "unleashed onto the figure of the subaltern woman," while the upper caste woman's body remains a site of protection and control by male authorities.[39] Swathy Margaret, in her account about her entry into the space of a university, foregrounds how she was haunted by the fraught histories of her own body that was "Dalit" and "woman": "The stories of Dalit women being used and thrown by upper caste men, told and retold by my mother came back shouting loudly in my ears."[40] Anupama Rao analyzes how forms of public chastisements, such as the stripping and parading of Dalit women, are constitutive of the sexual economy of caste that "prohibits all men from viewing all women as potential sexual partners, but also gives upper caste men the right to enjoy Dalit and lower-caste women" (2009: 235). Thus the crux of the problem is not per se in the practices that position the bodies of women as spectacle, "But what that spectacle is chained to, that is the operation of caste as *social* authority" (Vasudevan 2015: 55). In my analysis of the figurations of the sex worker and the lesbian, I attempt to tease out how practices of visibility—of seeing and being seen—acquire meaning and value according to the differential positioning of women's bodies in public, in a structure where dominant caste women's bodies are configured as in need of sheltering while Dalit women's bodies have historically been more available to a sexualized gaze. I reflect on how the account by a sex worker, Nalini Jameela, complicates existing frames of analysis.

Moving back to the site of the night vigil, although people of different age groups participated in this protest, public attention was focused mainly on the younger people, who were disapprovingly described as products of a neoliberal economy. The *Deshabhimani* news report narrates how as the dusk darkened into late night only the younger people were left, and it is then that they staged their "love scenes." Shailaja's writing is an attempt to bring this misguided youth back into the mainstream of the Kerala model of social development. Shailaja marks the distance of these younger people from the "other" women who occupy the city, mainly under the "cover of the night": "In the cover of the night, in bus stands and other public spaces, organizations involved in flesh trade are in the business of commodifying sexual immorality. Even the small gestures in a protest area would give license to such people" (2008: 28). If "domestic" women do not behave in a controlled manner in the night and in public, then there is the risk of slipping into the other category of the public woman on whom the pornographic gaze is a sanctioned one.[41]

Shailaja sees the sex worker's visibility as a sign of moral degradation and victimization and blatantly ignores the political discourse around sex work that has emerged in the last three decades in Kerala. Her feminism actively marginalizes the political claims of the "public woman." In this book, I will demonstrate that while thinking about the dominant Kerala woman and the modes of politics available to her, it is essential to engage with sexual "others" like the sex worker whose relationship to the night, the city, and visibility is markedly different. Reading these contemporary struggles side by side will enable us to produce a more complex picture of the processes of voicing and visibility. My analysis of the night vigil as a public event is crucial to an understanding of the negotiations, risks, and possibilities of sexuality politics. This book shows that strategies for claiming political representation in a mediated public sphere are not ones of stepping out of it, for there is no outside to step into. I will analyze how political activism on sex work and lesbianism produces texts and practices in which cultural tropes are remembered, reenacted, and transformed.

Region as a Sexual Field

Scholarship on gender, sexuality, public sphere, and cultural practices in different linguistic contexts in South Asia speak to the central concerns in this project.[42] Public controversies and legal trials about literary texts by writers such as Ismat Chughtai in the 1940s have become significant to contemporary explorations on the politics of sexuality (Patel 2004; Gopinath 2005). Placing "sexual events" such as the high-pitched debate over Kamala Surayya's[43] sensational autobiography *Ente katha* (My story, 1973) alongside controversies from the early twentieth century, such as the 1911 ban on the new edition of Muddupalani's *sringara* (erotic) poetry *Radhika santwanam* (Appeasing Radhika; see Tharu and Lalita 1993), can generate modes of theorizing that take into account disorderly circuits of desire. In the chapters that follow, I will further engage with scholarship that shows how sexuality, gender, cultural production, and politics have a long and ruptured history of being interwoven and co-constitutive in South Asia. I carry forward the nonlinear impulses in these interventions to analyze a vernacular context that has not been extensively studied so far using this approach.

Anjali Arondekar asks whether epistemological projects focused on a specific regional location can tap into the "imaginative possibilities offered by sexuality" (2012: 246) in order to undo the ideological certainties of the present. The critical spirit of *Unruly Figures* is aligned with this impulse. The links between sexuality and spatiality has been the focus of significant interventions in the field of queer studies and "present the opportunity for a developed understanding of the local, the nonmetropolitan . . . and the situated" (Halberstam 2005: 12). This call to shift the focus from the global to the local and explore "place in all its contradiction" (12) is heeded in this book.[44] Journeying through the maze of sexual narratives, transactions, and events that I assemble in this book, readers will be compelled to pause, lose their way, and undo the dominant frameworks through which sexuality is often mapped, conceptualized, and studied. I demonstrate that cultural events, forms, and texts that are prominent in the public sphere of Kerala, including materials produced and circulated by the state and activist groups, function as an important and rarely investigated vernacular terrain to reflect on sexual subjectivities that exceed the boundaries of categorization.

Thus I posit the regional as the ground through which questions can be asked about the past, present, and futures of sexuality politics in India. *Unruly Figures* brings a substantial body of Malayalam-language scholarship, literature, and media texts on gender, sexuality, and social justice (which do not usually travel across the language divide) into conversation with current debates on sexuality studies and feminism in Asian and Anglo-American academia. It is often presumed that sexual subjects situated in nonmetropolitan spaces shape their subjective negotiations through a transnational and metropolitan vocabulary of rights, identity, and recognition. I push against this pedagogic vision of sexuality politics in which regional sexual acts and actors are evacuated of history and displaced from the contingencies of their location. I put forward a reading practice that examines public cultures of sexuality in Kerala, "a small place" in the geopolitical dynamics of the nation and the globe, as *the* site for theorizing the political.

A significant body of scholarship has emerged since the 1990s that moves beyond the domain of sexual violence to critically analyze the politics of sexuality in India.[45] Several scholars have also specifically examined the mobilizations by sex workers and queer activists in post-1990s Asia and the ethical and political challenges raised by these struggles.[46] This body of work that focuses on political practices that have the potential to trouble the architecture of the state-sanctioned unit of the heterosexual family is of crucial significance to this book. Geeta Patel observes that "queered reading of time" disturbs incremental and calibrated temporal frames and turns away from the accumulative logic of nationalism, capitalism, and reproduction (2016: 265). I analyze how "perverse" subjectivities that cannot be mapped onto temporal frames of "proprietary heterosexuality" (268) are fabricated through tropes drawn from popular cultural practices in Kerala.[47] By focusing on peripatetic movements that catalyze the unruly figurations of the lesbian and sex worker, such as wandering and haunting, I argue that the regional public itself is an unruly formation. I will analyze how queer acts are staged through vernacular visual and literary registers of romance, intimacy, grieving, and mourning that disrupt the linear plotting of space and time.

This is not in any way to suggest that the region is a pure space of rebellion or resistance; in fact transgressive sexual desires and acts are often domesticated to fit into the governmental and developmental agendas of the Kerala state. Puar's influential theorization of homonationalism points to how queer bodies can work "*through* the nation and not against it" (2007: 50). National and regional "imaginative geographies" (46) and their generative relation to sexual identity politics form an important area of investigation in this book. For example, in the comparative reading of two films on lesbian desire in chapter 3, I point to how differing spatialities of the region and ways of inhabiting it present contrasting visions of sexuality politics.

Multiple scholars who examine the intersections of postcoloniality and globalization have critiqued the teleological imperatives of discourses of globalization and the demands on queerness to be represented in globally recognizable forms.[48] This book troubles the unidirectional discourse of sexuality in which "the West, Western cultures and the English language stand in as the 'origin' of cultural exchanges and non-Western societies occupy the discursive position of 'targets' of such exchanges" (Cruz-Malavé and Manalansan 2002: 6). There is a definitive move in this book to theorize practices of subject formation without falling into the trap of cohesive and bounded identities. Naisargi Dave's study on queer activism in India provides the significant insight that the trajectory of the formation of the lesbian as a political subject is a process of extraordinary invention that was also dogged by "moments of necessary loss— the containment of a range of possibilities into new codes for right behavior" (2010: 608). It is not merely an erasure of undisciplined feelings that Dave gestures toward but a corresponding misfit of certain actors, often small-town and underprivileged bodies, that are written out of the dominant script of LGBT politics. Shifting the attention to nonmetropolitan spaces in India makes it possible for me to locate a much more troubled and troubling dynamic of queer politics, inhabited by subjects freighted with a sense of history and possessed by memories that they cannot shed. In the chapters that follow, I will throw into relief a fractured terrain of sexuality suffused by the affective processes of subject formation.

This is one of the first books to bring into the same frame the political struggles for representation by the sex worker and the lesbian in Kerala. Scholars have noted how sexual identity categories emerge in the matrix of the economic liberalization machinery of the Indian state, the vast network of NGOs that shapes modalities of activism, and the circuits of multinational funding and interventions specifically linked to HIV/AIDS (Dutta 2013).[49] I examine how even as the state and public health agencies work toward plotting and managing the population by creating a grid of sexual categories such as CSW (commercial sex worker) and MSM (men who have sex with men), disruptive bodies appear, cohere, break down, and return from the edge of disappearance. I propose to show how the failure of both the sex worker and the lesbian to fit into governmental frames draws attention to the process of framing itself. The consistent attention to "everyday processes of looking at others and being looked at," what Mitchell refers to as "visual reciprocity" (2004: 47), is central to the conception of sexuality politics that I undertake in this book. In terms of the structure of the book, chapters 1 and 2, which focus on the figure of the sex worker, and chapters 3 and 4, which focus on the figure of the lesbian, are held together through my analysis of operations of framing and presencing, which maps the complex linkage of cultural practices and the politics of sexuality. By examining the interlinked and constitutive workings of visuality and legibility—how images and words mediate social relations and subject formation—this book aims to put forward a relational and memory-driven conception of the political subject.

The focus on the sex worker and lesbian in juxtaposition with the idealized domestic Kerala woman enables me to foreground starkly differential access to cultural and material resources that facilitates legibility and legitimacy. My aim is to give a critical account of the nonlinear movements of subjects who exceed the given paradigms of the state *and* progressive politics. From the haunting power of oral narratives on lesbian suicides to the affective responses evoked by a photograph of a murdered prostitute, this book is orchestrated through texts and events that are marked by their irresolution. This book will demonstrate that practices of memory and haunting shape queer politics in regional contexts in India and should not be papered over to consolidate an "agential" subject. Analyzing the instability of the cultural realm makes us aware of the power and possibilities of ephemeral acts and twilight zones of resistance.

I seek to ask in the chapters that follow: What resistances and everyday struggles go unmapped when we look only through the liberal lens? In my discussion of the oral narratives about lesbian suicides, if we apply a trajectory of empowerment, these subjects whose struggles end in suicide can only be seen as victims crushed by social pressures. But my reading of the interviews aims to tease out the political stakes of retaining the space of tension between agency and passivity, visibility and invisibility, through the spectral figure of the lesbian. *Unruly Figures* examines the close links between social death and literal death in Kerala and the danger of social questioning that literally pushes individuals to self-annihilation. Discussing how markers of *streetvam* (feminine essence) is a pre-requisite for women to acquire legitimacy in the public sphere, Sreekumar observes, "With it the ordinary woman gains the worth and dominance of respectability. Without it she endangers her social self" (2009: 21). Life narratives of sex workers, transgender people, and lesbians point to the proximity of death when certain lives are rendered illegible. Debates and reports in the last two decades on the recurring suicides of young women in lesbian relationships, brutal violence against transgender persons in Kerala, and "family suicides," in which a family commits suicide as a result of sex scandals, point to the thin line between life and death in contemporary Kerala. When the social self is devalued, life itself becomes a questionable zone, literally and metaphorically. In order to forge a locally relevant sexuality politics, it is essential to engage with how material conditions and possibilities of mobility are radically different for underprivileged women (see Rowena and Christy 2006).

This book speaks to dilemmas in differing fields such as sexuality studies, gender studies, and Dalit studies that seek to challenge the universal conception of the rights-bearing political subject.[50] This must not be mistaken as a claim that an easy dialogue is possible between these fields. In fact, Nitya Vasudevan (2015) rightly observes that some of the crucial impasses between mainstream feminism and Dalit feminism in India have been on issues related to sexuality, such as bar dancing and sex work. As I discussed earlier, Dalit feminist scholars have critiqued the reductive reading of the visibility of women's bodies in public as a sign of sexual liberation.[51] On the other hand, Dalit feminists who have been actively involved with sexuality rights mobilization in Kerala, such as Rekha Raj, also speak of the censure faced by Dalit women when they align themselves with such groups and participate in public events on issues of sexuality. She draws attention to an incident in 2013 in Trivandrum, where a group of Dalit women who sang folk songs at a protest event in support of LGBT rights were attacked for sullying those "authentic" folk songs and Dalit identity.[52] In her experiential note, Raj reflects on the complex negotiations undertaken by Dalit women as sexual subjects and political actors in the public sphere who have to carefully calibrate the ways in which their bodies and actions are read by people both within and outside their communities. Rather than solidifying the boundaries between studies on caste, gender, and sexuality, this book suggests that we can give an account of sexuality politics within a regional context only by being attentive to the ways in which political subjectivities are constantly made and unmade in a cultural landscape in which all bodies are materialized within the dynamic and power-ridden workings of caste, class, ethnicity, community, and gender.

Retaining Unruliness
Sexual Sites

This book demonstrates that it is essential to navigate a wide cross-section of cultural, political, and governmental realms and the interconnections between them to map the relationship between sexual figures and the process of subjectification. My methodology shows how the "registers of representation and of materiality are not actually separate" (Poovey 1995: 5). I analyze a selection of public health campaigns, pedagogic tools, and documentaries produced by state agencies such as KSACS (Kerala State AIDS Control Society), as well as documentation and interviews by activist groups such as Sahayatrika. I also examine a wide range of printed texts such as novels, autobiographies, film reviews, literary criticism, screenplays, and newspaper reports. The visual materials I investigate are popular Malayalam films, film posters, news photographs, public health posters, and documentaries. I also reconstruct significant public events and their mediated reception.

In conventional approaches to literary or filmic texts, the object, whether it is a novel or a feature film, is the primary document of scholarly analysis. Other factors—such as the historical setting in which the novel is produced, the identity of the writer, the political significance of the text, or its geographical location—are significant frames through which the novel is approached. But the hierarchy between the text and its context is still maintained in most literary criticism. My project, in contrast, is primarily concerned with the cultural networks in which texts are produced and circulated. I also select texts in which the notion of the author is undermined and revisioned. For example, both versions of Nalini Jameela's autobiography are collaborative projects that question the basic premise of the autobiographical form, which conventionally hinges on the conception of a unitary subject who narrates his or her life story. Similarly, the interviews conducted by Sahayatrika reconstruct through the memory of the community the lives of two women who committed suicide. But they are mediated at one more level, as the oral interviews are transcribed and edited for publication. Thus the binary relationship between author and text is dismantled as I track how cultural production occurs in a larger network of interconnected actors.

The specificities of print and filmic forms in Kerala and the representational trajectories of both these media inform my readings of cultural networks. In my discussions of cinema, I examine formal devices and codes of representation. Shot-by-shot analyses of cinema and close readings of literary texts are linked to an exploration of how specific genres and media are positioned in a regional public sphere. These close readings contribute to my analysis of cultural circuits because I place cinematic and literary codes in relation to a larger network of vernacular cultural production. For example, in my interpretation of *Deshadanakkili karayarilla* (1986), I draw on codes in Malayalam cinema about romantic couplehood and show how this film adopts these conventions in order to disrupt them. My analysis of formal devices enables me to place cultural forms in the field of aesthetic judgments in the region. Depictions of a heroine writing a love letter with literary flourishes and nature imagery in *Sancharram* (2004) can be understood only if we read it in the regional cultural milieu where poetic expressions of interiority and romance are valorized. Instead of taking for granted generic categories such as soft porn, romance, or realism, I give them substance and specificity by interpreting them locally, placing them in relation to the configurations of those categories in the Kerala public sphere. I demonstrate that the analysis of representational practices and formal readings have to go hand in hand with a mapping of the particularities of the vernacular public sphere in which these texts materialize and circulate. Paying attention to how each of these texts are embedded in regional structures of feeling allows me to expose the uneven topographies of the politics of sexuality.

The Labor of Return Journeys

The intensive phase of the research, on which this book is based, was primarily between 2006 and 2010. Therefore, when I refer to the post-1990s period, my main focus is on the two decades between 1990 and 2010. There have been significant events, texts, and political movements on sexuality in Kerala after 2010. Transgender identities and issues have gained more prominence in this time period.[53] A detailed analysis of these recent developments is beyond the scope of this book. But in the concluding chapter I reflect upon how the theoretical and methodological insights that emerge in this book might provide a framework to analyze the shifting sexual languages of post-2010 Kerala. The conclusion focuses on how cultural practices, the relational workings of memory, and tenuous modes of doing politics continue to shape regional imaginations of sexuality. For the pre-1990s period I focus in detail on texts and events from the 1970s and 1980s. I also refer back to texts, genres, and literary movements from the late 1940s onward that dealt with questions of sexuality, such as Vaikom Mohammed Basheer's novella *Shabdangal* (Noises, 1947/2007), which lead to a burning debate on homosexuality and the protocols of literary representation.

In order to track how cultural texts and events are mediated through popular memory and access the local contours of political struggles around sexuality, I returned to Kerala multiple times between 2006 and 2010 as a researcher and spent sustained periods of time observing and participating in political meetings. The ethnographic aspect of my project was necessary to record and analyze the generative relation between the subject and the figure. I attended meetings such as "Idam: Convention for Sexual Minorities in Kerala" (September 2008) and the Feminist Kerala Network meeting in Varkala (2008). I also went to campaigns organized by KSACS, such as the Red Ribbon Express campaign. The posters of soft-porn films pasted on the walls of busy streets and the family-planning and AIDS-prevention messages in railway stations were familiar sights that I recorded with more alacrity on my research visits to Kerala. I had informal conversations with outreach officers and other members of NGOs who worked with sexual minorities. I also connected with feminist and queer collectives and conducted interviews with media persons, artists, and activists who were involved with the campaigns and events that I analyzed.

For example, to reconstruct the Kunjeebi case, I interviewed feminist activists who mobilized against her custody murder, the photographer who recorded her death, and the sex workers who were her friends and supporters. To provide a thick description of how this case and the political mobilization surrounding it animates the present, I found it useful to juxtapose print and visual media accounts with oral narratives of people who were involved in this event. My conversation with artist and activist Aryakrishnan in 2015 is central to my analysis of the intersections between politics and art practices in the concluding chapter. Prior to the publication of her autobiographies, I had met with Nalini Jameela in 2003 to discuss the cultural and political interventions by sex workers in Kerala. Thus, in this book I examine not only the ways in which events are constructed and kept alive but also how history making is an ongoing and quotidian process.

During my research in Kerala, some of the people I interacted with asked me, "Why on earth did you go all the way to the US to study your home state?" Others saw me as a political ally whose investment in the region had not waned. But there was also an underlying anxiety about the unequal balance between them and me in terms of funding, mobility, and access to structures of knowledge production. "We are ready to help everyone, but there is no one to help us," Sanjesh, a sexuality rights activist in Kerala observed when we met for the first time. The KSACS media manager was reluctant to give me access to their campaign materials. He feared that my US location would affix a stamp of authority to my interpretation of their campaigns. This process made me more reflective about the different realms of knowledge production that I was mediating—the regional, the national, and the transnational—and the need to question the "naturalized hierarchies between these sites of knowledge production" (Lukose 2009: 14). During the time period of this research, my travel between the two locations that I straddled, the US academy and the public spaces of Kerala, was not in any way smooth and fluid. Each location made different demands on me and forced me to undertake different acts of translation while resisting some of the labels under which I could be easily slotted, whether it was that of the "detached

US-based researcher" or the "native informant." Tejaswini Niranjana observes that "the importance of moving in and out of languages, of being always between languages, indeed the importance of translation, needs to be acknowledged as a way of keeping open the space of criticism" (1998: 144), especially in the postcolonial context. She argues that simultaneously holding on to and negotiating different sorts of languages, linguistic as well as conceptual, is a necessary condition for feminism in the postcolony. My positioning in the US academy from 2004 to 2011 and in different academic institutions in India, outside of Kerala from 2011 to 2017, heightened this awareness of "existence-in-translation" (135). My navigation of multiple linguistic, cultural, and political worlds both in the United States and in India, and continued relationship to Kerala as a researcher, has shaped this book in palpable ways.

Unruly Figures is in many ways a return journey to a landscape that is familiar and formative. What changes when one returns "home" as an academic researcher? Returning home as a researcher, based in a more privileged academic space, demanded a critical distance from a familiar set of discourses. As a researcher I occupied a negotiated space between familiarity and distance, straddling the interstices between the "inside" and "outside." Feminist postcolonial theorists such as Gayatri Spivak, Trinh Minh-Ha, Chandra Mohanty, Kirin Narayan, Piya Chatterjee, and Kamala Visweswaran have examined the limits and hierarchies of projects of knowledge production in which the postcolonial researcher is positioned as a "native informant" who is also an "authentic subject" (see Spivak 1999). Often researchers who work on unfamiliar parts of the world or marginalized cultures have the inordinate burden of being completely identified with their research projects. While acknowledging personal investments, how can we practice modes of knowledge production that trouble the binary divide between the self and the other and between the West and the rest? Feminist scholarship has questioned the authority of the unitary, knowing subject and has pointed to how all projects of knowledge production are located and function through modes of identification and distancing.[54] Kirin Narayan's (1993) "How Native Is a 'Native' Anthropologist?" argues that the extent to which anyone is an "authentic insider" is questionable. In this historical moment she says that the insider/outsider paradigm is too reductive, and it might be more apt to view anthropologists in terms of shifting identifications. Thus rather than fix the researcher as an "authentic" subject whose autobiographical investments lead to a project of self-discovery, I propose that a reflexive, feminist methodology of knowledge production requires shifting modes of identifications and critical reflections on the familiar. This is the situated method of engagement that I work toward in this book. In the fourth chapter I analyze interviews conducted not by me but by the Sahayatrika team. My methodology and theoretical interests make it possible for me to use interviews conducted by an activist group, for my aim is to examine how lesbian suicides are mobilized in the public sphere. I ask, how do they circulate and produce a recognizable lesbian subject? I analyze how the framing of these interviews in a published format and how the circulatory context makes these suicides crucial events in the history of sexuality in Kerala.

Thus, there are many intermediaries in my plotting of the Kerala public sphere. These include activists who document and investigate lesbian suicides, journalists and academics who comment on texts and events, reviewers who categorize films and frame them for an audience, artists and activists who memorialize the death of fellow activists, and filmmakers who see themselves as intervening in the social. I position myself amid an array of commentators, but I also try to be aware of the particularity of my own position and how it differs from other actors in the scene. For I am a participant who is interpreting these cultural circuits and thus has to occupy a critical distance from the events on the ground. While activists have to resolve the political problems that they are confronted with and work on their feet to come up with strategic moves, cultural theorists can step back and provide a view of the situation that retains the tensions around irresolvable issues. The aim is not to come up with quick solutions, but to intervene in discursive formations so as to forge new models of thinking about the political. This ability to occupy a third position, which involves a suspension of quick judgment, is a valuable one that I try to retain in this book. My position as an interpreter of cultural networks allows me to participate in the process of reenvisioning the sexual geography of Kerala. But I see this writing as a collaborative process. I am in conversation with other political and cultural actors who constitute the Kerala public sphere. Through this awareness I try to undermine my position of author-ity.

A Small Place?

For many of the readers of this book, located in metropolitan spaces in India and abroad, Kerala will be a world apart from the immediate realities of their lives. There are many ways in which "small places"[55] can be unmoored and made mobile in this global economy. We are in an age in which diversity is valorized, as long as the center remains unshaken by the predicaments of the periphery. As Stuart Hall succinctly puts it, "To be at the leading edge of modern capitalism is to eat fifteen different cuisines in any one week" (1997: 181). As a focus on globalization and its structural impact replaces postcolonial studies in the Euro-American academy today, many cultural theorists explore the possibilities opened up by global flows and new "media-scapes" (Appadurai 1996). In the midst of such celebrations of fluidity and permeability, it is all the more important to emphasize how small places run a greater risk of being flattened or co-opted under a global umbrella.

Within the national schema, Kerala has a place of privilege because of its political, cultural, and economic history. But in the transnational economy, it is a small place that runs the risk of being framed in a snapshot fashion, with all of its complexities bled out. For example, *Sancharram* circulates transnationally as a lesbian story from an exotic, faraway land of lyrical charm. "In a land steeped in tradition . . . A secret love," says the blurb on the film poster.[56] When activists and academics "discover" resistant texts or lives and translate them for circulation in a global economy, they risk freezing these texts so as to fit them within the dominant registers of what agency or resistance should look like. When scripts of liberation become indiscriminately mapped onto all parts of the world, they lose their power to affect change and become hegemonic instead. Mary John's note of caution that "postcolonial and feminist theorists need to become more aware of the partial and composite characteristics of the theories they depend upon" (1996: 2) has only acquired greater significance in the last decade. She observes that emancipatory programs such as that of feminism have not been immune to a configuration in which the West has the "ability to project its influence beyond its geopolitical borders" (2). The flow of knowledge forms is also controlled by the flow of global capital. Rather than package an "incredible" or "forever oppressed" India for the academic marketplace, my attempt is to invite the reader to undertake with me a journey to spaces that disturb the certainties of a liberal humanist politics.

This is a risky task of cultural translation I undertake as a scholar. I make available for transnational academic analysis the cultural world of Kerala. In writing about an all-too-familiar/familial world, but approaching it through the critical lens of a dominant academic discourse, I struggle to point to the limits of translation, to reflect on what is gained by foregrounding incommensurability. "To pass through what is difficult and unfamiliar is an essential part of critical thinking within the academy today, an academy whose dedication to 'comparative' work is not a field or subfield of its operation but a fundamental and irreversible condition of communication itself," writes Butler (2003: 199) in her commentary on the power of encountering knowledge that is estranging and not quickly translatable into familiar forms. Encountering a project that presents a different context can be intellectually productive when the field of investigation has the power to point to the limits of one's tools of analysis. The challenge of my return journey was how conscious I could become of my own knowledge formations and how they are rendered insufficient by what I initially assumed was a familiar world. These moments of vulnerability, when the dominant paradigms of the public, of agency, of rights, and of resistance are reconfigured by regional discourses, are productive tensions in this project.

Scholars who take on projects on burning political issues are often asked: How will your analysis change things on the ground? Will it reduce AIDS? Will it stop lesbian suicides? These are not merely questions that are imposed from outside. Embedded in structures that valorize clear paths of action and strategies for empowerment, there have been moments of crisis when I ask myself these questions. But then I tell myself that the value of an intellectual project is not in producing blueprints for action or setting applicable targets. In a global economy that is so entrenched in a desire for clarity, for data and numbers, for target population and behavioral change, for progress in forms that can be recognized as progress, it is important to produce local accounts of sexuality that open up rather than foreclose models of political action. This book passionately believes in the need to muddy the ground, the need to strive for an academic practice in which cultural and political practices are not neatly packaged through key words like "agency" or "empowerment."

What it demands instead is a suspension of quick judgment, an ability to "turn the critical gaze upon ourselves, to leave open the possibility that we may be remade through an encounter with the other" (Mahmood 2005: 37). The labor of this project is to move away from a world that demands strategic action and political foreclosure to assert the value of a nuanced narrative of subjectivities suspended between action and passivity, resistance and submission, life and death. The chapters in this book are fragmentary[57] accounts of a region that aim to render vulnerable the certainties of dominant theories and paradigms of action.

The Body of the Book

Here are quick peeks into what will unfold in this book. Chapter 1, "Tracing the Prostitute: Between Excess and Containment," analyzes momentous representations of the prostitute figure in pre-1990s popular media and the afterlives of this figure in the post-1990s period. I focus on the visual, print, and oral documentation of the police custody murder case of a prostitute, Kunjeebi, in 1987 and the unprecedented protests that followed, which positioned the sex worker as the pivotal site for a feminist struggle in Kerala. I read this event in conjunction with the shifting cultural circuits of the cult Malayalam film *Avalude ravukal* (1978). I demonstrate that the tensions in the figuration and subjectification of the prostitute can be unpacked by focusing on the volatile traffic between visual and literary forms that traverses divergent registers of realism, melodrama, and pornography. Through tracing the incomplete and anxiety-ridden attempts to control and contain ways of seeing cultural texts, I argue that the prostitute figure as a seething site of contradictions signals the unfinished project of policing sexuality.

Chapter 2, "To Claim the Day: The Sex Worker as Subject in the Time of AIDS," is a critical analysis of the dual autobiographical project by a sex worker and activist, Nalini Jameela, in 2005, in conjunction with state-produced AIDS awareness materials. Jameela's first book was celebrated as the first-ever autobiography by a sex worker in modern India. Shocking the Kerala public, she published a revised version of her life story in a gap of six months, arguing that she was not satisfied with the style and political positioning of the first book. I read the narrative infractions in Jameela's repeated experiments with the form of the autobiography as public performances of a sex worker's negotiation with regimes of visibility, voicing, and legibility. This chapter takes a close look at the formal strategies of state-produced pedagogic materials in order to examine how the sex worker is addressed as a responsible agent within the AIDS machinery. I argue that Jameela's stuttered project of self-narration inhabits and takes shape within neoliberal modes of governance but tactically disturbs these structures. Her compositional acts of self-making positions the sex worker as a recalcitrant subject of governmental power and rewrites the links between women's bodies, region, and nation building.

Chapter 3, "Wandering in the Vernacular: Divergent Visions of Queerness," is a comparative reading of two Malayalam films, *Sancharram* (2004) and *Deshadanakkili karayarilla* (1986), as representative of differing trajectories of queer politics. I place the two films in different historical contexts—in terms of modes of circulation, reception, and the altered political and critical discourse on queerness—and deploy the pre-1990s film *Deshadanakkili karayarilla* to interrogate the limits of a universal language of sexual identity politics. For this purpose I undertake a close reading of the cinematic codes of both these films, especially their spatial arrangements and romantic tropes. The concept of *deshadanam* (wandering) is key to my reading practice in this chapter. I argue that the location of *Sancharram* in the dominant LGBT discourse in India and abroad makes it so enmeshed in setting up an established meaning for the term "queer" that the process of queering becomes one of stabilizing a chosen form of desire as the ideal one. *Deshadanakkili karayarilla* does not consolidate a particular subject position as the desired ideal. It stages the movements of wandering women in order to trouble the naturalized construction of the heterosexual couple, and injects a sense of instability into the social sphere itself.

Chapter 4, "Living Together, Dying Together: The Politics of Lesbian Hauntings," examines the public discourses on lesbian sexuality that have at their center the event of suicide and the specters of women whose lives could have been saved. I do a close reading of published interviews of community members conducted by an activist group in the wake of multiple reports on lesbian suicides in different parts of the state. I also zoom out and analyze the practice of using oral narratives on lesbian suicides as the grounds for a queer movement. A rhetorical analysis of the interviews and a critical understanding of the memory-making impulses of the activist organization Sahayatrika demonstrates how haunting is a mode of narrating social exclusion when the bodies at the center of the discourse are marked as out of bounds in multiple ways. I deploy the term *bhootham*, which in Malayalam carries the double meaning of "past" and "ghost," in order to analyze how political practices blur the linear ordering of time. I aim to create reading practices in which suicide as an act demands a suspension of quick judgment and a willingness to hold together the threads of divergent scripts through which the subject is made and annihilated. From tears to blood, stillness to haunting, I traverse the corporeal and spectral terrains of these multilayered narratives to reenvision the political.

Chapter 5, "'What You Think Is Fire . . .': Unspooled Movements and Suspended Readings," focuses on the memorialization of the transgender activist Sweet Maria, who was murdered in 2012, and locates these practices of doing politics as a tenuous and affective terrain that cannot be reclaimed for an identity-making project. This chapter underlines how the precariousness of acts of living continues to shape sexuality politics in regional contexts in India, even while there is a heightened investment within the more visible face of the LGBT movement on stable identities. It reflects on how *Unruly Figures* points to new horizons of possibility offered by practices that do not foreclose and define modes of being a political subject. I underline the crucial significance of producing suspended reading practices that allow us to engage with the haunting power of fragmentary spaces and unruly acts. In the spirit of the nonlinear organization of the book, the concluding chapter argues for the significance of the vernacular cultural archive to imagine queer futurities.

CHAPTER 1

Tracing the Prostitute

Between Excess and Containment

TWO SEXUAL EVENTS:

> A film poster of a young woman dressed only in a flimsy white shirt
> that clings to her body. Wet hair scattered around her face as she pulls
> up the shirt to examine a scratch on her thigh. Glass bangles on her
> hands. Lowered eyes that do not meet the viewer's gaze.

> A black-and-white news photograph of a woman's dead body in a police
> lockup. Her rope-like sari forms the noose around her neck. The
> camera is positioned behind her body. A long strand of plaited hair and
> dangling feet meet the viewer's eyes.

These are two images that have an iconic value in the public sphere of Kerala. They are controversial visual texts at the center of two foundational events that brought questions of sexuality to the fore in pre-1990s Kerala. This chapter brings together and analyzes these two events that occupy opposing positions in the regional and national discourse on gender and sexuality. The film poster is from I. V. Sasi's cult film *Avalude ravukal* (Her nights, 1978) on the life of a prostitute. This film was a huge hit at the time of its release and there are multiple contentious circuits through which it has lived on in public memory. This is one of the most notorious films produced by the Malayalam film industry, perceived as launching soft-porn cinema as a genre in the nation. But the film underwent a dramatic transformation in its public positioning as it was recouped as a realist depiction of the life of a struggling prostitute in the post-1990s period. The news photograph is of the murder of a prostitute, Kunjeebi, under police custody in 1987, and this haunting image plays a crucial role in the memorialization of Kunjeebi. The Kunjeebi case resulted in organized feminist protests that resonate in Kerala history. Bodhana (Awareness), the organization that led this protest, has acquired a different institutional form and is now named Anweshi (Seeker) Women's Counseling Center. Anweshi is currently one of the prominent feminist organizations in Kerala. The Kunjeebi case is a milestone because it was one of the initial political incidents in the history of Kerala that positioned the prostitute as the central figure of feminist mobilization.

The *Avalude ravukal* debate in conjunction with other pre-1990s political and cultural events, specifically the death of Kunjeebi in 1987, raises the following questions: How do cultural circuits that coalesce around the prostitute disturb the alignment between femininity, domesticity, and respectability that is central to regional identity? How does the process of tracing the prostitute produce a history of cultural practices in Kerala marked by the tensions between excess and containment? What are the links between sexuality politics and the afterlives of cultural texts? Forms that can make evidentiary claims associated with the human rights discourse, such as photography and the realist novel, are currently the dominant mode through which the representation of the prostitute can gain recognition and legitimacy.[1] But human rights documents, couched in the language of rationality, can slip into the territories of melodrama and pornography. On the other hand, popular cinema that is labeled as titillating can be realigned as a realistic depiction of suffering and exploitation. Thus, I analyze how the two public events that I focus on in this chapter create a dynamic field of representational practices that oscillates between excess and containment.

My analysis troubles the standard categorization of the *Avalude ravukal* debate and the Kunjeebi case as disconnected occurrences. I will demonstrate that the unruly trajectories of the prostitute can be traced through the productive transactions between different mediums such as literature, cinema, and photography. *Avalude ravukal* and the Kunjeebi case are both cultural occurrences from the past that have afterlives in the present, and I examine the political significance of the process of remembering. My analysis of these cultural sites takes me back to raging public debates on the Progressive Writers Movement in early twentieth-century India wherein the figure of the prostitute raises fundamental questions about gender, sexuality, and the form and function of art. Thus, this chapter juxtaposes momentous public debates from different time periods on the representation of the prostitute. The past is recalled here in a material fashion to "incarnate conflicting forces activated in the present" (Zapperi 2013: 28). It is the resonances of these debates in the present that make them productive sites to trace the uneasy terrains of sexuality and representation.

Representing the Prostitute

Scholars have analyzed how within the legal, economic, and epistemological shifts associated with colonialism and the nationalist movement in the late nineteenth and twentieth century, a vast array of sexual practices and actors outside the regime of conjugal domesticity are clubbed together, stigmatized, and recast under the sign of "prostitution" (Gupta 2001; Wald 2009). The prostitute became a target of upliftment in reform movements in this time period as women were harnessed to the project of fashioning the family, the nation, the region, and the community (Anandhi 1991; Banerjee 1998; Waheed 2014). Ashwini Tambe (2009) demonstrates that lawmaking and law enforcement on prostitution in nineteenth- and early twentieth-century Bombay was a productive process. She analyzes the role of the colonial state in promoting specific forms of prostitution while simultaneously increasing coercion of prostitutes (xviii). She demonstrates that the criminalized and pathologized prostitute was a target of governmental and juridical power (18). Svati Shah analyzes how the perceptions and practices that organize the routine life of sexual commerce in the streets of contemporary Mumbai disturb the binaries of invisibility/visibility and speech/silence and question the "foundational assumption that prostitution is knowable" (2014: 79). The Indian state's position on prostitution is currently governed by the Immoral Traffic Prevention Act (ITPA) enacted in 1986, a legislation that mainly aims to prevent exploitation of minors and forced entry of women into prostitution. Prostitution is not a criminal offense per se in India, but there are multiple provisions in this act that "criminalizes the outward manifestations of sex work" such as soliciting, brothel keeping, and trafficking (Menon 2007: xxxv). Thus the ambivalent workings of law also point to the "spectrality of paid sex" (Shah 2014: 97) in India.

The prostitute is a figure magnified by the currents of transformation in the history of cultural practices in India. Performance forms and rituals that involved the display of the bodies of "public women," such as the *devadasi* (temple dancer) and the *tawaif* (courtesan), have functioned as scenes of contestation since the nineteenth century (Srinivasan 1985; Nair 1994; Arondekar 2012). The tensions posed by sexualized feminine figures such as the actress, the dancer, and the prostitute are pivotal to the emergence of modern forms of entertainment such as novels, theater, and cinema (Tharu 2008; Majumdar 2009; Shandilya 2017). In highly influential literary movements such as the Progressive Writers Movement in early twentieth-century India, the prostitute is a recurring figure emblematic of the ills of a society organized on the grounds of gender, caste, and class inequality. Yet these fictional narratives engender controversy because they take the reader to uncharted terrains of sexuality, labor, and commerce that dislodge women's bodies from the sphere of domesticity. Intense controversies and highly publicized court cases in different linguistic contexts in India foreground the centrality of the prostitute in debates on obscenity, realism, and reform in early twentieth-century India. Iconoclastic writers of the time, such as Ismat Chughtai and Sa'adat Hasan Manto, insisted that the writer's task was to name "the existence of that which others will not speak about," and the prostitute, likened by Manto to the "sewers and drains" in every city, comes center stage in this act of turning the gaze toward urban decay and sexual exploitation (quoted in Gopal 2005: 119). This mandate of literary forms to capture all aspects of social reality, including its dark underside, is not a neat gesture of holding up a mirror to society. As Priyamvada Gopal observes, these literary movements stage "exposé as a fraught act" (40) and are driven by the recognition that "representation is not so much a given as a problematic to be engaged with" (4–5). These heightened public debates show how the representation of the prostitute is a challenging project.

Texts and events on the prostitute figure in Kerala speak to debates in different linguistic contexts in India about gender, sexuality, and representational practices. In my exploration of *Avalude ravukal* I focus on how the prostitute takes shape in the push and pull between containment and excess that is central to the dynamics of cultural forms that explore the knotty terrains of gender and sexuality. As I reconstruct the Kunjeebi case through photographs, news reports, and oral narratives, the precarious transactions involved in remembering the prostitute come to the surface. Vernacular cultural practices disrupt the attempts to place the prostitute in a singular register, either as seductress or victim, and dislodge the fixity of this figure. Through tracing the prostitute as subject and figure, I open up for analysis the unstable formations of sexuality in the region as codes of respectability are continually made and unmade.

Contentious Circuits of Cinematic Reception

At the time of its release, *Avalude ravukal* was lampooned as a disgraceful film that soiled the name of Kerala as a region. It was labeled as a film about prostitution that aims to titillate and gross money through the indecent exposure of the female body. Journalist and film critic E. V. Sreedharan's initial report, "The Walls Feel Ashamed," written in 1978, captures the anxiety over how this film tarnished the good name of Kerala in the neighboring state of Tamil Nadu, whose capital is Madras: "As this film became a major hit in theaters in Kerala it was also released in the big city of Madras. The walls of this major city were adorned with posters of Raji examining the scratch on her thighs. . . . At that point I wrote that this girl who came from the Kerala coast is destroying the respectability of the walls of Tamil Nadu. Malayalis there have to bend their heads in shame. If these walls had life they would have shooed this girl away" (1999: 3). But since the late 1990s, the film has been recouped as a bold, progressive portrayal of the subaltern prostitute, and in 1999, Sreedharan backtracked and critiqued his own hyperbolic report on the film.

Actress Seema, as Rajamma (Raji), the seductive and outspoken prostitute in this black-and-white film, is one of the most memorable characters in Malayalam screen history.[2] *Avalude ravukal* presents the life story of a young Hindu woman, Raji, who loses her parents at a young age and enters into prostitution as a means of survival. The film does not make explicit the caste of the heroine and thus insists on class as the structuring vector of Kerala society. The film shows her everyday struggles as she works as a prostitute who has sex with men in hotels and other semipublic spaces. In significant sequences of the film, the heroine criticizes social structures that push her into prostitution and then label her as a "bad woman."

During the course of the film, her younger brother dies through police torture. A schoolteacher, Chandran, who is indirectly responsible for her brother's death, tries to have a sexual relationship with her, but she refuses his advances. The object of her love is Babu, a student of English literature working on his masters degree, who lives close to her house. She seduces him in tantalizing ways but steadfastly refuses to have sex with him without romantic involvement. Throughout the course of the film, Babu does not reciprocate her declarations of romantic love, but toward the end of the film, in a dramatic turnaround, he offers to marry her. The film ends with her entry into an affluent, upper caste (Nair) domestic setting, but the narrative overall focuses on her life as a prostitute.

The prostitute as a cultural figure has a long history in Kerala, and *Avalude ravukal* draws on and reworks the accepted modes through which this figure is represented in literature and on screen. The prostitute straddles the doubleness of the female body as threatening and seductive, oppressed and rebellious. In significant Malayalam texts by women writers, such as Lalithambika Antharjanam's "Prathikara devatha" (Goddess of revenge, 1966), a Nambudiri (Brahmin) woman seeks revenge by deploying the material markers of her sexual encounters to tarnish the reputation of the powerful men who are the upholders of the community that chastises her. In "Pavappettavarude veshya" (The Prostitute of the poor, 1952/2008), Vaikom Muhammad Basheer criticizes the moral high ground taken against prostitution and shows how individuals are crucified while social structures are not the target of criticism. In Malayalam cinema in the 1970s, the prostitute is often positioned as a victim of social inequality who deserves sympathy and not chastisement. For example, P. A. Bakkar's *Chuvanna vithukal* (Red seeds, 1977), a story about two sisters caught in the net of prostitution and police harassment, won much appreciation in the state. But unlike *Chuvanna vithukal*, categorized as art cinema, the public anxiety that *Avalude ravukal* evoked can be linked to the commercial success of the film and its huge popularity in states outside Kerala. Alleppey Shereef, the screenplay writer, recollects the opposition the film encountered during the time of its production: "When the film was completed and previewed in Madras all the reigning kings of Malayalam cinema predicted that people would tear apart the seats in the theater if we took this film to Kerala. The film was banned by the censor board. Then it was after much difficulty that [the producer] Ramachandran got permission for exhibiting the film" (1999: 4).

Thus during the preview, the prediction was that the "enlightened" audience of Kerala would violently disapprove of a titillating portrayal of a prostitute's life. But contrary to such expectations, the film was a big hit in Kerala and in other states in India. The film is consistently mentioned in discussions about Malayalam cinema's investment in the production of soft-porn films. In 1978, an article in the Bombay-based English language film magazine *Filmfare* uses *Avalude ravukal* as an example of how Malayalam cinema was becoming increasingly sex oriented. It observes how this film was a box office hit in the neighboring state of Karnataka and changed filmgoers' taste to such an extent that even people who could not understand the language flocked to the theater to watch the film for its "indecent exposures" (*Filmfare* 1978: 10). In the *Encyclopedia of Indian Cinema*, the authors describe it as "originally a poignant if sexually explicit love story featuring an orphan brother and sister, notorious in a dubbed version titled *Her Nights*" (Rajadhyaksha and Willemen 1994/1999: 192). This notoriety that the film gained in the first two decades, mainly through its national reception, plays a significant role in its cult status in public memory.

These disapproving sentiments are also reflected in 1978 Malayalam film magazines, but the debates are more nuanced, and at the time of release the film had mixed responses. Renowned Malayalam film star Prem Nazeer observes that the "sex wave" in Malayalam cinema began after the success of *Avalude ravukal*. But he goes on to explain that this was because of a misreading of the film's popularity: "Many people mistook the reason for the success of *Avalude Ravukal*. They thought it was its depiction of sex. . . . But that was not the reason for the film's success. It succeeded because of the novelty of the theme and the enjoyable way it was depicted" (quoted in Mannarkat 1981: 281). Some of the reviewers granted an ethical impulse to the film in its commitment to lay bare the economic inequalities in society: "*Avalude Ravukal* is the story of a girl who is pushed into prostitution because of circumstances. These artists show how a commercial film can be made artistically" (Nakshathrashala 1978:

27). I. V. Sasi's ambiguous positioning as a director who made commer-
cially successful films but also had a commitment to realism contributed
to the contested history of *Avalude ravukal* in Kerala's public sphere. But
these complications were erased as the film gained notoriety in the
national context, and until the late 1990s, even in historical accounts of
regional cinema, *Avalude ravukal* was regarded mainly as a sexually titillating soft-porn film.

Since the late 1990s, attempts have been made to retrieve the film as
a bold portrayal of a prostitute that was far ahead of its times.[3] In 1999,
two decades after the release of the film, Imprint Books published the
screenplay of *Avalude ravukal*. E. V. Sreedharan, the journalist who vehe-
mently attacked the film at the time of its release, wrote the preface for
the first edition of the screenplay in which he regrets his earlier lack of
judgment: "Today I believe that we should seriously examine the human-
interest issue put forward by the film in 1978" (1999: 1). In 2004, almost
twenty-five years after the theatrical release of *Avalude ravukal*, Mathrubhumi Books, a reputed publishing house, published a new edition of
the screenplay. "This film was the story of a *thevadisi* [prostitute] in the
language of those days, in today's language it would be described as the
life-story of a sex worker," observes film critic Premchand in the introduction to the second edition of the screenplay (2004: 9). This shift in terminology points to the changing position of the prostitute in the Kerala
public sphere. By the late 1990s, the discussion about sex work in Kerala
entered a different phase because of the emergence of the sex worker as
a political actor and a participant in AIDS awareness programs. While
Sreedharan in 1999 retrieves the film primarily on the grounds of realism, Premchand in the later edition draws both on realist aesthetics and
the human rights claims of the sex worker in India.

Critical studies on practices of film exhibition and circulation in South
Asia point to how the division between categories such as art-house cinema, soft-porn cinema, and action cinema are often unstable and shifting (Srinivas 2003; Liang 2005). Ratheesh Radhakrishnan, in his study
on soft-porn cinema as a category in Kerala, observes the frequency with
which "serious" films that deal with sexually charged issues are given an
A certificate, and art house films, whether European or Indian, are reconfigured as pornographic through shifting categories of circulation (2010:
203). Also, through the commonplace practice of inserting uncensored

or deleted footage, known as cut-pieces, into films during exhibition, the erotic content of any film can be heightened (Hoek 2013). As Lotte Hoek observes, through "practices of including, excising or re-editing during the screening of a film" (2010: 49), celluloid itself becomes unstable during exhibition in theaters. Thus it is difficult to fix an insulated, stable category of soft-porn cinema in South Asia because it is a shifting category formed through modes of circulation and exhibition.

In fact, the need to control and streamline cinematic categories hinges on the uneasy recognition of the dispersed modes of production and reception of cinema within national and regional publics. Cinematic categories are value laden, and charged public debates are staged around the process of labeling and classifying "good" and "bad" cinema. As I discuss in the introduction, the Malayalam film industry oscillates between categories that are perceived as two extremes. It has produced directors who played a significant role in the development of art cinema in India, mainly distinguished by realist aesthetics. But Kerala is also seen as the state invested in the production of soft-porn films that are dubbed and circulated in all parts of India. As a result there are anxiety-ridden attempts within the Kerala public sphere to maintain the hierarchical boundaries between high and low cinema. Debates on sexuality, spectatorship, and forms of representation are foundational to regional identity formation.

All attempts to recoup *Avalude ravukal*, whether in the past or the present, have emphasized its gritty, realist aesthetics. The Progressive Writers Movement and the theatrical movement lead by Kerala People's Arts Club (KPAC), in which Left-associated artists aimed to produce a "new popular" that would address "the masses" (Joseph 2013: 115), influenced the definition of realism in Malayalam cinema.[4] In the 1940s and 1950s, under the umbrella of the Left's cultural interventions, it was purported that art's real mandate was to depict the life worlds of the masses—their sufferings, joys, and struggles. More than a singularity of aesthetic form, what defines realism in Malayalam cinema is a commitment to educate and transform the very masses whose lives are seen as the source of art. Jenson Joseph in his study on social realism and 1950s Malayalam cinema comments on the hierarches that are set in place within this form of cinema: "What is striking in this outlook is a certain valorization of working class life as the only legitimate source for the progressive art to draw from, and a simultaneous imagining of the toiling masses—the primary target audience—as susceptible to 'false consciousness' which prevents them from realizing their own class interest, and which thus necessitates their 'awakening' through progressive art" (120). Thus realism as an institutionalized category is defined by its pedagogic mode of address. Within Malayalam film criticism and other structures of recognition like state funding and awards, directors who delineate forms of oppression and articulate the need for social change have reigned supreme. Many of the celebrated films in Malayalam, such as *Neelakuyil* (The blue cuckoo, 1954) and *Odayil ninu* (From the gutter, 1965), are based on the work of novelists such as Uroob and P. Kesavadev who were committed to this framework of realism.

There is also an implicit distinction between two kinds of audiences in these debates about cinema—the unenlightened audience who sees a film through a smutty gaze, and sensitive viewers who can read a political message in the film. This is in keeping with Madhava Prasad's argument that realist cinema is marked by a secure positioning for the viewer who can be a distanced, "sympathetic consumer" of the spectacle of suffering (1998: 204). It is this detached vision of the secure, spectatorial position of realist cinema that Sreedharan invokes when he calls for "a new viewing eye—an eye that can recognize life's misery" for reviewing *Avalude ravukal* (1999: 4). But I argue that these strategies of distancing are difficult to apply to a film such as *Avalude ravukal*. Its conflicting textual codes and diffuse modes of circulation produce an inherently unstable viewing position. The motivation to fix the gaze of the spectator as a realist one is symptomatic of the need to sanitize the regional space of Kerala—to project a vision of a public sphere in which the figure of the prostitute is viewed only through a rational gaze, not smudged by desire or titillation. But the anxiety engendered by Raji's graphic image on the film poster cannot be completely exorcised.

The contradictory affective responses and codes straddled by this film text and its extratextual materials signal the incomplete attempts in the public sphere to control ways of seeing cultural texts. Mazzarella argues that the anxieties and fantasies that are at play in the discourse on the visceral tendencies of cinema point to the "public cultural dialectic of containment and excess" (2013: 221). He observes how mapping the relation between "unruly affect" and "public reason" "straightforwardly onto a division between subaltern lifeworlds and bourgeois publics" (24) will not allow us to engage with how "deliberative reason of the bourgeois public sphere, notwithstanding its own ideology, rests on both routinized and emergent currents of public affect" (25). Thus cultural texts centered on the prostitute figure emerge as a significant site for tracing the affective dynamics of the public sphere of Kerala. Rather than reading *Avalude ravukal* as a niche site of sexual excess, I locate it centrally within the deliberations in the regional context regarding the fashioning of gendered and sexualized bodies.

Excess and Containment

S. Sanjeev, in his analysis of the dominant rhetoric of film criticism in Kerala since the 1970s, points to the dichotomy between "art" cinema and "commercial" cinema, in which commercial cinema is denigrated because of its excessive investment in the body: "The transformation from commercial cinema to art cinema is envisioned as an evolution from surface reality (body) to interior reality (soul)" (2002: 67). The textual codes of *Avalude ravukal* and the dynamics of its reception stage this conflict between body/soul and commercial/art cinema. The film is made in black and white, and this adds to its aura of documentary realism.[5] Many of the early sequences of *Avalude ravukal* fulfill the criteria of a realist text. The spectator's gaze is aligned with that of the central character of the film, Raji, as she sees the city. The spectator sees fleeting glimpses of shop signs and pavements as though positioned inside a slow-paced rickshaw. This is cut to a closeup shot of Raji's face followed by her narration of her life story. She recounts how after her parent's death, with an infant brother to fend for, she started begging on the streets. The film shows us a flashback of Raji wandering in the streets with her wailing infant brother in her arms. "Boys who did manual labor hugged me and went to sleep on cold nights. I don't know when I got spoiled, or how. By the time I realized I was a grown-up woman, I had lost what a woman is supposed to guard," says Raji's voice in the backdrop while the viewer sees her asleep, embracing a boy on a grimy pavement. The voice in the backdrop and the personal history give psychological depth to the character and establish spectatorial identification with Raji. The documentary humanism of realist cinema is evident in these scenes in which the spectator watches and sympathizes with the spectacle of suffering. The sexual and bodily excesses in the film are constantly contained through the film's turn toward psychological depth and social commentary.

The opening sequence of the film, before the title cards appear, is a shot of Raji dressed like a celestial dancer. This is cut to a shot of a man with a long black whip, lashing it against her body. Her ornamented body, clothed in sequined attire, moves in a choreographed manner, even as she tries to escape from the men who surround her with whips. The camera tracks her movements as she runs desperately, twirling away from the men who surround her. Her body seems to spill out of the screen and fall toward the audience. Then the film cuts to a closeup shot of her face, asleep in bed with a customer in a hotel room, and we realize that the earlier, high-pitched sequence was her dream. Even before the spectator is introduced to Raji as a character in her day-to-day life, we are given access to her dreams and nightmares. Thus the film establishes a mind/body divide and gives us access to the interiority of the character before we encounter her in her profession as a prostitute.

The title of the film captures its restless shuttling between exteriority and interiority, body and mind. At a quick glance, *Avalude ravukal* is an invitation to witness the unveiling of the sexual escapades in a prostitute's life. The night here refers to the time set apart for illegitimate sexual transactions. But "night" is also evocative of the dark, unknown, and mysterious mind of this generic "her"—that which is beyond the visible, the known, the day. It is a promise to take the audience through a cinematic trip through what keeps "her" awake in the night—her dreams, nightmares, anxieties, and memories. The film is as invested in giving the audiences glimpses of what is beneath the surface, the fantasies and interior workings of a prostitute's mind, as it is in documenting the sexual encounters of a prostitute's life. The pivotal song sequence in the film from which the title emerges, "Nidraaviheenangalallo, avalude raavukal" (Sleepless are her nights), encapsulates the differing aesthetic modes through which Raji's body is represented in the film.[6] This song is a fantasy sequence in which an extreme close-up of Raji's face is the transition device to the palatial setting in which she dances dressed in a white, flowing costume (figure 1.1). The figure of her as the dancing woman is transposed onto the close-up of her face, eyes wide open. Thus the eroticized representation of her body is shown as conjured up through her own gaze.

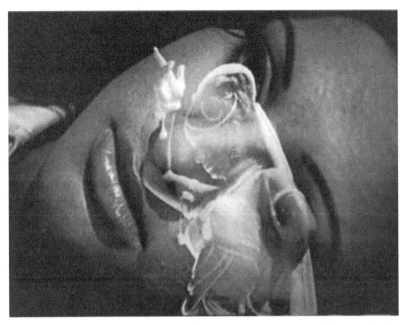

1.1   Close-up of the heroine's face as transition device: frame grab from *Avalude ravukal* (1978).

1.2   Fantasy dance sequence: frame grab from *Avalude ravukal* (1978).

The magical dream that follows uses mirroring techniques and translucent fabric that veils and unveils her. She strikes multiple spectacular poses and seems immersed in her own sensual movements, entangled in the enveloping flow of fabric (figure 1.2). In these fantasy dance sequences, "the image tends to float free into a register of sensual auto-erotic presentation" (Vasudevan 1989: 46). Since this song is staged as a dream sequence initiated by Raji, she seems to participate in and derive pleasure from the inhabitation of her body. Though this song sequence reminds the spectator of the opening sequence of the film when the dancing heroine is violently curtailed by whip-wielding men, in this sequence she comes alive through her gliding movements and directs them in ways that seem more pleasurable to her. These shots of the sensuous and glimmering dance of the heroine's body are intercut with more muted, dimly lit shots in which the heroine's body is presented in disembodied silhouettes against the expanse of the setting sun and the sea. The latter adhere to the conventions of lighting, cinematography, and setting of Malayalam art cinema sequences. The effect of natural lighting and the outdoor setting of these shots are in sharp contrast to the focus on the bedecked female body in an ornate, palatial space.

The silhouette shots of the heroine function as a containment strategy to balance the excesses of the sensual dance sequences and scenes of seduction that she initiates. In the deployment of the markedly artificial mise-en-scène of studio shots intercut with those captured in natural settings, there are multiple formal and identificatory modes at work in the same song sequence. This holds true for the rest of the film as well. The prostitute's body is disruptive and difficult to fix because it functions as the spectacle of suffering, the site of viewing pleasure, and the embodiment of sensual autoeroticism. But in the film, as in its reception, there are constant attempts to control the excesses of the heroine's body and her awareness of its seductive power by focusing more on her suffering and victimhood.

The *Avalude ravukal* debate points to the blurred boundaries between categories such as realist art cinema, soft porn, and family melodrama. There were many films produced in 1978 and the early 1980s in Malayalam that circulated as soft porn and used the term "night" (*rathri*) in their titles (e.g., *Hemanda rathri* [A sweet-scented night, 1978], *Urakkam varatha rathrikal* [Sleepless nights, 1978], *Sathrathil oru rathri* [One night in an inn, 1978]). This citational practice shows the impact *Avalude ravukal* had on the production of the soft-porn film as a genre. Tracking the aesthetic and thematic connections between *Avalude ravukal* and other soft-porn films in Malayalam is beyond the scope of this chapter, but from the vantage point of the present, the film becomes a central reference point in the debates and historical accounts of soft-porn and Malayalam cinema since the late 1970s. The film has tropes from erotic scenes in Indian cinema that now seem familiar, such as Raji's long shower sequence with a jazzy background score, the rain-soaked heroine in a flimsy white shirt seductively posing for the hero, and her stripping and posing seminude for a client. The film does not explicitly present sexual acts on screen, but the heroine's body is presented in tantalizing scenes through tropes that have been recouped into the genre of soft-porn cinema today.[7]

The film appeals to familial sentiments even though the protagonist is outside the conjugal family setting. Her relationship with her younger brother is a significant emotional angle in the film, and it takes on the elements of a maternal melodrama. She also often expresses her desire for marriage and conjugality, even when she is aware that this might be impossible in her life. In one sequence Raji enacts the role of a wife with the schoolteacher. She dresses accordingly, cooks food for him, and serves him, saying that "this is the first time I am being taken care of by someone and I am cooking and serving food for someone, both these things will not happen again." There is a theatrical quality in these scenes by which the nights of a prostitute's life are contrasted to domesticity through utopic song sequences and a "family drama." The film deploys these familial and romantic sentiments in order to set up a divide between the mind and the body, and presents a prostitute who declares, "Only her body has strayed, not her mind." Most critics who assert the artistic value of *Avalude ravukal* adhere to the hierarchical mind/body dichotomy that operates within the film itself, and the thinking, feeling heroine is recouped while erasing her sexualized embodiment.

It is clear that the "pornographic" in *Avalude ravukal* has to be actively denied in order to redeem this film, and this makes it important to understand what is at stake in this disavowal. Linda Williams (1991: 3) in her discussion of Hollywood cinema groups together horror, pornography, and melodrama as genres that signify systems of excess that have a bodily impact on the spectators. The optimum distance of the sympathetic consumer of realist cinema is in sharp contrast here to the unruly viewer who has an intimate relation to the screen that produces bodily excess. While the generic divides that Williams points to are located within the Hollywood film industry, the contentions between the aesthetic modes of excess and containment are crucial to Indian cinema as seen in the discussion about realism and melodrama (Vasudevan 2010). Film theorists have argued that in postcolonial India, cinema is pivotal to the making of the modern nation because realism as a form calls forth on the legal, rights-bearing citizen subject as its addressee: "Realism . . . is a mode of cultural production that is tied to the fiction of the social contract" (Prasad 1998: 196). Thus realist cinema is embedded in the imagination of a bourgeois public sphere made up of individual subjects who have a controlled gaze. However, Prasad highlights the constant negotiation between realism and melodrama as social and aesthetic forms in Asia. He notes that the melodramatic mode has persisted and dominated in Asia, unlike "its steady absorption into the realist framework in the West" (2001: 2). The popularity of a film like *Avalude ravukal* points to the conception of a viewing collective whose intimacy with the screen is visceral and unbound. The reference to the pornographic brings in elements of fantasy and pleasure whose meanings cannot be fixed in advance. As Laura Kipnis states, "Pornography begins at the edge of the culture's decorum . . . carefully tracing the edge gives you a detailed blueprint of a culture's anxieties, investments, contradictions" (2006: 120). Kipnis's call is an important one because it asks for a serious engagement with the pornographic, not to dismiss it as "perverse" or "obscene" but to explore it to mine the anxieties and contradictions at work in a cultural context.

Geedha observes that the cinematic form of *Avalude ravukal*, mainly in terms of its cinematography—the frontal portrayal of the heroine's body and the play of looks it triggers—acknowledges the utilization of women's bodies for a commercial purpose: "In *Avalude Ravukal* in every instance when Raji becomes naked in front of the men who buy her for a price, her body that becomes visible on the screen becomes a whiplash on the spectator's mind" (2013: 16). Thus, she argues that this film is more critical of social structures and gender hierarchies than recent films in Malayalam that feature the sex worker as a central character. But my aim is not to argue that *Avalude ravukal* was more progressive than recent representations of the sex worker; the enterprise of evaluating a text in such a way runs the risk of reifying it. I suggest that it is the contrary impulses in the film to expose the body of the heroine for a sexualized gaze and yet tell a realist narrative of suffering and exploitation that makes it useful in throwing light on the processes of the figuration and subjectification of the prostitute in Kerala.

The film fractures the opposition between the realist gaze of the distant spectator and an embodied relationship to the screen because of the intermeshing of scenes of bodily exposure and realist pedagogy. In one of the sequences of the film, the viewer watches Raji strip and pose semi-nude before the schoolmaster. The music is fast-paced and the camera focuses on her cleavage and bare shoulders as she lies down and bites her lips seductively. "I am beautiful, right?" she asks Chandran, the visibly aroused schoolmaster. The camera slowly pans over her naked legs. But when Chandran bends down to touch her, she abruptly changes mode. She abuses him and refuses to have sex with him as revenge for his role in her brother's death. Thus her fragmented body is presented before the viewer even as her angry words deny Chandran's claims to it. The sequence consists of graphic shots of her thighs, legs, and breasts, inter-cut with close-up shots of her face as she asserts that as a prostitute she is using her body to take revenge on the unforgiveable injustice done by Chandran. Here the viewer has to negotiate the contradictory impulses of watching the heroine's body as a sight for consumption and of recognizing her anger and her attempts to wrest control over her body.

The figure of the prostitute, functioning as the dual site of reform and sexual pleasure, point to the larger question about "public affect management vis-à-vis modern mass media" (Mazzarella 2013: 12). Tracking the history of the cinematic medium in India, Rajadhyaksha observes how institutions of social governance from the early years of cinema have noted the social and economic consequences of cinematic "excess" and how "cinematic exchanges trigger off something that can spill over into extra-textual and other social spaces" (2009: 7). He argues that a particular kind of public is produced through celluloid by the twin regulatory mechanisms of containment and excess—containment being a formal requirement for the film frame and a social requirement of the movie theater. While Rajadhyaksha is focused on the unstable public engagement with celluloid, I analyze how negotiations between excess and containment comprise a process through which the formation of the public takes place, and in tracking these tensions I produce a ruptured representational history of sexuality in Kerala.

Policing the Social Body

From popular accounts of the reception of the film at the time of its release in Kerala and outside, it does seem to have been perceived as sexually raunchy and therefore not suitable for a "family audience," a euphemism for women and children. "It All Started With . . . ," Babu Jayakumar's blog entry on the history of soft porn in India, endows *Avalude ravukal* with a forerunner status in establishing soft-porn cinema as a category.[8] He describes in an anecdotal fashion how throughout the seventies and eighties, the "Malayalam movie" gained salacious overtones.[9] His comments on the moviegoing practices associated with sexual films draws attention to the assumed gender segregation at work in film reception in the seventies and eighties: "Malayalam movies had come to denote a stag party, an all-men affair at certain cinema halls that were shunned by women . . . thus starting a new trend in film watching itself. It was the steamy scenes alone that warmed the hearts of men who watched them in the cavernous halls and discussed them at their local tea shops." Film theorists have questioned the assumptions behind such blanket assertions and pointed to how the anxiety over soft-porn cinema in Kerala is grounded in a need to police public morality. Radhakrishnan observes that in film historiography and public judgement, "Soft porn becomes the most visible non-family form of cinema, a kind of cinema that is frequented by (mostly lower class/caste lumpen) men" (2010: 205), and that the urge to control viewing practices is linked to the protectionist attitudes toward the family and the domestic woman anchored within it. Reading the heterogeneous strands of *Avalude ravukal* and its diffuse modes of circulation over a span of time challenges fixed assumptions about the category of soft-porn cinema and its gendered and class-based reception.

Publicity materials such as posters and film reviews have different modes of circulation from the film itself. Elements of the film like the songs and the screenplay can become unmoored from the film and acquire a more respectable status. From the 1990s onward, *Avalude ravukal* has been available in VHS and VCD format. It has been shown on Malayalam television channels, and clips of the film are available on YouTube and on Malayalam cinema websites. The conception of the audience as a body of people who watch a film in the theater was broken even prior to the video, TV, and DVD revolution because a film's publicity is staged primarily outside the theater. The debate around this film suggests a more dispersed realm through which a film circulates, so much so that an "A film" that is meant primarily for a male audience can enter the mindscape of a child or of women. If one takes into consideration the publicity materials and the songs—which includes one that belongs to the most feminine of all genres, the lullaby sung in a maternal voice—then the reasons for its popularity point to the particular modes of circulation of cinema as a heterogeneous medium that can cut across gender and age barriers, even as moviegoing practices may have excluded women from going to a theater to watch an A film.

There is an imagined audience that is projected when censors give this film an A certificate, and a journalist comments, "This was the first time a Malayalam film had a poster like this. The women of Kerala saw the poster, said 'chee' with a slight smile and bend their head in shame. But male desires were inflamed by this poster" (Sreedharan 1999: 2) (figure 1.3). In this statement there is a conjuring up of a social body, consisting of men and women, who should be protected from such a shameful or titillating poster.[10] This anxiety about the affective pull of film posters is played out in the discussion about the poster for *Avalude ravukal*, seen as irredeemable and as the most disgraceful aspect of the film's publicity.

This film creates a debate about representational forms, specifically the links between the visual and print media and the possible responses elicited by these two forms.[11] The preface to the first edition of the screenplay ends with the exhortation that as this screenplay is sure to give reading pleasure to the audience, it be admitted into the realm of "literature." Sreedharan celebrates the powerful dialogues, "the words born in

1.3   The front cover of the 1999
edition of the screenplay of *Avalude
ravukal* that uses the image from the
controversial film poster.

Raji's mouth" (1999: 4), that become a weapon against the inequalities
in society. The distilled verbal contents of the film become the core that
is resurrected in order to claim a new position to the film. Even though
Sreedharan reclaims the film script as a tragic narrative that captured
the "scent of real life" (4), he holds on to his opinion that the poster for
the film was an offensive one. The 1999 edition of the screenplay does
use the controversial shot from the poster as the book cover, but in the
2004 edition, a different shot from the film is used.

Sreedharan does a comparative reading of the film sequence and the
poster depiction of the seduction sequence. In the film Raji comes out
after a bath wearing Babu's white shirt and stands before him, rubbing
a scar on her thigh, saying, "When I jumped the gate, the nail scratched
me." He argues that screenplay places this act within a narrative, while
the poster functions as pure image divorced from the realist appeal of
the film, aiming only at titillation. Thus the screenplay brings *Avalude
ravukal* closer to a realist text to be appreciated by the right kind of audience. The image runs the risk of being appropriated and misused by a
larger public "attracted to the nudity and sexuality of the body being
sold . . . used for satisfying bestial sexual hungers" (Sreedharan 1999: 4).

The theater is marked off as a dark space to which people go on their own volition to watch films, and there are gradations between theaters that are more family-oriented and those that are dominated by men, but the poster that accosts the viewers in public spaces has a ubiquity that is the cause of more anxiety.[12]

Avalude ravukal strategically recalls other instances of cultural production in Kerala that incited debates on what can be the subject matter of art. Raji mentions her fascination for the writing of Vaikom Muhammad Basheer during her first visit to Babu's house, but the more direct link between her life and Basheer's writing is established when the police come to arrest her at Babu's house.[13] In a dramatic turn of events, the police barge into the house in pursuit of her because Babu betrays her and informs the police of her whereabouts; and at that instant she is engrossed in reading Basheer's novella *Shabdangal* (Voices, 1947/2007).

Thematically *Avalude ravukal* claims similarities to *Shabdangal* because they both portray lives from the grimy edges of society.[14] First published in October 1947, after the declaration of Indian independence and prior to the formation of the Kerala state, this novella is a scathing account of a soldier's life experiences in the backdrop of World War II. At the time of publication, *Shabdangal* set out to challenge what the writer perceives to be the meaningless façade of morality. This is the first well-known and highly controversial text in the history of modern Malayalam literature that depicts sexual acts and desires that shatter the mold of heterosexuality. The narrative is in the form of a first-person account of a soldier telling his life story to a writer. It begins with the soldier's feverish pursuit of a prostitute. He is tantalized by her feminine charms, heady with the scent of her body. Intoxicated with desire, he is in the heights of gratification when he embraces and kisses her. Yet in this scene of sexual intercourse there is a sudden shift when he is shocked and mortified to identify the markers of a male body: "I got up and held the breasts. They were bags filled with cotton! . . . bags filled with cotton! I sat there like that . . . hours could have passed. Or else just a few minutes. I removed the breasts slowly along with the bodice. A man's hairy chest. I kept the bodice with the cotton breasts on the bed. Beautiful breasts!" (Basheer 1947/2007: 43).

In spite of his sense of recoil and a series of conflicting emotions—"sympathy, anger, a little fear. A sense of disgust," in the dark blinded by "lust, alcohol and love"—he goes ahead with the sexual act with "she—it—he" (Basheer 1947/2007: 45). In retrospect the soldier regrets his self-degrading behavior; indeed, the whole story is presented as his confession. Though in the causal logic of the narrative the soldier is punished for his transgressive behavior by contracting gonorrhea and syphilis, *Shabdangal* remains a significant intervention in Malayalam on the representational practices of sexuality. The quilted fabric of the narrative compels the reader to enter into a messy realm of unmoored bodies, smeared with the touch, sight, and smell of desire—where disgust and attraction can interpenetrate and coexist in disorienting ways (47). The impetus of the text is not to create boundaries between the licit and illicit, moral and immoral; rather, it is to dislodge the structuring logic of morality itself. The world of fractured subjectivities and broken acts that are cobbled together here do not fit into a project of reform and upliftment. Basheer's edgy and disturbing novella can be placed alongside the experiments by progressive writers such as Manto, who put pressure on the radical discourse by "forcing an unusual engagement with *male* bodies and sexualities" (Gopal 2005: 12). Indeed, scholars such as Geeta Patel (2002) argue that the explicit or "excessive" focus on sexuality became a cause for crisis even in the structuring of the Progressive Writer's Movement, as it gets more established in the 1940s. Authors such as Miraji, Manto, and Chughtai had a difficult relationship with the literary movement because of the ways in which they explored sexuality: "naming a literary piece 'excessively sexual' was a way of devalorizing it as well as labeling it deviant" (103). Within the history of Malayalam literary production, and even within Basheer's oeuvre, *Shabdangal* remains a text that is difficult to categorize and incorporate because of its visceral explorations of sexuality.[15] At the time of publication, the novel was sharply criticized by the high priest of Malayalam literature, Guptan Nair, who regretted that "this book is populated with many wastrels and their fornications. . . . Homosexuality is a serious problem in our society. I feel that to write about it in such a casual fashion is a criminal offence" (1947/1994: 153). Literary battles were staged as critics argued about what liberties representational practices can take under the umbrella of progressive writing.

Avalude ravukal, in telling the life story of a struggling street prostitute, claims to participate in a similar project of documenting the gruesome realities of raw life. The visual reference to *Shabdangal* and the depiction of a reading prostitute immersed in this book are moves that establish the director's realist and literary credentials even as he is crafting a commercial film. This intertextual moment becomes a testimony to the pivotal role of social acts of reading and viewing films in producing the figure of the prostitute. When *Shabdangal* surfaces in *Avalude ravukal*, it functions as a mirroring moment. It draws attention to how circuits of cultural texts that occupy the gray zones between obscenity and realism become the mobile networks for the figuration of the prostitute. The multiple representational codes within these texts and their diffuse trajectories of circulation posit a prostitute figure that disturbs the ordering of the rational public sphere. The dynamic and cross-historical intersections between texts, events, and audience create an unruly network of excess and containment in which sexual figures are located.

The publisher's note for the 1999 edition of *Avalude ravukal* equates this film text to the literary experiments of the Progressive Writer's Movement that challenged the conventions of morality: "Like *Anju Cheetha Kathakal* [Five Bad Stories] in Malayalam literature, in film *Avalude Ravaukal* was described as a 'bad film' when it was released 21 years ago" (Rahim 1999: 1). Originally published in 1946, *Anju cheetha kathakal* (1946/1996) was a highly controversial collection of short stories in Malayalam by well-known progressive writers.[16] The book was banned on the grounds of vulgarity after a few copies were sold and the police sealed the press, People's Bookstall, which published the first edition of the book (Kumarankandath 2013: 180). Through its provocative title, the book is upfront about how it is playing with the sensitive borders between social realism and pornography. *Cheetha* as a term that refers to multiple significations of "bad." It can refer to what is seen as unclean and filthy, the detritus of society.[17] It can also at the same time refer to sexual transgression; a woman outside the sanitized realm of conjugal reproductive sexuality can be referred to as a *cheetha stree* (bad woman), like a "bad apple" that has decayed and should be eliminated from society. The 1996 reprint edition of *Anju cheetha kathakal* came fifty years after the first edition of the book. Its preface recounts the controversy the book had created: "That was a time when morality was given a lot of value. There were unwritten rules that all stories should be moralistic. . . . This book wanted to prove that for human knowledge, all kinds of emotional stories should be told. The editors declared it to be 'bad stories'; only those who liked it needed to buy it" (Varkey 1946/1996: 8).

Stalwarts of Malayalam literature, who feature significantly in the literary canon even today, wrote all five short stories.[18] The gender dynamics of this enterprise is made evident by Thakazhi's comment about the making of this book: "We had initially planned to have six bad stories. The sixth one was to be one of Lalithambika Antharjanam's short stories. That was a time when all six of us were luminaries at the peak of our careers. But we were worried about the controversy that would arise if a Nambudiri [Brahmin] woman wrote in such an anthology and finally gave up on that idea" (Varkey 1946/1996: 1). Thus, for male writers this enterprise was controversial, but to have an upper caste woman participate in this literary act was so risky that she had to be excised from the project entirely.[19] The ambiguous positioning of all these texts in the Malayali cultural realm points to how what is seen as dirty circulates within the public sphere, and the attempts to sanitize and monitor modes of reception are constantly under threat. *Avalude ravukal* is a text that gets labeled as pornography and revisioned as a realist text, but the slippages between these categories are evident in the history of the film's reception and a reading of the film itself. The cultural policing of frames of seeing hinges on the awareness that texts and bodies circulate in a disorderly public sphere, where the boundaries between morality and immorality, the rational and the affective, are shifting and unstable. These slippages in modes of address, textual codes, and practices of reception are also central to documents that are at the core of human rights discourses on the prostitute.

The Afterlife of a Photograph

The aesthetics of realism is central to the viewing practices associated with the human rights discourse, and the prostitute is quite often positioned as an object of sympathy in this discourse. But the trajectory of *Avalude ravukal* shows that the prostitute is an inherently unstable figure whose reception is marked by excess. It is in the cross-section of different forms such as realism, melodrama, and soft-porn that the prostitute as a figure becomes possible in contemporary Kerala. This instability comes to play in a different way in the reportage and memorialization of the custodial death of Kunjeebi in 1987. The violent death of Kunjeebi constituted a founding moment for the feminist movement in Kerala and produced print and visual documents that straddle the thin line between realism and melodrama. The Kunjeebi murder case is reconstructed in the public sphere of Kerala within the rubric of the post-1990s human rights and identity politics discourses on the sex worker. It is within the new imagination of the sex worker, produced through public health and human rights interventions, that differing figures of the prostitute are called back into the post-1990s public sphere. If figures such as Raji have afterlives in public memory as sites/sights of erotic desire and sympathy, then Kunjeebi is embedded in narratives of violation, victimhood, and compassion. The afterlives of the prostitute in the contemporary show how even as there is an attempt to produce the figure of a sex worker squarely within the rights discourse, there are other imaginations that disturb this configuration.

Velutha nizhalukal (White shadows, 2006), a documentary film produced by the members of Vanita Society in Partnership Sex Health Program, a self-help group for sex workers in Calicut supported by Kerala State AIDS Control Society (KSACS), reenacts in a docudrama format the story of Kunjeebi. The actors in the films were also members of the organization. The film opens with the mirror shot of the actress who plays the role of Kunjeebi saying, "By now all of you must have forgotten me." This is an admonition to a public that has an obligation to remember Kunjeebi. They might have forgotten her, and this is a call to remember. The documentary film channels Kunjeebi's spirit to narrate the history of struggling sex workers who have recently mobilized to better their conditions. Her story of denied justice is recast as a tale of martyrdom that animates the current era of collective struggle: "I see how after my martyrdom, you have awakened and organized. I bear witness to all this. I am still here with you, your Kunjeebi." The aim of a film such as *Velutha nizhalukal* is to produce a story of transformation—from the violated prostitute of the past to the politically conscious sex worker of the present. The spirit of Kunjeebi becomes the conduit for such an awakening. The body of Kunjeebi was a site of a significant political agitation in the 1980s itself, but this is not the central focus of the film. How does the violated body of Kunjeebi get reassembled and circulated in the early

2000s when the sex worker emerged as a significant node in AIDS prevention? What do these practices of remembering tell us about the figuration of the sex worker in Kerala?

I recount here the details of the Kunjeebi murder case. A divorced Muslim woman, Kunjeebi did sex work and supported her family. She lived in Bangladesh Colony (now renamed as Santhinagar colony), a poverty-ridden, urban settlement in Calicut. She was arrested on September 7, 1987, and taken to the Vanita police station in Calicut. Paradoxically, since this all-woman police station did not have a lockup room available, she was shifted to the lockup room in the city traffic police station (Ajitha 1987: 13).[20] Her body was found hanging in the police cell by the morning of September 11, 1987. Conflicting accounts by the police and statements by witnesses suggested that her death was the result of police torture, but the police claimed that she had committed suicide. An investigation was ordered due to public pressure and this led to the suspension of the sub-inspector and head constable of the Vanita police station (13). The investigation process conducted by the district collector produced a report that did not indict the policemen involved, and the case was squashed before it could reach the stage of a judicial enquiry.[21]

A newly formed women's group in Calicut, Bodhana (Awareness), took this up as their first case, and they organized a protest movement with sex workers and other residents from the Bangladesh colony under the banner of Kunjeebi Action Committee. Their aim was to expose the brutal police violence that lead to Kunjeebi's death while she was in custody. Sex workers formed a bond of solidarity with feminist groups, and "for the first time in the history of Calicut we organized a rally of hundreds of these women," said the noted feminist activist Ajitha in a conversation with me.[22] She marks September 18 as an important moment—when women who were humiliated and subjugated in society came out into the public space and joined the protest march on Muthalakkulam Maidanam at the center of the city "with their heads held high" (Ajitha 1987: 14). A tenuous link between feminists and sex workers was formed in the late 1980s using the language of rights. "This was our humble attempt to alter the situation where no one asks a question when any violence is done to women on the street," said Ajitha in the interview with me in 2008. She also opined that what had happened in the police cell was rape and murder by state authorities; because of that they

1.4 Protest march by friends and neighbors against Kunjeebi's custodial death. Reproduced with permission from the *Madhyamam* newspaper archive.

managed to get public support on the grounds of human rights violation.[23] Within the rubric of this case, Kunjeebi was presented as a woman who was economically deprived and therefore an easy target for police violence. Her class status as a "woman on the streets" is emphasized in the feminist reconstruction of this case.

When sex workers who were Kunjeebi's contemporaries reminiscence about this event, they say they came out in solidarity because she was a woman like them (figure 1.4). I spoke to a former sex worker who is now part of an NGO that addresses sexual minority rights issues, Federation for Integrated Research on Mental Health (FIRM) in Calicut.[24] She spoke about how it was a clear case of police torture: "We went and saw the body hanging in the police station, with black and blue marks of being kicked on her spine. I was not very brave then. I was very young, but I went out for the public protest against her death. She was one among us." In this recollection of Kunjeebi's death there is a sense of identification between the speaker and Kunjeebi: the interviewee claims Kunjeebi as part of a group to which they all belong. Witnessing the signs of violence on the body and participating in the protest are connected together as acts she did for someone akin to herself. There was also an evocation of how the incident impinged on her life in material ways, for "after this incident in the jail the police would take away our sari and underskirt; we would be left only with our underclothes." The staging of Kunjeebi's death as a suicide using her sari lead to other sex workers being deprived of articles of clothing in the police cell. The routinized impact of this death on the lives of other sex workers and the everydayness of encounters with the police and coercive state structures comes through in these observations. The memory of this staged death is inscribed on their bodies through a stripping of clothes as they continue to inhabit jails—which emerge as an unavoidable space in sex workers' narratives (Jameela 2005a; Shah 2014).

The police system as a coercive form of power operates in producing the figure of the prostitute and the sex worker. Foucault argues that the triangulation of "sovereignty-discipline-government" (1994a: 243) as forms of power that have the population as its primary target have historical continuities, and different modes of governance of a population coexist at a particular point of time.[25] Therefore the practices for embodying the sex worker and the prostitute are not mutually divorced. As we will see in the next chapter, everyday forms of violence and negotiations with the police and punitive structures of the state are crucial to the formation of both the prostitute and the sex worker. The representational tropes and regulatory mechanisms used in the pre-1990s period recur in the post-1990s globalization era, too, and the next chapter explores these interlinkages in more detail.

The media coverage of the Kunjeebi case, mainly through reports in Malayalam newspapers, played a significant role in putting pressure on the political administration and garnering sympathy for the case at that time. There was a renewed interest in the Kunjeebi case in connection with an exhibition of the work of news photographer Choyikutty in the Lalita Kala Academy Hall in Calicut in 2004.[26] The photograph by Choyikutty of the hanging body of Kunjeebi in the prison cell triggered public attention on this occurrence yet again. Choyikutty, in a conversation with me, observed, "If the photograph had not been published, this incident would not have become an event in history." His comment draws attention to the multiple mediations between acts of documentation and memorializing necessary to produce an event, and to the power of the medium of photography.

My conversation with him in February 2009 was in a small, dusty studio in Calicut where he also conducted photography classes for teenagers from Bangladesh Colony. He mentioned that he feels a sense of closeness to Kunjeebi from having recorded her tragic end, a sense of responsibility that troubles him even today. Even after her death, her funeral was marred by difficulties. Her estranged husband and family did not claim her body. Since the police did not provide the necessary documents, the authorities of two Muslim graveyards in Calicut were unwilling to accept Kunjeebi's body (Ajitha 1987: 14). The police were in a hurry to end this controversy, so they cremated her in a public ground with only police and media persons as witnesses. Choyikutty mentioned that Kunjeebi was buried without proper rituals as an "orphaned corpse." This unclaimed status makes him feel that it is essential to produce and circulate documents of her death. The role of a news photographer as a keeper of memories and his relationship to practices of recording vulnerability are posed in Choyikutty's reflections about this iconic photograph.

Kunjeebi's photograph has traveled through time and become a "freeze-frame" (Sontag 2003) in the public memory of Kerala.[27] It is not only the mechanical quality of the photographic medium recording the "reality" of an event but also its affective pull that makes it function as a powerful artifact in the public sphere. This photograph is referred to and republished in all contemporary discussions about the Kunjeebi case. It is the central document of human rights violation, and it also becomes the core around which a moving story of exploitation is narrated.

Figures 1.5 and 1.6 are a series of black-and-white photographs taken by Choyikutty in 1987 of Kunjeebi's lifeless body resting on the bars of the prison door.[28] In the frontal shot, her face and body are vertically fragmented by the bars of the prison against which her body leans. Her face is smudged because of the impression of the prison bar. Her hand dangles through a gap between the prison bars, and it almost seems to jut out of the surface of the photograph. In the second shot, we get a back view of her inert body as the camera is positioned inside the cell. This shot gives the viewer a better sense of the surroundings; we see the prison door, the blackened floor, and also the length of the sari attached to the ceiling. We can see a group of three people, including one policeman, looking at the body; the policeman who is in the foreground is recognizable because of his uniform. As viewers we are placed inside

1.5   Frontal shot of Kunjeebi's death in the police lockup. Photograph by Choyikutty. Reproduced with permission.

1.6   Back shot of Kunjeebi's death in the lockup. Photograph by Choyikutty. Reproduced with permission.

the police cell looking at the dead body from behind and also at the onlookers peering through the bars. The camera's perspective places us behind the dangling body; we see details like the plait of hair, her wristwatch, and the anklets of her feet that hit the floor. We are simultaneously looking at Kunjeebi and at the policeman who is also looking at her body. Thus there is a play of looks triggered within the second photograph, which draws attention to practices of looking itself. How does the spectator distinguish his or her look from that of the policeman—the representative of the state authority held responsible for this death? How does photography work at both an evidentiary and an affective level? What ways does this photograph set up a relationship between death, memory, and politics?

In thinking about the form of the photograph and its lesson for history, Cadava draws on the German philosopher Walter Benjamin's insights about the evocative potential of the medium of photography: "The possibility of the photographic image requires that there be such things as ghosts and phantoms" (1997: 11). The very act of photographing makes us aware of the fact that the subject before the camera is touched by death and the photograph will survive the photographed—that "the photograph is a farewell. It belongs to the afterlife of the photographed" (13). Thus the photographic image harbors within it traces of its own death: "The photograph dies in the photograph because only this way can it be the uncanny tomb of our memory" (11). The disturbing power of a photograph of a corpse, as in this case, may be because it functions as "the living image of a dead thing" (Barthes 1981: 79) and thus has the power to haunt the present and disrupt the linear movement of time. The peculiar force of the photographic medium can also be read in its dichotic relationship with death; it is a frozen moment marked by the sense of what has been and yet can live on and animate the present. The current formation of the sex worker thus becomes imbued with the afterlife of a recorded image of the death of a prostitute. In the fragmented practices of remembering Kunjeebi through a photograph, the edges of the figures of the sex worker and the prostitute become smudged.

On one level these photographs functioned as evidence to counter the police claim that this was a suicide and not a murder. Here, the purportedly objective, mechanical quality of the photographic medium (i.e., its ability to produce a "record of the real" [Sontag 2003: 26]) becomes central. R. Srivatsan observes that one of the effects of the news photograph is that it is seen as providing "solid evidence of truth" (2000: 46) that displaces other less reliable accounts, such as those of word of mouth and print. Detailed attention was paid to the photograph with regard to the positioning of the body so as to determine the cause of death. The fact that her legs hit the floor and the positioning of her hand, as though it was placed on the bar, suggested that this was not a suicide. The scattered alcohol bottles and cigarette stubs on the floor of the prison, seen in the second photograph, also functioned as clues to what happened in the prison cell prior to Kunjeebi's death. The photographic medium's ability to recreate a scene of crime is operational here.[29] But though these photographs have the character of forensic photography, in their circulation in different moments, they have been embedded in narratives of sentiment. Also, unlike crime photography, which is usually used by the state for purposes of regulation and punishment, this photograph was used to expose the injustice and violence of the police itself.

On September 12, 1987, *Madhyamam*, a Malayalam newspaper, first carried the news photograph following Kunjeebi's death. This report titled "Woman dies in the lock-up room: Controversy over the burial" focuses on the circumstances that led to the hasty burial of Kunjeebi's body by the police in a public funeral ground. Eighteen years after her death, this photograph was reproduced in media accounts of the Kunjeebi case, and the visual evidence thus has had an afterlife in public memory. A news report on the photo exhibition by Choyikutty in *Mangalam* newspaper focuses on his controversial pictures of Kunjeebi's death: "When Choyikutty used his camera to capture the picture of Kunjeebi's death, that picture became the first witness for the murder case" (2003). According to V. C. Hareesh's reconstruction of the Kunjeebi case in the newspaper *Kerala Kaumudi*, "Even after Eighteen Years Kunjeebi's Sobs Do Not Cease," Kunjeebi's dead body communicates what she could not say, as "this picture of the dead body leaning against the bars of the prison, will silently speak to you and tell you what happened there the previous night" (Hareesh 2005). The paradoxically "silent voice" that the reporter attributes to the photograph is on one level evidential, but on the other hand it is the animating power of the photograph to reach out to the readers and communicate a powerful story of injustice. There is an affective pull conceded to the photograph that exceeds its function as an image that operates as evidence.

News photography has a pivotal role to play in revealing acts of atrocities and can become the basis of a human rights protest, as in the Kunjeebi case. There is also a long history of sensationalism, tabloid journalism, and photography in India (Gadihoke 2011). Thus, like the televised news footage in the night vigil episode that I discussed in the introductory chapter, this photograph also generates multiple codes of viewing. In fact, the photograph leads to a rights claim by also functioning as a spectacle of suffering and pathos. The scene of violence, the dead body, and the presence of the policeman saturates the photograph with the aura of death, the sense of violence that has been. The complicated responses that the photograph calls forth show how a news photograph may position the viewer in such a way that the realist gaze is disturbed by affective excess. In her reflection on the function of war photographs, Sontag observes, "There are many uses of the innumerable opportunities a modern life supplies for regarding—at a distance, through the medium of photography—other people's pain. Photography of an atrocity may give rise to opposing calls. A call for peace. A cry for revenge. Or simply the bemused awareness, continually restocked by photographic information, that terrible things happen" (2003: 13). The distant, controlled, "bemused" observation of a photograph of an atrocity is one demanded of a realist spectator, a mode of observation in which the photograph does not disturb the spectatorial position.

But in the case of this photograph, the ability to position the viewer in the scene of violent death—the disturbing proximity we see from the perspective within the jail cell—could be what makes the spectator vulnerable. There are many ways in which this affective excess is managed in the framing of this photograph. It is positioned as realistic evidence but also harnessed to a narrative in which the viewer can occupy a position of sympathy. Compassion, as a mode of viewing the "pain of others," can function as a way of stabilizing the viewer's position and creating a modicum of distance from the spectacle of suffering: "In operation compassion is a term denoting privilege: the sufferer is *over there*" (Berlant 2004: 4). Compassion, as Berlant suggests, can work as a way of managing emotional distress so that the spectator can become an ameliorative actor not implicated in the structure of oppression.

"Even after Eighteen Year Kunjeebi's Sobs Do Not Cease," (Hareesh 2005) uses the language of sentimentality to create sympathy in the minds of the reading public toward the prostitute figure. The report starts with an account of how even after eighteen years, some policemen say that they hear Kunjeebi's cries echo from the lockup. The emphasis on her tears and cries shows how the report aims to create a sentimental link between the reader and the image of the prostitute. "When we discuss the pitiable situation of sex workers, one image might appear clearly in some of our minds—Kunjeebi," he writes, setting up Kunjeebi as representative of all sex workers who are helpless victims in need of pity and compassion (Hareesh 2005: 10). It draws a sentimental pageant of Kunjeebi as the loving, all-sacrificing mother, as "some of the older people in the colony can still remember the image of a mother who held her beloved daughter close to her chest, as she showed her the moon and fed her rice" (10). Kunjeebi's arrest and police torture is reconstructed as a tragic narrative of a mother who is torn away from her young daughter, a mother whose "only desire was to bring up her daughter in comfort" (10). Through the trope of destroyed motherhood, Kunjeebi's life story is linked to that of a sex worker in the present who was arrested while she was buying milk for her young child. "The law keepers and the judicial system do not think of the baby crying for milk. When this mother returns, where will this child be?" (10) is the emotional plea in the end of the report.

This image of the prostitute as an object of pity is a repeated trope through which the prostitute is materialized. Thus the human rights discourse, whose addressee must have a controlled gaze that views suffering and responds with an "*average* affect" (Barthes 1981: 26), is fused with the sentimental tropes through which the reader is asked to sympathize with the prostitute figure at a distance. My reading of representational practices point to how the prostitute as the figure of rights and figure of compassion are both produced through incomplete processes of controlling the affective excess of the public eye.

The ideal viewer of *Avalude ravukal*, the distant, contained subject who will sympathize but not be seduced by the erotic scenes, is also not a given in the case of a news photograph that circulates as a document for social justice. Other than functioning as evidence or producing an ameliorative sense of compassion, the photograph may also disturb the spectator's stable positioning through its haunting quality—its power to place the viewer in the scene of death. The photograph functions as a tear, a cut, and a splice—a possible slash in the linear narrative of history. In spite of the different narratives that attempt to stabilize this photograph, it still exceeds these frames, and the inert body of the prostitute raises questions about how we can conceptualize and raise the question of political representation while staring at the face of a violent annihilation of life. This unresolved question about the political subject that emerges at the event of death is further developed in the last two chapters of this book, which focus on memory, mourning, death, and queer politics.

My analysis in this chapter suggests that the challenging task for researchers working on the trajectories of unruly figures is be sensitive to the layers, impressions, and conflicting emotions lingering on the surface of objects, bodies, and spaces. How can practices of research and writing retain the tensions and unresolved movements within texts and documents that we decipher? It is difficult to predict in any exhaustive fashion the possible responses triggered by both *Avalude ravukal* and the Kunjeebi photograph. The excesses in the purview of documentary and filmic realism point to how the process of figuring, tied to practices of print and visual culture, retain a level of instability. The crisis produced by the representations of the prostitute is not countercultural, nor is it in the future. It is a part of cultural practices that unfold in affective publics. In the afterlives of *Avalude ravukal* and the Kunjeebi case, the emphasis is on harnessing these texts and events for a human rights discourse that privileges the aesthetic of realism, which has a distant, sympathetic viewer as its addressee. But a mapping of the circuits of this film and the Kunjeebi case signals to the fractures in the aesthetics of realism. Pulling out these contradictions from the vantage point of the present makes possible the creation of a regional history in which the formations of gender, sexuality, and the public sphere are not rigid and foreclosed.

My analysis in the next chapter will demonstrate that the sex worker's struggle to claim the position of a political subject in the post-1990s cannot be divorced from the longer history of the ways in which the prostitute is rendered legible within the public sphere of Kerala. The sex worker is intimately linked to regional histories of the prostitute, who coheres and scatters within an economy in which she is both a sexualized spectacle and a symbol of exploitation. Thus, chapters 1 and 2 in this book work together to foreground how the permutations of genres such as soft porn, news photography, autobiography, and realist fiction, all centrally concerned with the excess and containment of feminine bodies, function as a canvas to analyze the fraught and compositional practices of the making of the prostitute and the sex worker. The modes of representation in the post-1990s scenario, when the sex worker claims political presence and is recruited in public health programs, have both continuities and differences from the earlier representations of the prostitute. I will now move on to a discussion of the dual autobiographical project by Nalini Jameela in order to examine the modes of subjectification available to a sex worker in post-1990s Kerala. The contradictions in the representational genealogy of the prostitute make it possible for a sex worker to experiment with the form of the autobiography in Kerala. The tangled, shifting linkages between the subject of politics and cultural practices is crucial in the next chapter.

CHAPTER 2

To Claim the Day

The Sex Worker as Subject in the Time of AIDS

THE AUTOBIOGRAPHY BY NALINI JAMEELA WAS ONE OF THE KEY
events that signaled the arrival of a new mode of configuring the sex
worker in India.[1] She published her first autobiography in 2005 and a
second version after a gap of six months. This iconoclastic move of a sex
worker to take on the status of an author in India and demand respect for
her profession made her dual autobiographies the center of media attention. While distancing myself from the rousing reception of Jameela's life
narratives as a radical move and its denouncements by its detractors, I
argue that these acts of self-composition point to how a marginalized
subject has to engage with the state discourse but also critique it in
order to give an account of the self. Jameela's acts of narration that I
analyze in relation to AIDS awareness materials function as a screen
on which I track the fraught trajectories of the sex worker claiming political subjectivity.

The AIDS awareness and prevention machinery played a crucial role
in shaping political mobilizations by sex workers. Since the 1990s sex
workers in Kerala have come together to form collectives to struggle for
their rights. By 1999 sex workers had created an all Kerala network, and
its first state level conference was in 1999 at Trivandrum (Menon 2005).
In this chapter I explore the visual and verbal tropes through which the
state addresses the sex worker within the AIDS discourse in the post-
1990s context. How does the sex worker as a political subject both
deploy and disrupt the new modes of address by the state? Sex workers
experiment with a rich range of visual and literary forms such as short

films, autobiographies, and theater in order to claim political recognition. From crime fiction to documentary cinema, the state deploys popular cultural forms to address the sex worker as part of its AIDS prevention campaigns. The forms of representation used by the state and the sex worker are crucial to my analysis because cultural production is the site in which the contesting discourses on the sex worker emerge.

Anandinte thirodhanam (Anand's disappearance) is a small pedagogic booklet produced by Kerala State AIDS Control Society (KSACS) specifically for categories of people classified as being at "high risk" of contracting and spreading AIDS (KSACS and HLFPPT, n.d.). This booklet is in the form of an illustrated detective story and uses comic strip conventions such as bright watercolor graphics and speech balloons. CID (Criminal Intelligence Department) officer Arjun and his team set out to investigate the suspicious disappearance of a high-profile television serial actor named Anand. The clues lead them to Vimala, a sex worker who had a sexual relationship with him. The climax in the story is when Arjun discovers that Vimala had unprotected sex with Anand. This is the root of all the mayhem that is let loose in the narrative. CID Arjun proves that Anand had absconded because he was HIV positive. Arjun's advice to Vimala, through which the detective aims to restore social order, is to tell her to use condoms even when she is with regular clients. In the crime investigation carried out by Police Inspector Arjun, the criminal act is not that of sex work but of not using a condom. He does not advise Vimala to give up her profession, only to practice safe sex. This sex-education material shows the state's approach toward the commercial sex worker as a population category that needs to be managed in order to guarantee the health of the social body. These modes of address and pedagogic forms are crucial to my analysis.

This chapter begins with an introduction of Jameela's dual autobiographical project and its controversial reception. This is followed by a comparative analysis of pedagogic texts produced for high-risk groups and AIDS campaigns that address the general public to understand the specific mold in which the sex worker is positioned vis-à-vis the state and the family. After giving the reader a complex sense of the figuration of sex worker within the public health machinery, I will return to the processes of subject formation as explored by Nalini Jameela's autobiographical project. Through a close study of the formal and thematic experiments staged through Jameela's self-narratives, I will analyze how the sex worker uses cultural practices in order to "claim the day." I seek to contribute to the ongoing feminist debates on sex work by delineating the tensions within the figure of the sex worker and its relationship to practices of subject formation. My primary focus on the dynamics of visual and verbal forms and their constitutive relation to the production of the sex worker as a political subject sets my work apart from the legal, economic, and sociological studies on sex workers' mobilizations in India.

Stuttered Acts of Self-Composition

I read Nalini Jameela's autobiographical project not as a linear process of voicing but as a series of stuttered acts. We pause when we speak, but a stutter is an unsettling pause where the speaker labors to produce the next word and that effort is made evident. An act of stuttering makes us acutely aware of the mechanics and texture of speech; it dislocates vocalization from any presumption of naturalness or ease. It disrupts the durational rhythm of speech—stretches it or slows it down, creates pregnant silences, half words, and repetitions. I argue that Jameela's reiterated and incomplete project of self-narration produces figurations that disturb the structures of codification of the sex worker precisely because self-narration here is not a smooth process of exposure. The pauses, breaks, and repetitions in this project enable me to engage with the labor of constructing the self. I use the term "stutter" to point toward how projects of self-production undertaken by marginalized subjects creates a sense of torsion and excess in the existing codes of language and representation that gestures toward what cannot be contained within it. Thus the power of Jameela's project is not that it brings to light or breaks the silence about the "reality" of a sex worker but that the rhetoric of these acts of narration have the potential to disturb the lineaments of the present.

Oru laingika thozhilaliyude aathmakatha (The autobiography of a sex worker; Jameela 2005b) by Nalini Jameela was published in June 2005 by D. C. Books, one of the largest publishing firms in Kerala. It was advertised as the first autobiography of a sex worker in Kerala. The first book came out in six editions in one hundred days, and she became well-known in Kerala because of the debates in print and visual media on the controversial book. Media reports labeled the book as a candid, defiant document of "the life of the silenced." She "reveals her sordid story with no trace of compunction. Within 10 days of its release, 2,000 copies flew off the shelves as Keralites lapped up the first autobiography of a sex worker in the country," says a report in the national news magazine *Tehelka* (Ittyipe 2005: 22). The book was packaged as a "burning, spine-chilling"[2] exposé of the life of a sex worker. It garnered massive attention and debate in the regional, national, and international media.[3]

From sexual curiosity to political solidarity, a range of motivations could have contributed to the phenomenal success of this book. The book publicity also focused on how Jameela deviated from the familiar profile of an "author" because of her underprivileged caste, class, and professional status. She grew up with limited means in a working-class family of the non-dominant Ezhava caste. Her formal education ended at the age of nine when she was in the third grade. She worked as a daily wage laborer carrying loads in a tile factory, and then later as a domestic worker, before she became a sex worker at the age of twenty-four. Within the public sphere of Kerala there was a "furious debate" on the book and its unconventional author in which "'inadvertent alliances' between voices from the conservative right and some feminists were formed" (Devika 2007c: vii). Some of the leading Malayalam authors and critics condemned the book as a "prurient money-spinner," and many middle-class feminists attacked the narrative of an unrepentant sex worker who refused to be saved (vii). Other feminist scholars and activists in the regional public sphere, such as J. Devika, A. K. Jayasree, Reshma Bharadwaj, and Dileep Raj, emerged as supportive voices that argued for the need to recognize the significance and complexities of a sex worker's rejection of "dominant Womanhood" (x). Jameela's own involvement in political mobilizations is linked to her participation in AIDS awareness programs since the 1990s. She worked as the coordinator of the Kerala Sex Workers' Forum and was also a member of Jwalamukhi (Volcano), a sex worker's organization. As part of a transnational AIDS awareness program, she visited Thailand and received training in documentary filmmaking. She made two documentary films, *Jwalamukhikal* (A day in the life of a sex worker, 2002) and *Nishabdaraakapettavarilekoru ethinottam* (A peep into the silenced, 2003), before her autobiography pushed her into the limelight at a regional and national level.

Six months after the publication of her first book in December 2005, Jameela brought out a second version of her life story, *Njan laingika thozhilali: Nalini Jameelayude aathmakatha* (Me sex worker: The autobiography of Nalini Jameela; Jameela 2005a). This was not merely a revised edition; she stated that the second book was the more reliable account of her life. There are multiple shifts in the voice and choreography of the events from the first autobiography to the second. As the title, *The Autobiography of a Sex Worker*, suggests, the first book presents itself as the autobiography of a representative sex worker; the emphasis is more on the identity of the sex worker than the individual subject, Nalini Jameela. But in the latter, the "me" as sex worker acquires prominence, and Jameela's name appears in the title itself. The book's covers also capture this difference.

As seen in figure 2.1, the first autobiography has a closeup shot of Nalini Jameela's face in a horizontal position on its front cover. We see her hand held close to her face and the pink blouse that covers the upper part of the body. The back cover shows her hand spread out on a mattress sprinkled with fragrant jasmine flowers, associated with the scene of sex. Reclining, she holds our gaze from the bed and promises to tell us a story of her profession. In the second book cover we have a closeup shot of half her face in a vertical position, and there are scribbled letters etched all over the page (figure 2.2). There is no explicit suggestion here of her profession; rather, what is foregrounded is the act of writing itself. The running lines of letters form a layer over her face, thus merging her interiority with the act of narrating.

"This autobiography writing is part of the many experiments I have undertaken. You shouldn't hope that all the memories of one person can be presented in one biography," writes Jameela (2005a: 3) in the introduction to *The Autobiography of Nalini Jameela*, anticipating the criticism about her decision to narrate her life a second time. The revisioning of her life narrative was an unprecedented move not undertaken by many writers.[4] Both these books were the result of collaborative work. She wrote the first book using longtime associate I. Gopinath as an amanuensis. The publication details of the first version (*Oru*) mentions that the book is "Nalini Jameela's autobiography retold by Gopinath" (Jameela 2005b). Her dissatisfaction with the first collaboration made her publish a second autobiography: "I wanted to write this version of my autobiography in a hurry, to remedy the damage caused by the first, inadequate draft that

ഒരു
ലൈംഗിക
തൊഴിലാളിയുടെ
ആത്മകഥ
നളിനി ജമീല

2.1 Cover image of Jameela's
first book. Reproduced with
permission from D.C. Books.

was published. I was so concerned about reclaiming my autobiography"
(Devika 2007b: 142). The second book was written with the participation
of a group of young activist and academic friends, with whom Jameela
says she shared a "very equal relationship" (143). In the first version,
Gopinath's voice plays a prominent role, in both introducing Nalini
Jameela through his preface to the book and imposing his frames of
viewing sex work onto her narrative. The collaborators' presence is not
intrusive in the second version, and their names do not appear in the
publication details. In an interview with Devika included as part of the
English translation of her autobiography, Jameela reflects on the process of rewriting her autobiography with the participation of N. Baiju,
Shaju V. V, Shameena P. V., Reshma Bharadwaj, S. Sanjeev, and Dileep Raj:
"I could express myself in my own style with them and they worked as a
group, which was very good for me, since their many questions reacti-
vated my memories and allowed me to tell a good story. This wasn't the
case with the first version. The person who worked with me didn't encourage the participation of others—it was only his effort that counted. And
I hardly ever participated in shaping the story" (143).

2.2 Cover image of Jameela's second book. Reproduced with permission from D.C. Books.

One of the main concerns in the reception of Jameela's books in Kerala has been around the differences in these two versions. The domineering presence of the scribe I. Gopinath in the first book—through his rendering of Nalini Jameela's life as a "liberated" sex worker and his attempts to achieve "a seamless unity between her life and the Sex Workers' Forum's political statements" by appending a pamphlet published by the Sex Workers' Forum in 2003 to her life narrative—was critiqued by interlocutors such as Devika (2006: 1681). In the first autobiography, the sex worker is positioned against "the feminist," who is branded as regressive by Gopinath, who writes, "Feminists who do not analyze in depth this sexually starved society and write many pages against men will not understand Nalini. We should walk a lot more to catch up with Nalini" (2005: 2). Gopinath's self-positioning as Jameela's "progressive" supporter, and the jabs and caricatures targeting feminism, are absent in the second book. Scholars argue that Jameela demonstrated not only her desire for a more complex rendering of her life in her decision to produce a different version, but also her struggle to resist the collapsing of her life with a liberal manifesto on sex work (Devika 2007c: xiii).

In spite of Nalini Jameela's withdrawal of the first version of her auto-biography, I still draw on it because I argue that these two books form a chain of events that points to the intricacies and labor of the process of marginalized subjects claiming the public sphere. Since the second auto-biography was translated into English, it has received more critical attention than the first one. Moving away from the dominant trend to dismiss the first autobiography and focus only on the second one, I examine both these texts as mediated sites through which a sex worker claims a subject position. When a marginalized subject takes on the task of tracking the trajectory of her subject formation, it is not a quick move-ment of claiming the public sphere or "baring it all." She has to struggle to find narrative forms to tell her fragmented story, which is not tailored to the conventional form of the autobiography. Since the "auto" or the "I" she sets out to plot is not contained or stable, the form of the autobiogra-phy stutters here; it is reconfigured and pulls at its own seams as she tells and retells her story. But this literary form does seem to provide her with a space for self-exploration unavailable in the human rights discourse or public health discourse. Hence, it is important to read both these texts as part of an ongoing and incomplete political exercise and place them in juxtaposition to state-endorsed representations of the sex worker pro-duced by the AIDS discourse. I seek to see how a "literary work *can* differ from the official narratives thereby interrogating them" because of "the different emphases it provides in the representation of a subject" (De Mel 2007: 203). Jameela's experiments in self-narration make the reader con-front the central problematic of subjectivity and representation; the stag-ing of the stuttered acts of self-making interrupts neat narratives of the "empowered" sex worker that emerges in the state discourse.

Framing the "Sex Worker"

Instead of the scattered and diffuse group of people who existed within the gray areas of state policy and legality, the sex worker is produced by the AIDS discourse as a hypervisible population category, a central node in the management of AIDS. Recent studies examine how the sex worker emerges as a nodal site of intervention in the era of the global HIV/AIDs pandemic (Sahni, Shankar, and Apte 2008).[5] The commercial sex worker (CSW), normed as female, though there is a limited recognition of male sex workers, is perceived as the primary nodes of AIDS prevention and control in India.[6] In fact the change in terminology from "prostitute" to "sex worker" is linked to the AIDS discourse and rights-based mobilizations by sex workers. This is through the formation of collectives and organizations, such as the Sex Workers' Forum in Kerala, after a series of public meetings in 1999 and 2000.[7]

Nalini Jameela's narratives intervene in the ongoing debates on sex work in India. Dominant feminist groups in Kerala see prostitution as a symbol of commodification of women's bodies, especially in the context of Kerala's increasing investment in tourism. Significant interventions from a Dalit feminist standpoint have pointed to the risks of legitimizing sex work and sexualized forms of entertainment because of the entrenched construction of Dalit women's bodies as sexually available (Rege 1995). Scholars have argued that forms of sexual labor and constraints to social mobility in India can be addressed only by engaging with the complex permutations of caste, gender, and sexuality (Patil 2014; Christy 2017).[8] In Kerala, sex workers' groups and their supporters have articulated the need to arrive at a complex understanding of the positioning of sex workers and their fraught relationship to domesticity and structures of governance. An important interlocutor of the sexuality movement in Kerala, A. K. Jayasree argues, "A paradigm shift is necessary to address the problems of sex-workers delinked from the problem of sexual morality. . . . Their right to enjoy bodily pleasure and to self-determination should also be valued" (2004: 66).

Several scholars have examined the mobilization and formation of unions and collectives by sex workers since 1990s in India and the ethical and political challenges posed by these struggles (Ghosh 2005; Kotiswaran 2011b; Shah 2014). Kotiswaran (2011a: 238) analyzes the combination of demands for both recognition and redistribution that is articulated in the sex worker's movement. The documents produced by the Sex Workers' Forum, Kerala—"Some Questions-Some Answers on Sex Work" (written in May 1999) and "100 Questions" (displayed at the Festival of Pleasure, organized by the NNSW in Trivandrum, Kerala, in March 2003)[9]—point to the key motives of sex worker's collectivization: recognizing sex work as work, combating criminalization and police violence, questioning the moral stigma of sex work, addressing economic inequality, and demanding better access to resources. The AIDS discourse and the interlinked mobilizations on sex work create new forums where sex workers come into contact with social workers, academics, journalists, and media persons in different regional contexts. The process of writing in partnership locates Jameela's autobiographical project in the landscape of post-1990s structures of state, development, and activism.

Condom Teachers: Sex Workers in the AIDS Umbrella

Jameela's negotiated process of producing a life narrative had many faltered beginnings. She reflects on how, although she spoke about her life incessantly, it was difficult for her to write it down: "Though I tried many times to write, it would not progress beyond a few sentences" (Jameela 2005b: 1). When one partnership did not produce satisfying results, she would move on to find an alliance with a group of activists who could capture her style of narrative more scrupulously. Collaborative textual productions, in which Jameela retains author status in spite of all these mediations, are possible within the new visibility of the sex worker and the alliances between sex workers and other actors in civil society. This happens through political meetings, cultural events, and rallies organized by sex worker's groups and through conventions of solidarity building such as the World Social Forum, conducted under the aegis of global NGO networks. I am not suggesting that this is an easy process and that in the current economy a sex worker is in a position of control where she can pick and choose collaborators. Her first collaboration placed her in a vulnerable position, and her visibility in the public sphere had multiple risks.

The claims for recognition by sex workers in Kerala must be placed in regimes of governance in which they are primarily positioned as "targets" to be managed in a cost-effective manner. As part of my research, in 2008 I went to *suraksha* (safety) centers,[10] such as the Vanita Society Suraksha Center, a state-supported organization that works with "high-risk" groups, which had a prominent chart on the wall that said "Target Group: Sex Workers" in the first column, and went on in the next column, "Number of people who are counted as part of the target group: 1717." The chart had numerical counts for the number of people in the target group who had been made aware of safe-sex practices and for the number of condoms distributed in different areas within Kozhikode district. These charts are compulsory fixtures in all the *suraksha* centers in Kerala. Thus there is a process of identification and statistical enumeration through which the category of the sex worker is consolidated within AIDS interventions. Employees in these organizations describe one of their preliminary jobs as "site assessment," where they go to public areas like bus stops, railway stations, markets, beaches, and theaters to identify sex workers and also to improvise methods of tallying a count for condom usage. Focusing on sex workers and the state in West Bengal, Swati Ghosh examines what she calls a "watch-care system" in which the prostitutes are included within the "purview of the paternalistic state" (2005: 55). Jameela's narratives give us access to the negotiations of the sex worker as a subject located within these structures of governance.

The impact of the AIDS discourse is especially significant in Kerala, a state that has no brothel system and therefore no spatially marked-out zones for sex work, unlike other states such as Maharashtra or West Bengal.[11] Many sex workers in Kerala solicit and work in public spaces like the streets, lodges, hotels, bus stations, and theaters. A. K. Jayasree (2004) says there are three main categories of sex workers in Kerala. The first are street sex workers who lack access to stable living spaces and solicit on the street. The second have their own homes and solicit in hotels or lodges. The third are called "family girls" because they entertain clients at their own homes with or without the help of agents (59). These are not neat categories; many women navigate differing conditions of doing sex work at different phases of their lives. Many marginalized women also move from different jobs in the unorganized labor sector, and the dividing line between sex work and more "'dignified work'—like domestic work" is very thin (Devika 2007b: 139).

AIDS control programs have played a significant role in the developmental rhetoric of Kerala since the 1990s. In their anthology on disease prevention interventions in different global contexts, Stacey Pigg and Vincanne Adams (2005:15) argue that efforts at sexual reform and intervention are linked to national and local projects of development. They observe how in the biological terrain central to new technologies of governance, "'health' and 'life' become nodes of control, dominion and erasure" (15). Foucault (1994: 207) makes the highly influential hypothesis that as neoliberalism seeks to extend the rationality of the market and its methods of operation to areas that are not primarily or exclusively economic, such as the family and birth policies, the mode of governing human behavior is that of managing populations for strategic, economically, effective ends. His interrelated conceptualizations of governmentality and biopower refer to government as tactics of management of a population, not for the "common good" (237) but for directing the flow of population into certain activities through mass campaigns "without the full awareness of people" (241). Partha Chatterjee observes how in the Indian context, "The postcolonial state deployed the latest governmental technologies to promote the well-being of their populations, often prompted and aided by international agencies and NGOs" (2004: 37). The sex worker as a target of governance emerges in a neoliberal economy in which governmental technologies are used by the state to manage population categories through "instrumental notions of costs and benefits" (34).

The deployment of the sex worker as a conduit for defending the social body from AIDS has placed a demand on the sex worker to be an actor within state programs. Sex workers are deployed to spread awareness about the need to use condoms, and "since spreading awareness about condom usage was their main activity they began to be known as condom teachers" (Jameela 2005b: 93). The sex worker is given the function of a participant and not just a target in AIDS awareness programs through the role of the peer educator.[12] In AIDS prevention interventions, especially in phase 2 of the National AIDS Control Program, which extended from 1999 to 2007, one of the important strategies has been targeted intervention through peer educators.[13] In Kerala, peer educators are used to identify other sex workers to spread awareness about safe-sex practices, to keep track of the changes within the community of sex workers, and to provide them with necessary services.[14]

AIDS awareness programs in Kerala are now at an advanced stage and have a dynamic history behind them. Sharmila Sreekumar observes that AIDS was a symbol of a civilizational crisis in the early phase of the spread of the disease in the late 1980s and early 1990s (Sreekumar 2009: 169). She argues that the sex worker is positioned as the "other" of the monogamous woman victim in popular representations of AIDS such as cartoons and advertisements that were produced in this period. The sex worker in this early phase of AIDS control is projected as "not merely the carrier of an irreversible destruction, but destruction itself" (169). In the 1990s, the sex worker was kept out of the sympathy-generating space of

AIDS awareness advertisements, "neither are they brought into their visual spaces or given speaking parts—not even an ambivalent, third person, auto/biographical speaking part" (171). But this mass panic around AIDS and the corresponding characterization of the sex worker as a figure of doom and destruction shifted after the first decade of AIDS management. After 2000 and the introduction of antiretroviral therapy, the emphasis has been more on AIDS as a manageable disease and the sex worker as a partner in state campaigns of AIDS control.[15] In the post-2000 materials produced by KSACS, there is a conscious attempt to locate the sex worker in her familial setting and call upon her to take responsibility for a better future. In contrast to the 1990s demonization of the sex worker, in current narratives produced by the state, the sex worker is framed through the language of agency and empowerment.[16] The cooperation of sex workers with AIDS awareness programs also comes with the promise of other benefits, such as help with starting a bank account or acquiring a ration card, and thus offers sex workers access to the institutions of the state such as banks, hospitals, and public welfare.

AIDS Awareness Materials: Addressing the Sex Worker

There are different pedagogical tools produced by KSACS that use mass media forms to configure and address the sex worker. KSACS produces educational materials that include games, playing cards, comic books, pamphlets, and documentary films that can be used by NGOs to spread AIDS awareness among high-risk groups. These materials are produced specifically for "those who benefit from the sexual health projects of the state" (Oomji et al. 2005: 1) and are the target of the state-run *suraksha* projects. They are markedly different from pedagogic tools that address the general public. These materials do not circulate profusely in public media networks such as television, radio, newspapers, billboards, or posters in crowded public spaces—the primary modes through which the general public is inundated with AIDS messages. Many of these materials have shared formats in national and international contexts, but there are increasing attempts to tailor them to local needs.

The head of the media and outreach section of KSACS, Ajai Kumar, spoke to me in January 2008 about the use of accessible language and the attention to the modes of representation as an important strategy for making AIDS a less stigmatized disease. He drew attention to the "imaginative and people friendly" naming of the different projects run by KSACS: Sneha: Snehathinte Thoovalsparsham (Love: The Feather Touch of Love), centers that prevent mother to child transmission, and Thanal (Shade), counseling and support centers for HIV-positive individuals. One of the doctors who worked as a project coordinator with KSACS explained how they shifted from clinical names to more *painkili* terms to add to popular appeal.[17] Ajai Kumar also mentioned that since local contexts are different from national ones, there is an attempt to "Keralise things." Many of the campaign materials draw on tropes of Malayalam cinema and use popular literary forms, such as detective fiction, to spread the message through modes that appeal to the public.

A pedagogic board game conceptualized and produced by an organization associated with KSACS, Partners for Better Health, for the education of male and female sex workers, is a useful tool for demonstrating the manner in which the sex worker is addressed in the AIDS discourse. The format of the game marks a distance from pre-1990s models of state pedagogy and public health mechanisms. There is a sharp distance in the positioning of the recipient in pamphlets and posters of health education used until the 1990s and the new methods used by KSACS. The pre-1990s public health campaigns had a sloganeering format in which information was given to the audience in a direct, top-down, pedagogic fashion. Even today, some of the public health campaigns on family planning deploy the same format of direct message transmission. The board game, in contrast, is an interactive tool of pedagogy in which the sex workers have to be participants in their own edification.[18] The philosophy of peer education is embodied in this game too. It is a community activity where the player interacts with other sex workers, and the board comes alive and acquires meaning only if the participants are ready to throw the dice and participate in the rules of the game. This is education that is also recreational; it is premised on the belief that the better learner is the one who actively participates in the process of education, in keeping with the global developmental agenda of women as "both agents and beneficiaries of development" (British Official Development Assistance, quoted in Eyben 2007: 73).[19]

Four people can play the board game at the same time, and the throw of the dice determines what column the player has to move to. The game is in the model of the popular children's board game Snakes and Ladders (Chutes and Ladders), but instead of the emblems of snakes and ladders that in the typical version of the game determine the progression of the player, here winning or losing the game is determined by the player's sexual practices (figure 2.3). The colorful board has square columns numbered from one to one hundred. At regular intervals the columns have sketches and messages about safe and unsafe sexual practices that determine the fate of the player. For example, the fourth column has an image of a man in the center hugging two naked women, with the words "you had sexual intercourse with more than one partner without using a condom, go back to square one."[20] This is a pedagogic tool for educating sex workers and other high-risk groups on safe health practices,

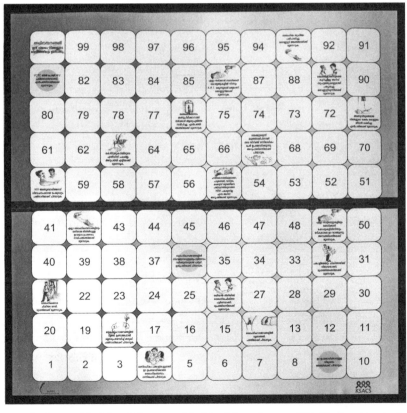

2.3   Snakes and Ladders (Chutes and Ladders) board game: KSACS education tool for "high-risk" groups (2007).

and for motivating them to take responsibility for their own safety and well-being.

The images in five columns are about signs of medical problems that need immediate medical attention. Showing symptoms of a sexually transmitted infection (STI) or not taking steps to get treatment immediately puts the player at a disadvantage: "Pus and swelling on your sexual organs that causes discoloration and emits a foul smell, go back to column twenty." The language here is stark and direct. Sexual organs of the male and female body are sketched in direct terms, visually and verbally. There are close shots of male and female sexual organs that shows signs of infection, as in column fourteen. The players of this game are primarily addressed as owners of their susceptible bodies and reminded at every throw of the dice that their choices regarding their health care and sexual practices will determine their progress not just in the game but in life, too. The last column of the game spells out this connection explicitly: "Congratulations! Replicate this success in your life too." Unlike the posters and campaigns that address the general public, there is directness in the sexual references here. Through pedagogic tools such as this board game, the sex worker is addressed as a risk-prone body, and it is within this framework that the sex worker acquires a shape and form in the AIDS discourse. By inviting sex workers into the ambit of a game in which safer sex practices "becomes the hand through which one gambles with death" (Patel 2016: 319), the board game links investment and risk-assessment as central to the technologies of subjectification.

Geeta Patel argues that the "techno-intimacies" at work in the making of subjects who are the conduits of safe-sex practices point to the production of personhood that is ensconced in embodied conceptions of "risk, loss, compensation" (2016: 318). The language of finance and insurance through terms such as "risk protection" seeps into the sinew of everyday living and bodily transactions: "Financial technologies are absorbed into the business of living. Life becomes about risk, credit, and equity (life-finance), even as those terms appear to belong to another order (capital)" (319). The modes of address and codes of representation in the documentary films that I will now analyze also point to how the production of the sex worker is enmeshed with the language of risk, loss, investment, and compensation.

Two documentary films produced for KSACS by Invis Multimedia, *Nanmakkayi* (For your well-being, 2006) and *Thiricharivinte koottay-makkayi* (For a collective through realization, 2006), reflect the maxim of progress through self-sufficiency and encourage sex workers to protect themselves and work for the well-being of the community. Outreach officers at NGOs mentioned that the documentaries were popular among sex workers because of their emotional appeal. *For Your Well-Being* tells the story of a young sex worker, Ramani, and her transition from risky sexual behavior to safe-sex practices. The film's opening shot is a close-up of Ramani's face as she dresses up in front of the mirror. Her young daughter watches her, and Ramani fondly pats her cheek as she steps out of the house. At the doorstep Ramani faces the camera and says, "I am Ramani. I am a sex worker like you. I am a little busy right now." The direct address, the conversational tone, and the bestowal of interiority through the closeup mirror shot establish audience identification with Ramani from the beginning. The voiceover in the film aims at creating a connection with the spectator: "Ramani is one among us, our vocation relies on our beauty and health. Let us take care of that." The film shows the sex worker in the role of a peer educator in Ramani's interactions with an older sex worker who learns about AIDS testing centers in the state and the necessity of practicing safe sex. But the film also positions Ramani as a peer educator whose journey into knowledge will enlighten the viewing community.

The film has a melodramatic and sentimental tone. It sets up Ramani as a suffering, single mother who is the "sole support for her aging mother, who has collapsed in the path of life, and her young daughter, who she loves more than her life." The dialogues are saturated with hyperbolic tropes about motherly love, and emotional mother-daughter scenes are staged with lilting background music. When Ramani resists an older woman's advice to go to a testing center, she warns her, "There will be no one to take care of your daughter if you get sick." This emotional appeal to her motherhood motivates Ramani to visit an AIDS testing center. The film's opening title says *"For Your Well-Being . . .* My safety, is my family's safety." Thus the film places the sex worker as a woman whose commitments to her family forces her to do sex work and foregrounds the need for her to adopt safe-sex practices so that she can fulfill these responsibilities. Ramani is also advised to take her partners to the testing centers, because if they have an STI she may get infected again. Thus the sex worker is addressed as an individual agent who should take primary responsibility for the well-being of herself, her family, and the social body.

The documentary film *For a Collective through Realization* captures this state-sponsored recasting of political problems raised by the sex workers in order to provide a developmental solution. This film is a celebratory account of one woman's empowerment as she becomes a member of Vanita Sahakarana Society (Women's Cooperative Society), a community-based organization (CBO) run by sex workers with the support of the state. The film shows us the trajectory of a sex worker, Geetha, who is arrested by the police, but the society bails her out and she becomes a new member in the organization. From then on we see an awestruck Geetha being introduced to this new world of progress through self-empowerment. She is advised to take regular medical tests and practice safe sex in the familiar AIDS awareness paradigm. But she is also taught how to start a bank account and save money. We see her navigating an urbanizing cityscape of Kerala, where the camera pans from billboards of nationalized banks like State Bank of Travancore to privatized, global banks such as HSBC. The music is upbeat and jazzy as she is warmly welcomed in institutions of modernity like the bank and the hospital. There are repeated shots of successful enterprises run by sex workers, which include a tea shop, handicrafts unit, laundry service center, garbage clearing services, and tailoring center. All these jobs are traditionally feminine occupations that bank on domestic skills of cooking, cleaning, and sewing, in keeping with Desai's (2002: 32) observation that economic restructuring through globalization uses existing patriarchal assumptions about women's labor and endurance abilities. When Geetha is suitably impressed with all these venues of successful entrepreneurship, her friend, who is a longtime member of the cooperative society, smiles and says, "You have no clue what other things are in store for you to see." In this tantalizing journey of progress, the possibilities are endless and presented as easily within the reach of this new entrant. If she follows the instructions given to her, she can continue to be a sex worker but also access all these supplementary economic resources.

The film spends limited screen time showing Geetha's interactions with her clients or her life as a sex worker. The only reference to this activity is to show her buying Kamasutra, a popular brand of condoms, after she decks her hair with jasmine flowers in preparation for doing sex work. There are repeated shots of women doing other forms of work, but the film only refers to sex work and never visualizes it. Geetha's journey to civic participation and economic empowerment is tied more to her supplementary economic activities, which have societal acceptance. By downplaying the complexities of doing sex work and the social stigma associated with that job, the film posits Geetha as a beneficiary of development; her journey to progress is devoid of any confrontations. This film puts forward the utopic promise of progress through the effort of a community of sex workers, made up of individual members who willingly subject themselves to norms of safe-sex behavior and economic productivity. This form of individual self-disciplining and "efficiency" is the crux of the market-oriented logic of development.

The final sequence of the film is a close-up shot of lush, green grass lit up by beams of sunlight. This pastoral shot is cut to a smiling Geetha sitting on the doorstep of her new house, and she exclaims, "Because I luckily reached a CBO, I am able to work and fend for myself without depending on anyone else. . . . This house is now my own. I am happy today." Geetha is a satisfied, docile beneficiary of state reforms. Her life story spreads the message of safe sex, but here we have a sex worker who does not challenge the normalized vision of the monogamous reproductive family. In a society where the domestic woman ensconced within conjugality has a privileged position and any other sexual arrangement is met with violent disapproval, this film accommodates Geetha by casting her primarily as an economic agent and a safe-sex practitioner. The gaping black hole in the film is that, though it is addressed to sex workers, it does not analyze the liminal position of sex workers within the social. It does not recognize their demands for social acceptance, which disrupts the arrangement of female sexuality as contained within the conjugal reproductive unit. In both these films, the anchoring voices are those of individual sex workers whose stories become exemplary narratives for other sex workers to follow. Thus there is an active attempt on the part of the state to facilitate identification with these ideal sex-worker protagonists. In light of the analysis of a sex worker's autobiographies that I undertake later in the chapter, it is important to note that the state aims to govern the subject formation of sex workers through these interpersonal modes of address.

Questioning the Familiar/ Familial

The structure of the family and the figure of the domestic woman is deployed and reworked in discourses on AIDS and sex work. In 2007–2008 the National AIDS Control Organization (NACO) engineered and executed a massive and innovative plan to spread AIDS awareness messages all throughout India. This was through the Red Ribbon Express, a specially designed, seven-coach train that traveled across 180 stations in India carrying HIV/AIDS prevention messages through the course of the year. This was described as an innovative national campaign to link HIV/AIDS into the mainstream of socioeconomic development, "an umbrella exercise to involve, inform and incorporate the people into a genuine mass movement against the disease"[21] The train was a mobile education and exhibition center that used high-tech devices like interactive touch screens and 3-D models to give the visitor a clear view of HIV/AIDS transmission and prevention.

On July 8, 2008, I went to the railway station in Calicut, Kerala, to see the exhibition in the train and the public reception of the Red Ribbon Express. When I reached the platform, I had to join a queue of almost three hundred people waiting to get on the train. It was a mixed crowd, men and women who cut across different age groups and class strata. There was a long, well-ordered queue of senior-level school children in uniforms, brought in en masse from school. This national-level pedagogic mission used new high-tech modes of communication technology coupled with the railway system—the latter being one of the foundational networks of India's entry into colonial modernity. The colorful awareness posters, vending units for Moods condoms (a popular brand), well-lit 3-D installations, and informational short films screened in the train were all aesthetically appealing and glossily packaged. The direct focus on disease prevention in the board game for use by sex workers was absent in the pedagogical tools for the general public.

The framework of the family as the foundation of a healthy nation was a repeated trope in many posters. For example, one poster showed the picture of a working-class family featuring the parents and two children, a girl and a boy. All of them pose in a stiff manner and smile at the viewers. The woman is dressed in a traditionally auspicious red sari, a sign of her marital status, with the tip of the sari demurely covering her head.[22] A blue sky and a green field form the backdrop to this well-arranged family photograph, and the inscription says, "A healthy Bharat begins from a healthy family: from all of you, from all of us."

This sex education through sanitized and beautified language and images that appeals to a large cross section of the public, including school-children, is a markedly different enterprise from the materials for high-risk groups. The modes of address used in both these campaigns are distinctive, yet they share some common ground. Both aim at creating a collective that will help the progress of the nation. "Come let us surge ahead together," says another poster in the Red Ribbon Express, and the appeal is both to the nation as a family and to the separate familial units that comprise it. With the sex worker, too, this trope of familial welfare is used, as in the case of *For Your Well-Being*, but there is an omission of how the recognition of the sex worker might question the arrangement of the normative family and thus the foundation of the nation. The sex worker's world as shown in *For Your Well-Being* is a self-contained one, and there is little overlap in the positioning of the sex worker and the domestic woman.

In sharp contrast, the autobiographies by Jameela disruptively yoke together the sex worker and the domestic woman. Her narratives question the arrangements of sexuality in which the monogamous wife is glorified as the anchor of the family, the foundation of the nation and region. In an interview with Devika in the English translation of her book, Jameela complicates the binary between the domestic woman and the sex worker, noting, "I look after my family, I also do social work, and when in financial need, as someone in my situation often is, I do sex work" (Devika 2007b: 140). She foregrounds her identity as wife and mother and shows how sex work becomes essential to support her family. Thus Devika notes how Jameela writes an "elaborate domestic" into the narrative of the life of a "public woman" (2007c: x). Important turning points in Jameela's narrative are structured by the needs of her family, especially her children. She enters into sex work to support her children after the death of her first husband, and later she goes back to sex work after a gap of almost a decade when her third marriage falls apart and she has to take care of herself and her young daughter.

The acknowledgement of how the sex worker often has responsibilities to the family, especially her children, is part of the new address through which the state speaks to the sex worker. My discussion of the documentary *For Your Well-Being* captures this emotional appeal to the sex worker as a primary caregiver and earning supporter of her child and aging mother. Though the sex worker is encouraged to take on domestic responsibility, she does not in any way critically comment upon the unequal structures of the patriarchal family. Jameela, on the other hand, pries apart the binary between the sex worker and wife/mother by showing the similarities between the domestic realm and the sphere of her work. When her friend introduces her to sex work after her first husband's death and explains the nature of the work, Jameela observes, "When my friend said I have to go with men who needed women, I understood these men wanted to *use* women like husbands used their wives" (2005a: 29). Here it is through the terms of sexual exchange within conjugality that Jameela understands the structure of sex work. She often notes the similarity between the domineering behavior of clients and husbands: "Those days clients had the behavior of husbands. We couldn't ask them anything, but they wanted to know everything about us. And if they did deign to say something then the attempt would be to prove how they are so above us" (39). She also contrasts the sexual and physical violence in her first marriage to the more satisfying sexual and emotional bonds that she develops with some of her clients. Nalini Jameela has also recently published her third book, *Romantic Encounters of a Sex Worker* (2018), a memoir that captures her relationships with her clients, which is beyond the scope of analysis of this chapter.

In the opening chapter of the first autobiography, "The Manifesto of a Sex Worker," she argues, "A sex worker is much freer than an ordinary housewife in Kerala. . . . During night-time and even during day-time who else can walk with some amount of security on the streets of Kerala? (Maybe women who wear the veil can do it)" (Jameela 2005b: 15). Here she challenges assumptions about the domestic women's protected status in society and exposes the entrenched forms of curtailment of women's mobility. Her rhetorical aim is to dismantle the assumption that the domestic, upper-caste Hindu woman, who is the "Kerala woman,"[23] is more liberated than the "other woman." She draws a list of the relative freedoms sex workers have in comparison to the housewife: "Sex workers are free in four respects. We don't have to cook for a husband; we don't have to wash his dirty clothes; we don't have to ask permission to raise our kids as we deem fit; we don't have to run after a husband claiming rights to his property" (109). Kotiswaran argues that the destabilizing potential of political articulations by sex workers lies in the fact that "their demand for recognition is not framed in terms of an authentic sex worker identity but is deconstructionist in that it challenges the institution of marriage" (2011a: 239). Nalini Jameela's statements have a prominent role in Kotiswaran's analysis of how sex workers place their work in relation to other forms of female reproductive labor—in the realm of domesticity and the unorganized sector—and of the structural inequalities that cut across these spheres (216). While scholars have analyzed the challenging propositions in Jameela's narratives, I draw attention to the formal strategies through which the sex worker is materialized as a political subject in these narratives.

We need to see the contradictions in the dual autobiographical project as centrally linked to the staging of the sex worker as a subject. Scholars have noted that the statements that criticize the unequal hierarchies of power in the sphere of conjugality are not borne out entirely by her life decisions of three marriages and her expressed desire for her daughter to enter into a suitable marriage. "How much then are Jameela's protagonist's pronouncements the taking on of a certain rhetoric that leaves her own life and choices quite untouched?" asks Ashley Tellis (2008: 8). I would suggest that this rhetoric becomes an essential strategy to trouble the entrenched hierarchies between the sex worker and the domestic woman in Kerala. Krupa Shandilya argues that in the case of the foundational nineteenth-century Urdu novels by Ruswa on the figure of the courtesan,[24] the "rhetorical dimension" of the text (2017: 81)—that is, the narrative oscillation between Umrao Jaan as a courtesan who enjoyed the company of men and a modesty-desiring woman who bemoans her fate—is "crucial to untangling the political representation of the courtesan" (80). Jameela's manifesto-like, declaratory statements as a representative sex worker, which coexist with contradictory accounts of decisions that push her into domesticity and conjugality, must be read as performative acts central to the assemblage of the sex worker as a political subject. These contradictions and oscillations—the stutters in the narrative—are crucial to her negotiations with structures of state governance also.

The Subject of Critique

Scholars and activists have analyzed the positioning of the sex worker within post-1990s structures of governance. Ashwini Tambe (2009: xvii) argues that these new modes of address and deployments of participatory language to enlist the support of the sex worker in AIDS campaigns is instrumentalist, and that the state is an interested entity performing for domestic and international audiences and funding agencies.[25] Kotiswaran observes that the "knowledge base on hitherto unexplored sexualities" (2011b: xvii) functions on a "utilitarian calculus that permits interventions amongst sex workers but only to the extent necessary to prevent the spread of HIV to the general population" (xvii). Social workers in Kerala who worked with state-supported sex worker's organizations claim that "sex workers are used as tools by the government . . . many of them don't have a space to sleep in the night. The government does not make any arrangements for their children to get a school education."[26]

An autobiographical project such as Nalini Jameela's demonstrates how new modes of address by the state, however instrumentalist, cannot be divorced from their attempts to claim a subject position. Jameela's project of self-narration inhabits and takes shape within neoliberal modes of governance but tactically disturbs these structures. Her narratives also show the slippages between the address to the sex worker as a population category and sex workers' own struggles to access the participatory position of the "citizen." While sex workers are "hypervisibilized" within the AIDS discourse and yet "remain invisible as social beings" (Amar 2013: 231), Jameela's autobiographical project posits a practice of narrating through which the sex worker emerges as an unruly and embodied presence.

Jameela's life narratives exemplify the spirit of critique that Foucault defines as "the art of not being governed so much" (1994: 265). He observes how within governmentality, critique is not a face-off opposition and a refusal to be governed at all, but a practice of negotiating and limiting the modes and aims of governance. It is not a full-fledged stepping out of the system, but "the art of voluntary insubordination, that of reflected intractability" (266). This definition of critique focuses on strategic planning, practice, and reflection, not a revolutionary stepping out of regulatory structures. This staging of infractions within the system can be used as a frame for Jameela's narrative of the life of a questioning sex worker. Jameela is a recalcitrant subject of state reform because even though she uses the language and beneficiary measures offered by the state, she exceeds the dominant frames in which the sex worker is placed. She is a subject of state reform who concedes to the benefits brought about by the AIDS discourse, but her self-narrative shows the interventions by sex workers to wrest control over the process of political and cultural representation.[27] The sex worker claims political subjectivity in Jameela's writing, and this complicates the mechanisms through which the sex worker is allowed entry into state structures as an entrepreneurial, self-sufficient agent or a population category. Jameela (2005b: 93), in the chapter titled "Projects" in her first autobiography, describes how the sex worker's organizations in Kerala began work focusing on human rights issues in 1995. The language of incremental change through set targets, as propagated by the AIDS discourse, is in sharp tension with the demands of sex workers for justice and social change.

Jameela records her struggles to claim recognition through state mechanisms. She documents her attempt to get a passport in order to travel to Thailand to attend a Media and Social Work Seminar organized by GAATW (Global Alliance against Traffic in Women). At the passport office they demand a ration card, and she realizes she does not have one.[28] Her father had immediately cut her name from the family ration card when she got married against his wishes: "My father knew the ration card had lots of value. I just thought I lost the monthly allotment of subsidized rice and sugar. I didn't know that I had lost my identity itself" (Jameela 2005a: 93). The power of the ration card to bestow legitimacy on her existence brings to the fore how processes of identity and subject formation are embedded in modes of recognition used by the modern state.

Jameela writes in the first autobiography about the interventions of activists who supported sex workers' rights movements: "We didn't have a ration card or any of the signs that a society gives to its citizens. The truth was that no one was even aware that all that applied to us also. No one recognized the term sex worker also. People called us other terms like 'veshyas' and 'abhisarikas.' . . . It was at that point that Paulson and his group entered into their midst and told us that we were human beings and had the same rights as others" (Jameela 2005b: 74). Here, different modes of representation get entangled, and one seems as important as the other in order to produce a better social position for the sex worker. The right to have a ration card, which is a sign of being under the care of the modern state, is as important a gesture as being called a sex worker instead of historically denigrated terms like *veshya*. Jameela's claims on categories of governance, like the citizen, demonstrate how political subject formation draws on and intervenes in established ways of recognition by the state. Jameela's narrative dwells on the mediated subjectivity of the sex worker who deploys modes of address put forward by the state, even as she raises discomfiting questions that disturb the positioning of the sex worker as a docile follower of state reforms.

Thus my aim in this chapter is not to put forward static diagrams of developmental practices and their impact on communities and individuals in different regional contexts. Neloufer De Mel (2017), in her study on developmental initiatives in the post-tsunami resettlement of Burgher women of Batticaloa, Sri Lanka, observes that at a macro level these development interventions did not radically alter women's access to substantive equality. Yet, she argues that "if subject formation is 'an effect of practice,' for the Burgher women who had never participated in the formal procedures of associational governance before the tsunami . . . democratic participation through debate, and consensus building and collective decision-making spelt a 'grammar of becoming' that should not be underestimated" (82). It is beyond the scope of this chapter to analyze how sex workers in Kerala as a community negotiate with the processes of development channeled through the AIDS machinery. My emphasis has been on the structures of identification that the state offers the sex worker in its pedagogic materials; this does not foreclose the possibility that sex workers in practice slip out of and exceed these frames. In fact, Jameela's self-narratives can be read as a "grammar of becoming" that inhabits and creates a sense of dissonance within official discourses.

The upbeat, utopic accounts of progress through self-empowerment as embodied through the protagonist Geetha in the documentary film are disturbed by Jameela's narrative, which does not gloss over the everyday violence faced by women in sex work, especially street sex workers, both from state authorities, in the form of the police, and from clients. Her entry into sex work is through her sexual encounter with a police officer, "a hegemonic male ideal" (Christy 2017: 103) with all the markers of an upper-caste man. He behaves with her tenderly in the night, like "the lover of my dreams" (Jameela 2005a: 31), but betrays her to the police the next morning. This was in 1977, at the time when India was under a state of internal emergency,[29] when disciplinary state power worked in a draconian fashion. Jameela's account of the event is a disturbing depiction of blatant state violence: "As soon as we got to the police station, the caning started. We were caned on the soles of our feet. In my anger and distress at this treatment, I shouted, 'Police to sleep with by night; police to give a thrashing by day!' In between beatings, the Assistant Station Inspector jeered, 'So what did you think? If you slept with *saar* at night, he wouldn't tell us?'" (31). The forms of violence are described in a stark manner, the details of the acts of violence and their infliction on specific parts of her body heightening the memory of physical pain. As she recreates this event through the lens of her memory, there is an interjection of her voice of desperation and anger even as her body becomes the site of subjugation. She does not depict the scene of violence as an instance of silencing; instead, in the retrospective narration there is a pushing back on her end through her desperate, verbal response. The "body in pain" here is a dynamic one that acts/reacts "rather than a passive entity inviting our assistance." (De Mel 2007: 100).[30] Thus the sex worker is not rendered immobile as a helpless victim who can be rescued only through outside intervention.

This sense of struggle in the face of day-to-day violence underwrites Jameela's narratives of the life of sex workers and links them to the political struggle around the 1980s police custody murder of the prostitute Kunjeebi that I discussed in detail in the previous chapter. She demonstrates how, far from being an aberration at the time of Emergency, police violence is a continuing reality in sex workers' lives in Kerala.[31] Jameela emphasizes the struggles in sex workers' lives as they have to strategize and maneuver their way through multiple everyday structures of violence.

The police as the law keepers become the most familiar face of the state for sex workers, and the protests against police violence become an important field in which the sex worker emerges as a political subject. By insisting that juridical forms of power continue to penalize sex workers, even as they are enumerated and incorporated within public health interventions, Jameela points to the paradoxical impulses within the workings of state power. A repeated thread in her narratives is the demand to be protected from police violence and to practice her profession without being abused by state authorities, as "most often when sex workers are arrested as part of a raid in a hotel room, the police prepare the charge sheet in such a way that the men who are with them are not punished" (Jameela 2005b: 85). The documentary *For a Collective through Realization*, which I discussed earlier, begins with the sequence of two sex workers fleeing from the police. The camera focuses on the running feet of the two women as the police jeep chases them. But the situation is quickly resolved with the intervention of the Women's Cooperative Society. Police violence in this documentary is presented as one of the structural factors that can be solved through incorporation into development programs. Jameela's narrative points to the diffuse networks of state power within which sex workers continue to face violence from disciplinary institutions of the state, even as they are recruited to spread AIDS awareness and given certain benefits and entitlements.

Beyond Victimhood

Jameela uses the language of rights to articulate her demands for equality, but her narrative posits a subject who is not the victim demanding reparation. As I discussed in the previous chapter, in feminist activism against violence toward sex workers in the 1980s, the emotional appeal was primarily through sympathy for the prostitute as a victim. Jameela's narrative makes a significant shift in the paradigm of the rights discourse by demanding equality and not sympathy. Her intervention in a seminar conducted in 2002 as part of the Kerala Social Forum (a series of public deliberations and meetings evaluating the impact of globalization conducted as a prelude to World Social Forum that was held in India in 2004) is a critical statement on the dominant rhetoric of the sex worker as a victim: "The heated debate began when a doctor remarked that in his imagination a sex worker was a dark, thin, poverty-stricken woman standing in front of a hut. The doctor did not know I was a sex worker. At one phase of the argument he was shocked when I asked him if I fitted the image he just described" (Jameela 2005b: 103). Jameela uses her body and self-presentation to complicate the monolithic representation of the sex worker as an emblem of deprivation. She also draws attention to the caste-ist overtones in this statement, the assumption that the "dark" woman from a non-dominant caste will be sexually available. Her interventions disrupt the imagination of the sex worker as a symbol of oppression, a dominant rubric through which the she is positioned in the public sphere. Wendy Brown argues that permanent identification with narratives of suffering have the "capacity not only to chain us to our injurious histories . . . but to instigate the further regulation of those lives while depoliticizing their conditions" (2005: 85). Brown observes that confessions of suffering become the norms through which "victims" are regulated and frozen in that narrative. Jameela struggles to move away from this "regulatory fiction" (91) of the sex worker as the perennially suffering victim.

In the public address she makes in Calcutta in connection with the celebration of Indian Sex Worker's Day organized by the Sex Workers' Forum, Jameela recounts how in contrast to other participants who recounted their exploitation and oppression, she spoke about how sex workers were different from other women. It is the relative lack of constraints in a sex worker's life in comparison to a married woman that she describes because "unlike everyone else who used the five minutes they got to recount the tragedies in their own locations, I felt more satisfied talking in this way" (Jameela 2005a: 92). She deploys a language of mobility and self-assertion, especially in her public speeches and interviews, to describe a sex worker's life in order to counter the common rhetoric of soliciting sympathy and pity. She marks these instances of addressing a large audience through public speeches or shouting slogans as significant moments of claiming recognition as a sex worker. The opening chapter in the first autobiography, "Sex Worker's Manifesto," asserts the sex worker's status as a laboring body and argues that this work must be treated with as much dignity as any other socially accepted job. In an interview with Dileep Raj, Jameela argues, "It is not essential that everyone does sex work because they like it. Most people do jobs they do not like to do. . . . Do people talk about rehabilitating individuals who do scavenging work in the most unhygienic conditions?" (Jameela and Raj 2005: 23). More than unequivocally celebrating sex work, she is also concerned about the stigma associated with this work that determines dominant approaches to sex work in Kerala. She observes how many people who declare solidarity with sex workers do not understand the real problems they face. A theater group from Thrissur made a documentary and staged a play on the life of sex workers. But Jameela disagreed with the premise of the play, which portrayed the pathetic life of sex workers and asked society to rescue them. She asserts, "I believe firmly that we do not need the kindness or sympathy of the society—what we demand is a position of equality with other sections of society" (Jameela 2005b: 82). This demand for equality draws on the political language used by rights-based organizations like FIRM and the Sex Workers' Forum of Kerala.

When women's organizations in Kerala organized a Make the Night Our Own demonstration in Trivandrum, she says that this itself was not the actual demand of sex workers, as the night always belonged to them. "Sex workers did not have to organize a protest to own the night. Their problem is to claim the day . . . That has been denied to them by Kerala society" (Jameela 2005b: 102).[32] Thus, she observes that sex workers have always been allowed to function in a covert manner, under the cover of the night.[33] But in broad daylight there is no open recognition or acceptance of them. Even when they are incorporated within public health mechanisms of AIDS control, they are often denied access to other institutions of society. This denial is demonstrated in her narrative of the lack of access to institutions of modernity like the home, hospitals, and schools. The "public" as a legitimate sphere of bonding and belonging is one on which the sex worker has a limited claim.

Her conflicted relationship to the sphere of the home and the family must be read in the context of how the home is an aspirational space, not guaranteed to the subaltern woman. The identical dedication in both her autobiographies, "To sex workers who have no space of their own and are forced to sleep on the streets at night," points to the unmoored position of the sex worker who does not have any space of rest or belonging. She is pushed into risky ways of living, where her privacy and safety are never taken into consideration. The articulations by sex workers who are hyper-visible and yet disenfranchised dismantle the assumption that visibility automatically results in recognition and autonomy. It forces us to ask how the linear trajectory from inside to outside, private to public, gets unraveled when we make the sex worker the focus of feminist and sexuality politics. The mobilizations against the ban on dance bars in 2005 in Maharashtra lead to an intense debate—on issues about the body, modes of exhibition, and forms of erotic labor—that disturbed the assumptions about the ideal subject of feminist politics (Agnes 2007; Sukthankar 2012; Gopal 2012). The articulation by the Bar Dancer's Union and the sex worker's organizations point to how the totalizing attack on the commodification of women's bodies results in a reification of a docile and disciplined feminine body and does not engage with the tactical ways in which women's bodies in public navigate structures of power.

In this context, it is important to note that Jameela stakes a strategic claim to recognition by writing and rewriting her autobiography. As I argue in the introduction, print cultural practices are crucial to the configuration of the public in Kerala as an interconnected, affective network. Thus there are specific regional linkages between cultural practices and the public sphere that make the autobiographical project a crucial one for a sex worker in Kerala to fashion her politics. A demand for rights and decriminalization of sex work is mainly directed at the state as the law- and policy-making authority. However, the publication of her autobiographies reconfigures the reading public as the addressee. This exceeds the demand for decriminalization of sex work and entitlements and becomes an appeal to the public for a new imagination of the sex worker and her position within the social.[34]

Narrative Infractions

Unlike a political speech or manifesto, the form of the autobiography allows the articulation of instability and contingency in the process of political subject formation. Within the form of the life narrative, the subject is always incomplete and shifting and forms a contrast to the contained, unified subject at the core of the rights discourse. Jameela's opening statement in her first autobiography brings to the fore the tensions of being not only a representative figure but also a shifting subject whose life story cannot be neatly told: "There is an upcoming revolution in Kerala, spearheaded by the lower-most sections of society, I am one of those who are part of that struggle. I was born as Nalini, at one moment in my life I became Jameela, today I like to be known as Nalini Jameela. Let me now muster courage to remember my life experiences" (2005b: 16). These shifting instances of naming and self-definition mark the distance of the autobiography from a rights-based political document.[35]

Her second autobiography approximates the conventional forms of autobiographies more than the first. There are certain conventions about how one can tell an intelligible story of one's life. As Butler observes, "The norms by which I seek to make myself recognizable are not precisely mine" and "there can be no account of myself that does not, to some extent, conform to norms that govern the humanly recognizable" (2001: 26). Butler draws attention to the norms in place that have to be negotiated if one is to produce a recognizable autobiographical narrative at a particular historical juncture. The temporal arrangement of a narrative is one way in which a life story becomes recognizable. One begins at the beginning, with the memories of childhood becoming an acceptable starting point. A childhood memory functions as the opening moment of the second version of Jameela's autobiography, which commences with her "first memory: I must be two and a half or three years old. . . . Even now in my mind I have the image of my grandmother standing on all fours and cooing to my infant brother" (2005a: 13). This is markedly different from the first version of her life narrative that begins with a chapter titled "The Manifesto of Sex Workers." Yet the form of both books is fragmented and episodic and does not follow the logic of a linear developmental arc. The endings of both the books are inconclusive and anticlimactic. The formal ruptures in this dual autobiography project are enmeshed with Jameela's precarious positioning within the social. The complexities of Nalini Jameela's task of giving an account of oneself, in which the "self is already implicated in a social temporality that exceeds its own capacities for narration" (Butler 2005: 8) is captured in the fifth section of the second autobiography, which includes a chapter titled "Nalini, Jameela."

This segment of the second autobiography is a montage of memories in which she looks at different media—photography, film, and literature—and her own encounters with these narrative and documentary forms. The narrative shuttles through space and time and strings together multiple instances. She records her experience of watching a film for the first time in her life when she was fourteen, her responses to well-known literary writings in Malayalam that she encountered as a child, and having her first photograph taken: "I had my picture first taken when I was twenty-one. I wore a traditional sari in it. When I looked at it, it was a lot like my mother's photo. Not like mine!" (Jameela 2005a: 106). This juxtaposition of different media as a means of creating memory is a move she reflects on in the second book: "That's the way my memory is. I remember the past in moving pictures, like a film, with scenes that are sharp in my mind" (Devika 2007c: 135). Linguistic practices here intersect with the workings of the visual in order to produce a tapestry of embodied memories. From the medium of literary narrative, she expands her reach and speaks of other significant representational practices and the emotional impact these media have on her.

The chapter about naming herself Nalini Jameela comes after she recounts these memories of encountering different representational media. Here she establishes the need to access different cultural forms of narrating in order to create a subject called Nalini Jameela. Her reaching for visual forms of representation even as she uses the verbal form of the autobiography is linked to how this is not a unified liberal subject who can be neatly mapped onto the existing form of the autobiography. The fractures and ruptures of her embattled subjectivity create a sense of torsion in the form of the autobiography and result in the invocation of multiple representational practices. Thus there is no "telos of represented object to representing subject" (Kang 2002: 27) possible in Jameela's experiments in self-narration. She is, to use Laura Kang's terminology, a compositional subject, "composed, composite and positional" (Kang 2002: 27). In order to give a circulatable, public form to her subjectivity, she uses visual tropes and creates cinematic instances even as she is verbalizing her life story—thus taking us to the realm of unruly figurations.

In interviews Jameela characterizes the second book as a corrective and a more authentic rendering of her life. She explains that she produced a second version so as to reclaim her autobiography and assert her voice. But in order to engage with the stuttered process of subject formation, it is necessary to read both the books as interconnected projects. The two versions of her life, shaped by different collaborative partnerships, are interlinked episodic explorations on the fragmented subjectivity of a sex worker that do not fit into a "liberal theory of resistance" (Amar 2013: 233). Both these texts are mediated productions, and the overlaps, the reiterated as well as incomplete processes, point to the impossibility of a contained theory of self-formation, when the subject from the margins lays claim to representation. It is not surprising that Jameela wrote not one but two versions of her autobiography and still feels her project is incomplete: "I should warn you I might write again in the future—'My autobiography, part II!'"(Devika 2007c: 143). The struggle to create a form within which she can speak as a subject is arduous and vexed. She has to speak multiple languages, tell conflicting tales, and reorder temporal and spatial plotting. She inhabits the paradigms of rights and citizenship and also accesses the AIDS awareness frameworks for the "sex worker," and even then, parts of her story remain unsaid and illegible.

The subject formation that Jameela performs in her narratives is a reminder of the precarious positioning of the sex worker in the public sphere. It reveals how ration cards and governmental recognition are only one mode of participation in the social. She seeks participation in these state mechanisms of entitlement. But what exceeds the documentary enterprises of state processes surfaces in Jameela's autobiography as a practice of self-making, which complicates the discourse of the sex worker as a victim, a medicalized body, or an abstract representative of a marginalized community. Her compositional style of juxtaposing the linguistic and the imagistic, and her turn to visual media even as she uses the literary form of the autobiography, places a demand on the reader and the critic to be open to these shifting modes and acknowledge the necessity of these restless movements for a subaltern subject to tell her life story.

Udaya Kumar in his monograph on first-person narratives in Malayalam observes that self-narratives must be seen as performances "located from the outset in a public exhibitory space" (Kumar 2016: 21). He demonstrates that while reading self-narratives, we need to look at gestures of extrospection: "Consider the inner world itself as inscribed on the surface of things, as produced through actions and utterances in a field of mutual exposure and unevenly shared visibility" (21). In Jameela's autobiographies, the iconic events of self-assertion are staged in public. This is a model of subject formation that marks its presence through interrelated modes of being face to face with a viewing other. Because of this constant awareness of a sociality in which the "I" exists in relation to a "you," Jameela's acts of affirming the self are always risky and tenuous. Ashley Tellis argues that Jameela's narrative turns every moment of interiority into a "matter-of-fact exteriority" and flattens "the autobiographical 'I'" into a connector with several other "I's," and he reads this as intricately connected to her fraught social position (2008: 6).

One of Jameela's powerful memories is about how as an eleven-year-old she participated in a protest march for land rights: "That picture is clear in my mind. . . . Me walking with the crowd holding a flag aloft, shouting slogans—feeling like someone who was getting noticed. Like we say a woman warrior" (2005a: 105). Later she describes realizing how people were staring at her because of her physical beauty. Though she was only eleven, her body had the shapely contours of a fourteen-year-old: "I just wore a short blouse and a skirt that reached my knees. Silk Smitha's clothes in later years. That's the only dress I had then" (105). In one memory, there are two oscillating frames through which she perceives how she is looked at—the first as a brave political protestor and the second as a sexualized body. The comparison to Silk Smitha is telling, because Silk Smitha was an actress who was the ultimate symbol of sensuality in South Indian cinema in the eighties.[36] The erotic tensions in the public gaze do not cancel out her sense of claiming presence and her appreciation of standing out in this march. Such statements by Jameela furthermore capture the repeated move we see in this book, where marginalized sexual actors draw on immensely popular "low" cultural forms such as soft-porn cinema and sensational fiction to script the processes of subject formation. Many of these cultural forms play on the multiple valences of acts of seeing and being seen, as I discuss in the introduction to this book.

In an interview she mentions how after becoming a sex worker, she started paying attention to the grooming of her body and dressing well so that she could make "an impression on a man" (Devika 2007b: 137). She states that this was not only to seduce the man in a sexual fashion and get him into bed: "It means that you exert an influence on people. The man is aware of your presence; he can't ignore you" (137). The significance of being seen and creating an impression on the viewer is recounted in both versions of her autobiography. During the early phase of her life as a sex worker, she worked at a hotel where the small room in which she had sex with clients had no electric bulb or any source of lighting. This was the arrangement in the hotel so that the client would not know the sex worker's identity and could not see her face. One of her regular clients wanted to see her, and after much insistence on his part, she stepped out into the lighted hallway. He was struck by her good looks and asked her, "You are so beautiful, why do you sit in the dark like this?" (Jameela 2005a: 35). Jameela expresses her surprise at his behavior: "Usually men went off and returned at night, that's all. It wasn't common at all for them to pay us compliments. . . . That amazed expression which lit up his face on seeing me for the first time remains stamped on my mind even now" (35). Here we see another instance when Jameela's image of herself is formed through the admiring gaze of the witness. His amazed face becomes the mirror through which she builds her sense of self-worth. The significance of an addressee, whether it is a watching crowd or one man who asks her to switch on the light, parallels the workings of autobiography in which experiences materialize by circulating in the interlinked public network, through the relational dynamics between the narrator and the reader.

The instances of her personal history that she presents as self-affirming provide new entry points to question the dominant assumptions about women's bodies, visibility, desirability, and beauty. By suggesting that the body of a woman can function as a material site of marking one's presence, she creates a sense of friction in the singular paradigm of the sexualization of marginalized women's bodies as objectification and erasure of personhood. Thus in her narratives the sex worker is a political subject whose claim to the public sphere and recognition does not rest on frameworks of respectability or victimhood. At the same time, it is important to note that she does not erase the violence and exploitation borne by subaltern women in the site of sexual and economic transactions. The impact of her narrative is that it forces the reader to reexamine set paths toward inhabiting the public sphere through contained and sanitized models of political subjectivity. The scenes of self-fashioning she presents compel us to take on board the erotic potential of bodies in public, even bodies that are participating in a political march. This fraught, fragmented, and incomplete exercise of a sex worker claiming the day gestures toward the stuttered process of compositional subject formation. The gaps, frictions, and irresolvable tensions in Jameela's dual autobiographies are productive to think about regional registers of sexuality and subjectivity in post-1990s Kerala.

This questioning of dominant paradigms of the political subject and its links to the recasting of narrative forms is central to my investigation of political interventions around the figure of the lesbian. This will be my focus in the next two chapters. In contrast to the hypervisible sex worker, the lesbian is relatively absent in state processes and public health discourses. But queer politics in India is located in the matrix of identity politics, sexual health management, NGO-ization, and human rights discourses. This is an important scaffolding for the emergence of the lesbian as an identity category in the present. I examine the possibilities and limitations of this framing. As the much-commented-upon public debates and mobilizations around Deepa Mehta's *Fire* (1996) have shown, cultural practices are a crucial field to map the politics of lesbian desire in India. In the next chapter, I analyze the representational practices of two Malayalam films, from post-1990s and pre-1990s, to reflect on the formations of queer politics in Kerala.

CHAPTER 3

Wandering in the Vernacular
Divergent Visions of Queerness

RELEASED IN 2004, LIGY PULLAPPALLY'S FILM *SANCHARRAM* (THE journey, 2004) makes an important political statement by portraying a lesbian love story in rural Kerala. *Sancharram* makes a strong claim for positive representations of lesbian desire in order to counter societal violence against sexual arrangements that are outside the frame of heterosexuality. It aims to create a cinematic space within which lesbian desire is openly affirmed. Labeled as the first Malayalam "lesbian film," *Sancharram* has been celebrated in reviews from India and abroad as inaugurating radical sexual politics within Malayalam cinema. This film, in which two young women defy societal conventions in order to embrace their desire for each other, is read as emblematic of the aspiration for sexual liberation in globalizing India. This is in keeping with a narrative of progress in which contemporary forms of representation and politics are often characterized as breaking the silence and making visible hitherto repressed forms of sexuality in the non-Western world. My aim in this chapter is to push against this narrative of progress. I will read *Sancharram* in conversation with another Malayalam film, *Deshadanakkili karayarilla* (The wandering bird does not cry, 1986), in order to mine the multiple sexual imaginations that are available within the public sphere of Kerala. While acknowledging the important intervention made by *Sancharram*, I interrogate the limits of a universal language of sexual identity politics in which this film is embedded. My analysis points to the dangers of valorizing a singular model of politics as universally applicable and as the only available mode.

My analysis in this chapter speaks to debates on the formation of queerness in India and how it is enmeshed in global, national, and regional networks of power. By reading a film text from the 1980s that does not circulate in the public sphere as a lesbian film, alongside a film like *Sancharram*, I open up the possibilities of a critical imagination of queer politics. I offer this comparative reading to reflect on the challenges of sexuality politics embedded in the precarious domain of regional publics. I aim to think through the central question of how cinematic practices can throw light on the fractured terrain of gender and sexuality in contemporary Kerala. This exercise is undertaken with the awareness that there is no a priori radicality to queer subjectivities. Possibilities of disruption nestle only in the practice of queering. I signal toward this potentiality by following the movements of cultural texts as they travel through space and time.

Wayward Readings

The opening shot of *Sancharram* depicts a steep, menacing cliff and a surging waterfall below. A young woman is precariously positioned at the edge of the cliff. The camera gives us a close-up of her feet as she suspensefully holds them out into thin air. Booming sounds of temple drums can be heard in the backdrop, making this a climactic moment of possible suicide, which the film returns to in the end, when we see the girl turn around to stake her claim on life rather than death. *Sancharram* is bracketed by this threat of suicide within both the film plot and the contemporaneous events to which the film responds. Pullappally says that she was motivated to make this film because of her concern about the series of lesbian suicides in Kerala: "I hope my film helps young gay people consider the option of moving ahead with their lives, instead of taking the devastating step that will resonate for years within their own families and communities, suicide" (Cheerath-Rajagopalan 2005). Preceding *Sancharram* by two decades, *Deshadanakkili karayarilla*, directed by P. Padmarajan, is one of the rare Malayalam films from the 1980s that touches on the issue of lesbian suicide.[1] This film ends with the double suicide of the two women protagonists. We see them in the closing shot in bed—entangled bodies in a final sleep. The acts of lesbian suicides and the debates and mobilizations around it point to a discourse of sexuality in Kerala within which some of the dominant assumptions around the public and the private, norms of desiring, and modes of resistance get troubled.

My readings of the two films, *Sancharram* and *Deshadanakkili karaya-rilla* (hereafter *DKK*) are both firmly rooted in the demands of the contemporary moment as the dominant frameworks of a global LGBT rights movement—like the politics of visibility, the concept of a counterpublic, and the desire for a solidified gay or lesbian subject position—get transfigured in the public sphere of Kerala. The transnational flows of AIDS funding and a globally circulating language of sexuality, with a set vocabulary of identity categories, inform the configurations of LGBT politics.[2] Lawrence Cohen tracks the history of sexual identity categories in India and its links to the global spread of "identifications, institutions and capital" (2005: 300). Analyzing the imbrications between processes of globalization and LGBT politics, Ashley Tellis and Sruti Bala argue that the narrative of queer subjectivity "cannot be disinterred from the debris of globalization and offered as a pure counter-hegemonic narrative" (2015: 17).

The recent direction of LGBT activism in India, primarily organized around the legal struggles to decriminalize homosexuality,[3] has been critiqued by scholars and activists who have drawn attention to the constitutive erasures in the making of a legible pan-Indian subject of queer politics who seeks recognition from the state (Manayath 2015; Sircar and Jain 2017). Akshay Khanna attempts to dislodge the liberal subject, who tends to get reified when forms of activism rely primarily on legal frameworks, and investigates the adoption and contestation of the "idiom of 'sexuality-as-personhood'" in queer politics (2016: 20). The contradictions in the process of naming and in the production of identity categories are central to projects such as Maya Sharma's *Loving Women* (2006), which maps a complex field of same-sex practices by recording the life narratives of working-class women in North India. Sharma observes that interactions of the researchers in "spaces fraught with . . . silences and half-truths" (2) rendered their "preconceptions of identity categories irrelevant" (6) as some of the working-class subjects did not identify as women and many of them were unfamiliar with the word "lesbian."

Commenting on the founding anthologies that brought together personal narratives,[4] experiential accounts by activists, and literary narratives in order to produce "gay" and "lesbian" subjects in the public sphere of India, Akhil Katyal observes that in spite of their avowed political goals, "These narratives do as much to establish sexuality-based subject positions as interrogate them" (2016: 171). He argues that the "doubleness of the concept and practice of sexuality" (170) and "the multiplicity of intersecting idioms of same-sex desire" (1) is traceable when we focus on the sphere of narration and cultural practices. The instability of the cultural sphere is crucial in this book because it questions simplistic celebrations of the liberatory potential of visibility. In this chapter, I posit the nonlinear juxtaposition of cinematic practices as a productive move to undo teleological narratives of identity formation. In the context of ongoing debates that signal toward the need to question the "definitional certainties" (70) that govern the field of sexuality, I tease out the disorderly circuits of regional articulations that reshape the dominant grammar of LGBT politics.

The slippages in processes of signification have been central to scholarship that focuses on literary texts that were the epicenter of high-pitched battles and legal trials on the grounds of obscenity during the colonial era, such as Ugra's Hindi collection of short stories, *Chaklet* (Chocolate, 1927/1953);[5] the Urdu anthology of short stories and a play *Angarey* (Live coals, Zaheer 1932/1990); and the writings of Ismat Chughtai (1915–1992) and Sa'adat Hassan Manto (1912–1955). These are key moments in the history of sexuality in South Asia because they place the representation of body, sex, desire, and intimacy as a central problematic in the public sphere. My explorations in the second half of this book speak to the reflections on "queer" as a methodological practice that emerges in this body of critical work. Scholars who have engaged with the poetics of sexuality in vernacular registers, especially in Urdu, have envisioned queer as a wayward and angular practice of reading that does not presume transparent access to identities or acts: "Queer, then, is not a mode that brings to light, illuminates in a transparent fashion. Queer readings celebrate the unfinished. They keep alive the possibility that when something is deciphered some small piece will escape or evade clarity, will remain obscure" (Patel 2014). Geeta Patel's conceptualization of "queer" foregrounds practices of reading that open up rather than foreclose the contradictions nestling in a text. This conception of queer as predicated on ways of reading that trace "crooked lines" is significant to the modes of analysis that I will adopt in the following chapters.[6]

The comparative as a paradigm of analysis allows me to juxtapose texts from two time periods to locate different registers of sexuality available within a region.[7] Gayatri Gopinath's (2005) comparative reading of Ismat Chughtai's short story "Lihaaf" (The quilt, 1941/1994) as an intertext to Deepa Mehta's *Fire* (1996) disrupts the developmental trajectory of sexuality and representation. Indeed, the ocular play in the story is augmented through Chughtai's account of the public trial in Lahore in 1944 on charges of obscenity, in which she was exonerated because she said that she did not use "four letter words" and claimed that the child narrator "did not know" about lesbianism (Kishwar and Vanita 1983: 5).[8] This story and the public trial, which are key to debates on lesbianism in South Asia, disrupt strategies of visibility, identity, and recognition. In the ending of "Lihaaf," the narrator stops short of revealing what she saw under the somersaulting quilt, and we as readers are also arrested in this moment of knowing and not knowing, seeing and not seeing. The "quilted effects" (Gopinath 2005: 151) of this oft-remembered story have poised the problematic of vision and voicing as central to the scene of sexuality and cultural practices in India.

My discussion of Basheer's novella *Shabdangal* in chapter one points to how the perpetual gap between sight and perception, appearance and reality, in the scene of sexual encounters is crucial to the making of one of the earliest queer texts in Malayalam. Rosemary Marangoly George, in her reading of Kamala Das's autobiography *My Story*, observes that the "slipperiness in her writing, resulting from a perennially unstable set of referential contexts, heightens the queer charge of the autobiography" (2000: 741). My analysis in the chapters that follow suggests that the challenging task for sexuality studies on South Asia is to engage with the political valence of reading and spectatorial practices through which we traverse erotic formations without rushing toward certainties.

Controversial literary texts such as *Shabdangal* and "Lihaaf" place us in the mis-en-scène of desire. The erotic friction between the reader and the scenes they witness cannot be plotted in a singular axis. This relationship between subjectivity and desire is crucial to cinema. The erotic charge of watching cinema is associated with the process of entering into a spatial domain and being set into motion by a force field of bodies, looks, and acts. Ceaseless movements that activate the screen shape the experience of cinema.[9] The queer possibilities of cinema are linked to its power to immerse the spectator in a sensory experience that can be transformative—not because it offers a singular node of identification but because it triggers the pleasure of inhabiting multiple positionalities (Kuzniar 2005). Wayward readings and spectatorial practices, routed through the unhomely inhabitation of space and time, are crucial to my engagement with the challenges of sexuality politics in India today. I argue that the critical potential of queerness can be kept alive only by engaging with the wanderings of vernacular sexual figures.

Circuits of *Sancharram* and *DKK*

Sancharram is a film that locates itself centrally within an international LGBT countercultural space. Sexuality in *DKK*, while definitely informed by a cultural discourse around desire and female friendship,[10] is much less solidified and therefore more readily available for multiple interpretations. I explore the political implications of the cinematic codes used by a director from the 1980s who might be aware that he is taking up a taboo theme but represents it so that the lesbian relationship is posited as one among other possibilities of desire.[11] This provides a productive counterpoint to a film like *Sancharram*, which is the product of a very different logic of cultural representation and wears its queer identity politics on its sleeve. The imagined audience and the circuits of reception of both these films are also markedly different.

Chicago-based director Pullappally's *Sancharram* has garnered critical attention, awards, and appreciation for being a bold film that breaks accepted boundaries.[12] *Sancharram* was honored with the Chicago Award from the Chicago International Film Festival, the Lankesh Award for India's Best Debut Director and the John Abraham Special Jury Award for Best Malayalam Feature Film. It has been lauded as "an incredible act of affirmation of queer desire" by well-known gay rights activists in India like Arvind Narrain.[13] It premiered in the Chicago International Film Festival and has been screened in film festivals in India and in many noted LGBT film festivals in the United States, Canada, and Australia. This is a film that locates itself in the visible LGBT networks in India and abroad through its publicity, its places of exhibition, and its networks of circulation. The DVDs of this film are marketed by Wolfe Videos, a well-known North American distributor of gay and lesbian feature films. This is one of the few Malayalam films whose copies at the time of its release could be easily picked up from American home video providers like Blockbuster or Netflix. It is one of the rare films to which audiences in metropolitan centers in the West and in India have had earlier and easier access than a Kerala-based audience. *DKK* was not labeled or marketed as a queer film at the moment of its production, but the intimate relationship between two women forms the crux of this film, too. Its context of production and circulation, mainly for a regional Malayali audience, is very different from that of *Sancharram*, which has not yet had a full-fledged commercial release in theaters in Kerala. A film like *DKK* that is historically positioned outside the current moment can be deployed in order to offer a new lens with which to examine the contemporary.

Whether it is through the metaphor of the closet or the paradigm of coming out, the questions of visibility and invisibility and the stakes of what it means for a sexual relationship to be public and recognizable have been among the persistent concerns of contemporary LGBT politics. A sexual relationship acquires social sanction as a legitimate couplehood only when it stakes a claim in the public sphere through an act like marriage or living together. The publicness of sex becomes intimately tied to the spaces that a couple occupies. In cinema we can track this by looking at the mise-en-scène and camera work that place characters within different spaces. There are also specific cinematic codes of representation through which a couple is established. These include certain gestures, ways of inhabiting space, and the positioning of the actors' bodies in relation to each other within a shot.[14] In the case of *Sancharram*, the exercise of producing such a film is itself mired in the language of visibility and invisibility, and a "breaking the silence" trajectory is one into which the film neatly fits. In contrast, the link between sexuality and the public sphere is explored in complex ways within the cinematic text of *DKK* so as to dramatize some of the strategic negotiations that the heroines in this film have to undertake in order to walk the thin line between visibility and safety.

The different conceptions of desire that these two films put forward are played out through the different spatial economies of these films. My spatial analysis in this chapter is twofold. I mainly analyze how spaces are framed within these two films, but I read this in conjunction with the different sites of production, circulation, and reception of these two films. My analysis demonstrates that a film like *DKK*, which does not make its heroines claim a queer subject position, manages to retain a sense of contingency of the term "queer." Through its more subterranean ways of working, it disrupts and queers the social sphere of Kerala in critical ways.

Reading against the grain of some of the more celebratory reviews of *Sancharram*, which describe the film as "queering" the terrain of Malayalam cinema, I demonstrate how this film actually puts into place a narrow and rigid definition of what the process of queering involves. In her influential intervention, Judith Butler writes that the assertion of queer must never purport to fully describe those it seeks to represent (1993: 230). She argues that to democratize queer politics and retain an awareness of the exclusionary ways in which discourses of power work, it is essential to emphasize the level of contingency in any notion of queerness. A critique of the queer subject should be built within a critical queer politics that is aware that a single trajectory of queerness cannot be universally applicable. "For whom is outness a historically available and affordable option? Is there an unmarked character to the demand for universal 'outness'? Who is represented by which use of the term and who is excluded?" (227), she asks, drawing attention to the complexities that are bound to arise when certain crystallized forms of queerness are exported universally.

David Eng, J. Jack (Judith) Halberstam, and José Esteban Muñoz (2005: 1) reassess the political utility of the term "queer" in the context of late twentieth-century global shifts that have led to the mainstreaming of gay and lesbian identity and the national manifestations of sexual hierarchies. In a more recent intervention, Anjali Arondekar and Geeta Patel draw attention to the geopolitical flattening that continues to shadow queer studies even as it turns its gaze to spaces outside the Euro-American context because the local/vernacular reappears "as incident, exemplar, or evidence, as spatial fodder for the queer mill" (2016: 155). My comparative reading of *DKK* and *Sancharram* suggests that we need to engage with vernacular cinematic practices so that the region is not reduced to mere "spatial fodder" but enables us to open up dominant categories of analysis. In assembling the critical vocabulary and epistemological frameworks for this analysis, I draw on vernacular concepts such as *deshadanam* (wandering) and deploy it alongside conceptual terms that have global traction, such as "critically queer," to draw out the transformative possibilities of such acts of theorizing.

Differing Scripts of Travel

Sancharram tells the story of two young women in a rural setting in Kerala, Kiran and Delilah (Lilah), whose friendship crosses accepted boundaries and enters the realm of the sexual. Kiran comes from a prestigious Nair family with a father who is an established journalist and a mother who comes from a wealthy background.[15] Delilah, Kiran's neighbor, is Christian, and her mother runs their household and rubber estate after the death of Delilah's father. The film shows the budding relationship between the two girls as they study together in the same school and share their everyday lives. Kiran is reluctant to express her sexual desire for Lilah, but when circumstances force her to do so, she discovers to her surprise that Lilah shares her feelings. They confess their love for each other, but a crisis develops when Rajan, one of their classmates who desires Lilah, sees them in an intimate moment and reports this to Lilah's mother. Due to familial pressure, Lilah agrees to an arranged marriage and Kiran is ostracized both by her family and in school when news about their relationship circulates in the community. Kiran repeatedly attempts to convince Lilah to cut ties with her family and run away with her, but Lilah refuses to do so. On the day of Lilah's marriage, a desperate Kiran contemplates suicide, but changes her mind in the last moment and turns back to embrace a new life. At the same instance, in a dreamlike sequence, Lilah rebels in the wedding hall and refuses to passively enter into a suitable marriage.

While the motif of an imposing home and its surroundings is prevalent through *Sancharram*, it is the motif of the journey that is central to *DKK*. Its title, *The Wandering Bird Does Not Cry*, refers to the figure of the migratory bird that roams the nation (or *desham*) and never cries. The film follows the trajectory of the lives of two young girls, Sally and Nirmala (Nimmi), who are in a strict boarding school run by Christian missionaries in Kerala. They are both seen as a disruptive presence in the school and are punished for breaking school rules. Sally is shown from the beginning as the more aggressive and assertive of the two, and she often takes the initiative for their escapades. The principal of the school even calls Nimmi "Sally's tail." Both the girls are shown to have apathetic families. Sally and Nimmi rebel against Devika, a teacher in their school. To take revenge for Devika's disciplinary actions, the two of them decide to run away from a school picnic organized by her. Things work according to plan, and their disappearance results in Devika's suspension.

The two of them take on new identities as tourists and research fellows and start to live in a youth hostel in a different town. Sally cuts her hair short, and her clothing style changes to jeans and shirt, a costume that in the eighties would be a marker of both Western modernity and an appropriation of masculinity. Nimmi finds a job in a handicrafts store. They seem satisfied in each other's company until the entry of an older man, Harikrishnan, into Nimmi's life. Sally is suspicious of this man, but Nimmi is clearly attached to him and looks upon him as her "father, lover and companion." He also seems to reciprocate her affection, but as the film progresses, we see that he is actually in love with Devika and hopes to marry her. He also wishes that Nimmi and Sally would return to their school and resume their education so that Devika can get her job back. Toward the end of the film, he convinces Nimmi to go back to school, while Sally resolutely refuses to do so. On the day before Nimmi is to return to her old school, Harikrishnan tells her about his plan to marry Devika. Nimmi is shattered at this news and attempts to commit suicide when Sally also packs her bag and goes away. But Sally returns at the right moment and tells Nimmi that she cannot go wandering off by herself. The film stages an intense moment of reunion between the two girls, but the narrative takes us to the following morning, when we see both girls dead in bed, hugging each other.

The Public Sphere and the Making of the Couple

Sancharram, through its textual politics, its marketing, and its circulation, positions itself as a "lesbian" film staking a claim for an expression of queer desire that goes against societal norms. On a quick analysis, this film seems to fit into what Michael Warner (2002: 86) terms a counterpublic discourse. A counterpublic is seen to be in a conflictual relationship to the dominant public and therefore operating in frictional relation to the norm. As Warner argues, "A counterpublic maintains at some level, conscious or not, an awareness of its subordinate status. The cultural horizon against which it marks itself off is not just a general or wider public, but a dominant one" (86). But through my reading, I argue that the "poetic-expressive character of counterpublic discourse" (86), or its transformative power to challenge the ordering of *the* public that claims universality, is not carried through in *Sancharram*. Pullappally's film works within the logic of a neat splitting of the dominant public sphere and a disruptive counterculture. In order to perform this dichotomous relationship, the film posits a traditional Nair home and a picture-perfect rural Kerala as the backdrop for its love story. There is a need to construct a calm river for a countercultural stone to create its ripples.

DKK, both in terms of its spatialization of desire in the film and the spaces it occupies through its circulation, undoes this binary between a dominant culture and a counterculture that sets itself against it. It makes visible the "contradictions and perversities inherent in the organization of *all* publics" (Warner 2002: 81). Unlike *Sancharram*, this film was screened in mainstream film theaters and also makes its way into domestic spaces later, through its transmission on Malayalam television channels. Padmarajan is seen as one of the established and highly popular filmmakers of Kerala whose films are nostalgically invoked as part of the "golden era" of Malayalam cinema. So there is a culture of aesthetic appreciation and film reception that places *DKK* as acceptable, "good" cinema. The circuits of circulation of this film as a mainstream film meant for "family audiences" show how the dominant public sphere can itself be an unstable space. Thus my reading of *DKK* suggests that films and cultural texts that circulate in the mainstream public sphere and carry the label of "good art" might at times have their own strategies of undoing normative codes of desiring.[16]

Of the three interlocking strands of desire in the film—the relationship between Nimmi and Sally, the marriage-oriented relationship between Harikrishnan and Devika, and the incomplete romance between Harikrishnan and Nimmi—it is the one between Sally and Nimmi that functions as its emotional fulcrum. The Harikrishnan and Devika relationship is shown as a "mature" love story of a man and woman who belong to the same caste and religious background and are shown to be eligible for each other. This relationship has the ingredients necessary for the making of a heterosexual couplehood that can lead to the establishment of the reproductive and economic unit of the conjugal family. But the film actively dislocates this story from its narrative center and reduces it, at best, to a subplot. The Harikrishnan and Nimmi relationship is shown within the diegesis as an interrupted love story, and the couple is never stably established because Nimmi's desire is not completely reciprocated by Harikrishnan.

As viewers we are stitched into the fabric of the film primarily through the affective links between Nimmi and Sally. There are sequences in the beginning of the film in which the camera movements and the spatial arrangements help to set up a bond between Nimmi and Sally. For example, there is one sequence in which both the women sit on the long steps in an open courtyard in the school and Sally unfolds her plan of how to foil a school entertainment event. The first shot is a medium shot of Sally, and then the camera tracks backward, both of them in the frame. As they talk, Nimmi clicks a photograph of the view before her. The camera moves behind Nimmi, and we see her hand and shoulders and then Sally as seen from her perspective. When Nimmi proceeds to take a photograph of Sally, we see her through Nimmi's gaze. The scene ends with a long shot of both of them now seated close to each other with Nimmi's hands on Sally's lap. They are placed together at the center of the long steps that extend to both ends of the frame. The spatial arrangement wherein they are framed by the long steps and planted in the middle structurally resembles the genre of a "couple photograph," and it enables the film text to establish them as a connected unit.

The song sequence, which celebrates their togetherness, is one that again follows many of the conventions of representing romantic couplehood in Malayalam films. Muraleedharan, in his analysis of sexualized bonds between men in popular Malayalam cinema in the 1980s and 1990s, demonstrates how "desire in contemporary India overflows contemporary heterosexist frameworks of reading" (2002: 191). In a song in *DKK*, we see Nimmi and Sally holding hands and walking together toward the sunset on the beach. The lyrics of the song describe them as nightingales that are in search of new shores. Sally puts her arm around Nimmi's shoulders as they walk in parks or go shopping in crowded streets at night. They go boating together on a blue lake. They run around playfully and try to chase each other and end up falling into each other's arms.

Nimmi drapes a towel over Sally's body as she comes out of the swimming pool. The song ends with both of them on a merry-go-round at a fair, another familiar space of the heterosexual couple. By placing them in spaces that are often marked cinematically as the space of the couple—like the beach, the park, and even the merry-go-round—and deploying body language that marks a sense of physical intimacy, this song gives them the position of a couple in the film. This is emphasized when we watch the second song that comes later in the film and is dedicated to the budding romance between Nimmi and Harikrishnan. Similar scenes are repeated against similar backdrops like the beach, the park, and the street, showing how the codes with which the filmmaker represents queer desire echo the ones he uses to put into place the heterosexual couple. This replication of representational codes and repetition of the space of the couple in the film makes it difficult to differentiate one couple as legitimate and the other one as illegitimate. One does not seem to be more or less impossible than the other in the cinematic space.

DKK weaves a crisscrossing network of relationships, where one organization of sexuality overlaps and throws a shadow on the other, in such a way that it disrupts the centrality of heterosexuality. It manages to do so by claiming publicness to the performance of sexual relationships. Ritty Lukose examines the "very fraught kind of public intimacy" through which young women in globalizing Kerala negotiate their navigation of public spaces, consumption, and education (2009: 98). She identifies romance as a significant domain for negotiating consumer citizenship in Kerala. Lauren Berlant and Michael Warner (1998) discuss the counter impulses within the discourses around sexuality and public culture. On the one hand, there are multiple mechanisms in place through which certain forms of sexuality acquire public recognition and legitimacy. This could range from approving smiles earned by a handholding heterosexual couple in suburban America to the manner in which landlords in most cities in India prefer to lease or rent out apartments to married couples. Contrary to this, there is an erasure of the public in sex when "sexuality seems like a property of subjectivity rather than a publicly or counterpublicly accessible culture" (560). Analyzing the current formations of queer activism in India, Nithin Manayath observes that the "deployment of global legal-culture notions of privacy to mark the legally defined private as a legitimate domain of erotic action" (2015: 267) is a move that further threatens public cultures of eroticism like sex work, cruising, and street-bound hijra livelihood. Thus, the contradictions around sex as both public and intensely private is one that is of much significance to queer politics today. These are questions that get staged in distinct ways in *Sancharram* and *DKK*.

DKK foregrounds the publicness of sexual relationships by making the couple through their positioning in public spaces. Thus couplehood is shown as a public construction with established cinematic codes. One obvious example of this is the mandatory song sequence into which the couples in this film, Nimmi and Sally and Nimmi and Harikrishnan, are fitted. These song sequences mirror each other. They show up the conventions of the making of the couple and reflect how cultural forms like cinema play a role in this construction. Often in films the rituals of heterosexuality are repeated so much that its ritualistic codes become naturalized. But when two women as a couple perform the codes of heterosexual couplehood, it opens up gaps and fissures that foreground the constitutive instabilities of romantic couplehood. The acknowledgement of the public construction of couplehood in this film undercuts the assumption that heterosexual couplehood is a stable or natural formation.[17] *DKK*, by drawing attention to conventions of the construction of heterosexual couplehood, manages to queer the public sphere of Kerala instead of setting up a separate niche that could work as a countercultural one.

A comparative reading of these two films exposes the different literary and cinematic conventions that make couplehood culturally intelligible.[18] *Sancharram* draws on existing literary and cinematic conventions of making the couple, but its impulse seems to be in opposition to that of *DKK* because it enacts both couplehood and the act of desiring as intensely private and subjective. The space of the couple as it emerges in *Sancharram* often appears as a dream space that is disassociated from the social or the public realm. The film is heavily invested in the visual and verbal discourse of romantic love in which sexuality becomes a "property of subjectivity" (Berlant and Warner 1998: 560).

The plot device that is used to kindle the romance between Kiran and Delilah is a familiar one from the Malayalam romantic writing dating from the nineteenth century and even earlier. Kiran's smoldering desire finds an outlet when one of their classmates, Rajan, asks her to help him pen love notes to Delilah in order to win her heart. "I like her as much as Kunjakko Bobban likes Shalini in *Aniyathi Pravu*," says Rajan, drawing on a popular Malayalam teenage love film to express his desire. Rajan's status as a misfit within this narrative of romantic love is complicated. For one, he is a man between two desiring women. But he is also not from a dominant caste background and lacks Kiran's cultural repertoire. He struggles to speak English, and his language of romance comes from delegitimized, *painkili* (sentimental) fiction.[19] At one point, when he decides to take on the task of writing to Delilah, his declarations of love with their over-the-top, sensual sentimentality, only serve to disgust her.[20]

Kiran, however, employs a high literary discourse of love when writing to Delilah. Her language comes from the romantic poetic traditions of Malayalam literature and is saturated with nature imagery and intense emotionality. Kiran is set up as the intense, introspective poet fairly early in the film. In a Malayalam literature classroom she interprets Sugathakumari's poem "Krishna nee enne ariyalla" (Krishna, you don't know me), about the lover-deities Radha and Krishna, as a poem about the hellish loneliness of love. It is through poetic words that Kiran and Delilah reveal their love for one another. The first poem that Kiran publishes is titled "Awakening" (Unnarvu), whose parallels to the American feminist writer Kate Chopin's novel *The Awakening* (1899), a classic evocation of sexual liberation stemming from a deep sense of selfhood or interiority, are hard to miss. Placing the love story in this high romantic tradition creates a reified object of lesbian love; in this idealized form, only certain privileged subjects can practice it.

The queering of the public sphere in *DKK* and the reification of lesbian desire in *Sancharram* are apparent in the contrasting spatial dynamics of both these films. On the official website of *Sancharram*, the director, Ligy Pullappally, gives an account of how the choice of theme of this film was triggered by an e-mail she received in January 2000 describing the death of a young woman at a university in Kerala, who committed suicide after rumors were spread on campus about her lesbian relationship. These reports made Pullappally want "to do something to draw attention to the alarmingly frequent incidents of gay suicide—to try to stem that tide."[21] By tracking newspaper reports for corresponding dates, I found that the specific case that *Sancharram* was responding to is the suicide of a Dalit student in Kerala Varma College, Thrissur, in

November 1999.[22] An MA student in political science, Mini committed suicide after she ran away from the hostel with another woman friend and was brought back home. The letter she left behind states that the baseless rumors spread on the college campus about her being a lesbian and a morally corrupt woman forced her to commit suicide (Sreenivasan 2000).

In the article "Lessons from Sahayatrika," V. N. Deepa (writing as Devaki Menon)[23] discusses this case and observes that what is noticeable here is the social norms that make "the public accusation of being a lesbian carry so much stigma as to drive a woman to suicide."[24] The report in *Sameeksha* by K. K. Sreenivasan, the responses of Mini's family, and the demands by the college's Dalit students association for a judicial enquiry into the circumstances that lead to Mini's death point to the unsympathetic and hostile manner in which the college administration handled this case as linked to Mini's caste identity. Based on assumptions of the moral looseness of non-dominant caste women, for example, the hostel warden checked Mini's bank account to see if she was working as a prostitute. The vilification and humiliation that Mini faced was shaped by her marginal position, her privacy and safety trespassed with impunity. Her suicide throws light on the ways in which exclusions around caste structure the violence faced by sexual minorities in Kerala. While the director specifically mentions how the suicide of the Kerala Varma College student motivated her to make *Sancharram*, the translation of the event into a cinematic text significantly shifts the caste position of the central character.

The central desiring subject of the film, Kiran, fits the mold of the model "Kerala woman." She is an educated, career-minded Nair woman whose intellectual capacity and creative faculty mark her as a promising future citizen. At the same time, Kiran is in many ways the icon of rebelliousness in this film. She is the one who takes the initiative to express her desire to Lilah and refuses to be crushed by social pressures. When Delilah says that she is willing to get married but simultaneously continue a relationship with Kiran, Kiran refuses this adulterous arrangement. The film ends with Kiran choosing life over death and walking ahead heroically to carve out a path of her own. But this sense of agency that the film bestows on Kiran seems to be tied up to an essentialized Nair identity that the film constructs for her.

This construction of the agential woman as a Nair woman taps into the formation of caste privilege in Kerala. Nair identity is valorized both because of its links to a matrilineal past and because of the community's willingness to embrace modernity in forms such as education and employment. Within literary writings since the late nineteenth century, the Nair woman is often given the status of an autonomous subject whose matrilineal history gives her an aura of individual rebellion. *Sancharram* taps into this history when Kiran traces her lineage back to her female ancestor who rebelled against social conventions in order to marry the man of her choice. In *Sancharram* desire is posited as unconnected to existing social structures, and it is enacted in its fullest only by Kiran, who is shown to have an external horizon of possibility. In the beginning of the film, she comes to Kerala from the metropolitan capital Delhi. At a moment of crisis, caused by the public revelation of her relationship with Delilah, she talks on the phone to her gay uncle in Delhi while considering a move outside of Kerala. Her access to markers of modernity, like the fluent use of English, sets her up as mobile and capable of functioning outside of the local setting. Pullappally's choice of the social location of her main characters cuts against some of the repeated patterns brought out by the Sahayatrika group in their study on lesbian suicides. The study has brought out the disturbing trend that many of the lesbian women who have committed suicide are from marginalized communities, especially Dalits, Adivasis, and Muslims. Many of these women have limited economic means and fewer opportunities to move to more urban centers in India.

The shift from a marginalized woman to a woman firmly located in a privileged, mobile milieu shows how the form of a romantic love story and a "coming out" narrative hinges on a protagonist who is a Nair woman. This is because the narrative conventions of this romantic story are woven around the conception of a desiring woman who is positioned as agential. While it is not easy for any woman to lead a non-normative life in contemporary Kerala, there is a greater availability of narrative forms within which an upper-caste woman can be presented as an autonomous, transgressive subject. For the "other" woman who belongs to the non-dominant caste or class strata, her ownership over her body is not a given, and there is a paucity of canonized narrative forms within which her story can be told. She does not fit into the model of the agential

Kerala woman, and her desire to desire does not find many celebrated precedents in narrative.[25] Samidha Satapathy argues that caste and gender intersect to limit the possibilities of transgression available to Dalit women and that it is important to revisit the concept of transgression in terms of accessibility and affordability: "Transgression has been acceptable only when those who can afford to transgress, transgress" (2006: 78). So it is not coincidental that a filmic rendering of high romantic desire between two young girls deploys the figure of the privileged Nair woman in Kerala as its central protagonist.

Deshadanam: Travel without a Final Destination

If we take a quick look at the titles of both of these films, what stands out are their invocations of movement and travel. Travel is a process through which space is rendered mobile. *Sancharram* literally embodies this sense of movement. *DKK*'s reference to travel is through the term *deshadanam*. As discussed earlier, it refers to the figure of the migratory bird (*deshadanakkili*) who seasonally wanders from one destination to another in search of a conducive environment. *Deshadanam* suggests ambiguities in the Malayalam language with reference to the concepts of space and travel. *Desham* as a term conjures up multiple imaginations of space. It refers to the macropolitical unit of the nation, but it can also be used in a much more local sense to refer to the spatial unit of a particular geographical region within Kerala.[26] *Deshadanam* is the process of traveling through the *desham* in a wandering manner, without necessarily having a destination in mind. It is more the journey itself that matters than the final destination. There is an element of quest or search that is built into such a notion of traveling.

It is through occupying space and encountering new experiences that one arrives at new meanings. Since the term *desham* can refer to the larger geographical unit of the nation and also to a specific region, it infuses multiple histories and spatial frames into a localized space. Layers of possibility are packed into one single space that is rendered mobile and unstable through ways in which it is occupied. The term *desham* parallels De Certeau's (1984) definition of a "space" as distinct from a "place." For De Certeau place carries an indication of stability wherein every object has a specific location in relation to each other. Space, on the other hand, "occurs as the effect produced by the operations that orient it, situate it, temporalize it." Thus he argues that: "*space is a practiced place*" (117).

The focus on *deshadanam* encapsulates the central proposition of this chapter that "queer" is a form of reading that is akin to modes of wandering—unglued movements that set the reader on a crooked path with no finite endings. One of the important distinctions I would like to draw between the spatial representations in *DKK* and *Sancharram* is how within *DKK* the specific area of Kerala within which the film is set becomes a "*desham*" or a "space" in flux, while in *Sancharram*, the location appears as a "place" that remains stable and frozen. Although the film is titled *Sancharram* (The journey), a sense of mobility is overturned by the rigid sexual politics that arise from the spatial dynamics of the film. One of the privileged sites within this film is the inside space of the home, which is represented through the image of the Nair *taravad*.[27] The film spends a lot of its energy in constructing this space of the imagined home as rooted in tradition. This is one of the chronotopes that the film uses repeatedly.[28] The opening sequence of the film is a shot of the ancestral home of Kiran's mother. The shot frames the outside of the home as a leaf falls in slow motion in the foreground, giving it an aura of having lived through the passage of time. The opening shot of the house seems arrested in time, resembling a still photograph. This is followed by two shots, one of the wooden pillars and the ceiling of the house, and then a close-up of a lamp that hangs from the ceiling, blackened by time and use. When the young Kiran enters the house, we have a high-angle shot of Kiran, who seems dwarfed—physically overwhelmed—by the house. The camera tilts up to show her reflection in the glass of old photographs on the wall. Then the camera tracks her exploration of the old house, museum-like: ornate woodwork, artillery on the wall, and replicas of paintings by Ravi Varma.[29]

Through these carefully chosen and arranged artifacts (e.g., black-and-white photographs and paintings by Ravi Varma), the film condenses time and produces an imagined cultural cocoon equitable to Kerala. Backgrounding the initial establishing shots of the house, a voiceover of Kiran's mother tells the story of the continued lineage of this Nair heritage as one that is sustained through women. The establishing shots of this house function as the transition device for Kiran and Delilah's move from childhood playmates to intimate adolescent friends. We see them as small children playing together in the garden in front of the house. As Delilah's mother calls out to her, she leaves reluctantly and Kiran enters back into her house. There is a long shot of Kiran's house in all its grandeur, and the camera holds still for a few seconds. This is followed by a dissolve into another shot of the same house and a grown-up Delilah rushing in to meet Kiran. Although the film exposes the heterosexual foundations on which this matrilineal tradition is built, it relies on a manufactured idea of Nair tradition that is portrayed as timeless and eternal and embodied in the iconic architectural structure of the Nair *taravad*.

"In a land steeped in tradition . . . a secret love," says the blurb on the DVD of *Sancharram*. The film constructs Kerala as a place that stands still and seems to be untouched by modernity. "All this is filmed against the lush backdrop of Kerala, the histories and customs of the *taravads*, the strong women who run the houses in this matrilineal society," says Vikram in a review of *Sancharram* that appears on the official website of the film.[30] The film thus establishes continuity between the idyllic landscape and the sphere of the Nair home, as both become emblematic of a rural Kerala. Other reviews of this film mention its "mesmerizing lyricism" and emphasize that what is different about the film is the eruption of same-sex love in a pristine, rural setting. Thus the film sets up an imagined, pastoral Kerala that is steeped in tradition. The film's construction of this frozen space is essential for its narrative of forbidden desire to seem radical.

The single scene of sexual intimacy between the two girls shows us how much the film relies on its idealized construction of a place in order to deliver its "queer" statement (figure 3.1). The scene is set in a secluded pond that has stone steps, and the sequence begins with a long shot of the pond itself. We see the lilac water lilies, the green water lapping the edges of the pond, and the reflections of the coconut trees. This is followed by the sequence of intimacy between the two women, shot in a series of extreme close-ups (figure 3.2). At the end of the sequence we get a close-up of Lilah's feet as they hit the water. The camera pans to give us a shot of the green water with fish moving in it. Then there is a cut to a long shot of the pond seen through the window, and the next shot shows a stone statue on the steps of the pond. The director thus sets up an idyllic setting within which the desire between the two women is staged. The

3.1 The prelude to the sexual encounter: frame grab from *Sancharram* (2004).

3.2 The kiss between Kiran and Delilah in the backdrop of the stone steps and the pond: frame grab from *Sancharram* (2004).

pond, the greenery, and the temple drums that form the audio-visual backdrop are the conventional pegs on which Pullappally hangs her "radical" love story.

Most of the scenes showing interactions between the two women are located in places that are marked by an absence of other humans.

Narrow pathways bordered by emerald-green fields, towering hills, bubbling brooks, a moonlit night—such pristine landscapes form the backdrop for the unfolding of their desire. Or, it is within the closed spaces of the house—the bedroom of either Kiran or Lilah—that we witness their interactions. This particular construction of a cinematic "place," to use De Certeau's term, makes the spatial terrain of this film a static one. The regional setting within this film does not acquire the layered texture of a *desham* but remains inanimate like a picturesque tourist postcard.

In sharp contrast to this, *DKK* is mostly set in Cochin, an urban center of Kerala, and in the public spaces in this city that are mobile and dynamic. Unlike the neat binary that *Sancharram* sets up between the stable realm of the home/homeland and the disruptive forces of desire that rock it, *DKK* sets out to map a fluctuating social field of an urbanizing Kerala. It is important that the director chooses Cochin as the destination point to which the heroines run away in an attempt to build a new life. Even today Cochin is seen as the urban hub of Kerala—embodying a heady mixture of anonymity, sexual activity, and criminality.[31] The film makes constant references to the dangers and possibilities that the city offers. When Nimmi and Sally come to a Catholic convent in Cochin and request accommodation for a night, Sally tells the missionaries that if they deny them accommodation, they may have to read about the gang rape of two young girls in the newspapers the next day. When Harikrishnan and Nimmi first meet, he refers to the multiple encounters between people in the city who meet and part as strangers. Sally and Nimmi capitalize on the fact that Cochin is a city of tourist flow and behave as if they are outsiders visiting Kerala. They rename themselves Maya and Eileen, speak in either English or broken Malayalam, carry cameras, and exude an interest in Kerala folk arts. As they navigate this new space, they are well aware of unpredictable developments. The unnamed desire and intimacy that is staged between the two women seems to be intrinsic to the lack of stability of the social sphere they occupy. The layered and mobile realm of the *desham* they inhabit is akin to the layered and mobile realm of their desire. Therefore queerness is not posited as a forbidden desire; rather, it is part of the messy contours and multiple possibilities within urban space itself.

While *Sancharram* unfolds in the home space and the realm of the family, *DKK* is marked by its absence of home or domestic spaces. In fact, all through the film there is not a single sequence in which either Nimmi or Sally is shown inside a house. They occupy a range of public spaces, and the film focuses on their negotiations of these spaces. These spaces form a shifting terrain as the two women move through and occupy them. The film begins in a highly disciplined boarding school run by Roman Catholic sisters, and we see the attempts of Nimmi and Sally to upset the order of this school through diverse pranks and rebellious acts. After they run away from school, the youth hostel marks their arrival in the city. Here they can don new identities and temporarily erase their histories. A place made for travelers and tourists is shown as a transitory space that can offer temporary shelter to the two women.

One of the high points in their journey together is when they feel that they have escaped the surveillance of the school authorities. A long sequence of both of them running together on the open road visually and aurally conveys their newly acquired sense of freedom. Initially as they cautiously open the door of the convent and step out into the street, the background music consists of reverberating drumbeats, and a sense of tension is conveyed through the music and lighting. There are shots of the two of them stealthily running in the dark, hoping to find an escape route. But as the sequence progresses, they move into an open road and it is the break of dawn. The two women merge with the morning joggers—another sign of an urban milieu. The background music shifts to a fast-paced symphony of multiple instruments: flute, drums, and violin. This sequence is in slow motion, and their bodies move in unison to the rhythm of the rousing music. We see them surging ahead, hair flying in the air, a broad smile on their faces. There are multiple closeup shots of their legs moving rhythmically as they run on the road that stretches before them. This sequence immerses the viewer in the exhilarating movement of two young women occupying the open space of the road.

The public spaces that these two women occupy reflect the everyday spaces of an urbanizing Kerala in the eighties. There are night shots of crowded streets with shops on both sides and political posters that festoon the roadsides. Phone booths, ice-cream parlors, public parks, bus stations, restaurants, and theaters give the audience a texture of the developing urban spaces in Kerala in that period. The two women's encounters in these public spaces are often tinged with a sense of danger. In fact, the first time we see them breaking a rule in school is when they go to a theater to watch a matinee and the news reaches the school authorities because they are harassed there by some men. After they run away from school, we see them negotiating the streets and using various methods to evade different men on the streets, including a policeman who targets them. In night scenes on public roads, men often follow to harass them, and Sally at one point voices in English, "They are getting on my nerves."[32]

The film speaks directly to the feminist debates in Kerala that have occurred since the 1980s about women's lack of access to public spaces and the high level of violence against women in such spaces. This is an ongoing debate and a matter of concern for activist groups based in Kerala. Deepa, in her observations around the responses to Sahayatrika, a support network and help line for lesbian and bisexual women in Kerala, mentions that many of the women the organization supported did not identify primarily as lesbians or as women loving women. They were "drawn to the potential of a political and social space where one could articulate issues and experiences of women's sexuality more freely" (2005:192). These responses to Sahayatrika show both the absence of locations where women can resist the "patriarchal ordering of their bodies" (192) and the continuing struggle of women to stake a claim on public spaces.

Thus the strategies staged in *DKK* of two women occupying public spaces do have a political resonance even today. In fact, the film retains a sense of ambivalence about what brings these two women together; is it their desire for each other or their common dream of an imagined space of freedom? Or is it even possible to distinguish these two motivations? They often express a shared desire for a safe space. This is the question that Nimmi asks Sally when they first come to the youth hostel: "Is this the place you told me about . . . the safe space far, far away?" But at no point in the film do they seem to attain this sense of reaching a destination. They are always on the run, always in search of another world. This is how they perform a *deshadanam*, a constant wandering within one regional location.

What is disruptive about the film is that it shows that the journey is a possible one. These women do manage to enter into public spaces usually closed off to women and to occupy them in strategic ways as a couple. When Harikrishnan first sees them in a restaurant eating ice cream and chatting, he mistakes them for a heterosexual couple. Later when he realizes that they are two women, he has no qualms over interrupting their shared space and even insinuating that they are immoral women because they while away their time in a public place. He interrogates them and tells them that he could easily inform the police of meeting two young women in suspicious circumstances. The ease with which he is able to disrupt the space shared by these two young women comes from the fact that the public space of the restaurant is not one that belongs to them. The film's tragic ending suggests the impossibility of safe spaces for two women. But in spite of this closure of possibilities, the whole film stages multiple enactments of two women's struggles to occupy the public sphere. "As the film concludes, a new journey begins," says the synopsis of *Sancharram* on the film's official website with reference to the ending.[33] I would argue that *DKK* begins where *Sancharram* ends; it actually sees the two women set off on a physical journey through the world and encounter the grittiness of life. It is a journey that ends in suicide, but what the film captures is the journey itself. By showing these two women performing this disruptive journey and occupying public spaces in unconventional ways, the film queers the social sphere in which it is located.

Strategies of Queering

A comparative reading of *Sancharram* and *DKK* and their strikingly different representations of spaces highlight the different discourse of sexuality within which these two films are located. Ligy Pullappally undertakes the project of setting up a visible lesbian subject and makes a claim for the expression of lesbian desire within the Kerala public sphere. As I and others have argued, Gopinath also observes that "the film's representation of queer female desire and subjectivity functions quite clearly within a global human rights-based framework; to that extent, it mirrors both the uses and limits of such a framework" (2007: 345). Pullappally's political agenda, as it is projected through her film, flattens the more tentative and conflicted political contours and strategies that emerge from Kerala-based groups like Sahayatrika. In *DKK*, through the journey of the two women, we see a dramatization of the tensions between visibility and invisibility and the women's attempts to deploy various everyday strategies of survival. After they run away from school,

Sally exclaims that they are free birds once they get out of the school uniform. "No one can say who we are now; we can decide that from now on," is her statement of celebration at the masking of their past identity. From renaming themselves to dressing differently and taking on new identities as tourists or researchers, there are multiple ways in which they erase their past and make use of anonymity in a new place in order to lead the life they desire.

In the political organization of sexual minority rights in Kerala, there is an implicit critique and a search for alternatives to the politics of visibility. Since the backlash against lesbian couples who come under media scrutiny is often tremendous, Sahayatrika organizers mention that they have to use a multiplicity of strategies to negotiate the tensions between visibility and safety. Deepa draws on the experiences of Sahayatrika to emphasize how "visibility continues to be both empowering and disempowering for sexuality minority groups, and we must all grapple with its contradictions" (2005: 192). Sahayatrika, in its early phase, had published public statements without having any visible spokespeople (194). In her introduction to the organization, Deepa highlights its tenuous nature and its strategic use of invisibility and/or anonymity: "Sahayatrika itself came to be perceived as representing a community and movement (one tabloid newspaper estimated our organization membership as being 1,000 women strong!) when in fact our contacts with women were sometimes tenuous and fleeting. This tenuous community had an invisible spokeswoman with a fake name and dubious identity—Devaki Menon—a pseudonym which sometimes represents myself and sometimes Sahayatrika workers collectively" (176). The organizational experiences of Sahayatrika point toward strategic uses of invisibility and anonymity, even as the organization fights for public acceptance of homosexuality. The lesbian subject position that is posited in *Sancharram* carries a much less conflicted relationship to the politics of visibility. It transplants the coming out narrative to the Kerala scenario in an unproblematic way.

The process of making the lesbian visible in post-independence India has been closely entwined with the trajectories of cinematic forms. The commercial release of Deepa Mehta's *Fire* in India in 1998,[34] the attacks against this film that led to theaters being vandalized and posters burned by Shiv Sena men and women in Mumbai and Delhi, and the unprecedented counterprotests in which queer activists, artists, writers, filmmakers, and politicians organized to support the film is often positioned as a founding event in the national discourse on homosexuality. Making a direct link between representational practices and political movements, Shohini Ghosh says, "The theatrical release of *Fire* gave visibility to the representational lesbian, and the subsequent controversy gave visibility to the 'real' lesbians" (2010: 101). A broad-based Campaign for Lesbian Rights (CALERI) was formed as a response to this controversy to build awareness that "discrimination on the basis of sexual orientation/preference is a violation of basic human rights" (quoted in John and Niranjana 1999: 584).

A personal account by two activists who organized the protest that took place outside the Regal Theatre in Delhi on December 7, 1998, brings to fore the act of breaking the silence: "By the morning of 8 December it had all happened. The word lesbian was on the front pages of every newspaper I picked up in Delhi. LESBIAN. It looked odd and out-of-place. Why was a word like that being tossed around? A word so loaded with fear, embarrassment, prejudice, a word shrouded in silence, a whisper that spoke of an identity that must be hidden from others, that frightening word that dare not cross any threshold, was on that winter morning landing at the door-step of millions of households in many parts of the country" (S. L. 1999/2000: 524). To capture the momentousness of this event, the writers take recourse to a kinetic prose that signals the sudden proliferation of a denigrated term in ordinary spaces—everywhere that a newspaper can reach. They declare the coming of the term "lesbian" in bold letters that leads to the breaking of what they term as a "social contract" of silence (525). While it is crucial to acknowledge the power and far-reaching impact of this event, it is also important *not* to deploy this moment to plot a singular narrative of lesbian politics in India as tied to paradigms of visibility.[35]

The practice of making visible and the call to claim visibility has been central to feminist and sexuality politics in India and other parts of the world; but following the interventions of scholars on gender and visual culture, my aim is to move away from the empirical sense in which visibility is used to the rhetorical and discursive connotations of visuality. It is important for sexuality politics to trouble an uncritical investment in all-out visibility and ask "how things are made visible" (Hayes 2005: 521). In fact, if one reads between the lines of the statement of coming out written by S. L., one can see the inherent tensions in this project of voicing and visibility. The account mentions the "great personal risks" taken by those holding posters in front of cameras and also points to the conflicts within the group about the language and use of terms such as "lesbian," "sexuality," and "women-women relationships" (S. L. 1999/2000: 525). The organizers themselves used the pseudonym "S. L." when they published this personal account.[36] While teleological accounts of sexuality politics compel us to brush aside these negotiations as small hiccups in an initial stage of the project of consolidation of a stable identity, my analysis points to the need to keep alive these tensions, to engage with the differential costs and struggles of subjects who may seek recognition under the umbrella of the term "lesbian." I suggest that processes of anonymity and spectrality continue to be tied to practices of queering—in both the sites of cinema and activism. We have to be wary of a smooth alignment between the "unambiguously visibililized" (Ghosh 2010: 135) lesbian subject and its correspondence to queer spectatorship. Cinematic attempts to "visibilize" the lesbian in uncertain terms may in turn run the risk of essentializing identities.

Ligy Pullappally, in her conversations about the making of *Sancharram*, draws attention to the ways in which her film is a particular process of translation. She draws on the frameworks of LGBT rights within a metropolitan Indian and transnational context and applies them to a rural setting. In an interview that appeared in the Bangalore-based newspaper *Deccan Herald*, she positions her film in the middle of the mainstream LGBT movement both in India and abroad in saying that *Sancharram* was her response to Deepa Mehta's film *Fire* (1998): "That film handled the subject of a lesbian relationship as well. . . . In addition, *Fire* is an English language film in an urban setting. I made my film to reflect the more *traditional* gay experience in India. My characters are unapologetically gay and speak a regional South Indian language" (Cheerath-Rajagopalan 2005, italics mine). A climactic moment in Deepa Mehta's film is one in which the two women protagonists bemoan the fact that there is no word in their language to name their relationship. Pullappally seems to function within this same logic of naming and making visible as she sets out to show how lesbian love in a recognizable form is alive and thriving in rural pockets in India. She highlights her choice of Malayalam as the language for the film. But this is an uncomplicated process of translation in which an already-processed concept of lesbian desire is neatly plastered onto a new context, which risks the freezing of cultural formations more than it queers the social sphere.

In her attempt to produce a "traditional" lesbian narrative, the film at times slips into an unquestioning valorization of a Nair identity and banks on a caste-based stratification to deliver its heroes. The film draws on the tropes through which Nair hegemony is consolidated in contemporary Kerala, like the caste group's claims of a military past with expertise in martial arts. In the beginning of the film we see Kiran as a young girl returning to her mother's ancestral home in Kerala and wandering around its huge, palatial rooms. It is in this place that the film embeds her. Even when her mother confronts her about her relationship with Delilah, it is her Nair identity that Kiran asserts to articulate her spirit of rebellion. "Isn't it the blood of the warriors that flows through me also?" she asks as she refuses to settle for any compromising marriage. Thus the film, in its attempt to set up a heroic female figure, resorts to the trope through which male heroes in Malayalam films are often made. Caste, religious privilege, and a noble lineage become the markers of heroic valor. The setting up of totalized identity categories in a film like *Sancharram* results in relations of power within which selected practices and subjects are privileged over others. The celebration of a high romantic lesbian desire and a singular lesbian subject position in cinema sets off a pattern of cultural exclusions and inclusions.[37] Thus this film sidesteps and reduces the complexities of the very issue of lesbian suicides that motivated the film in the first place.

DKK, because of the historical moment of its production and the circuits through which it moved, steers clear of a countercultural labeling. Padmarajan as a director was an important exponent of the genre of "middle cinema" that blended the conventions and concerns of commercial and art cinema and thus appealed to a larger audience base.[38] Though he was quite risqué in his representations of sexuality in some of his other films and writings, his attempt with *DKK* was primarily that of addressing a Malayali middle-class audience. The star casting in this film with the popular hero Mohanlal and successful actresses like Urvashi and Karthika and the attention paid to the song sequences are all markers of the fact that this was a film made for a mainstream theater release. Padmarajan in this film steers clear of graphic expressions of sexual desire, and this is distinct from some of his other films, such as *Thoovana-thumbikal* (Dragon flies in the sprays of rain, 1987) and *Namukku parkkan munthirithoppukal* (Vineyards for us to dwell, 1986). *DKK* is understated in its visualization of emotions and romantic feelings.

Even in the final emotionally charged scene in which Sally returns to Nimmi, her affirmation of her attachment to Sally is in the form of a question. "Haven't you understood me yet?" she asks Nimmi, leaving the audience to fill in the gaps of what either they or Nimmi understand and thus making possible multiple interpretations of the relationship. The process of queering that this film undertakes is not to set up a stable unit of the "lesbian couple" nor is it privileging a particular subject position as the queer subject position.

In Search of a Resolution

When filmmakers give a representational form to relationships that are considered to be outside the realm of the legitimate, the plot resolution or the ending of the film is often a point of crisis. *Sancharram* takes a conscious turn away from suicide as a possible ending and stages Kiran's decision to turn away from the abyss of death and toward the beginning of a new life. This is cinematically represented by the metamorphosis of a caterpillar into a butterfly that flies into the blue sky. At the same moment, Lilah's voice booms through the air as she cries out Kiran's name. Here the film suddenly cuts to the scene of Lilah's wedding in the church. As the wedding vows are read out by the priest, they are repeated multiple times, as if resonating in Lilah's mind. The camera gives us Lilah's point of view as she kneels down, and we see everyone around her elongated and blurred. Suddenly the church empties out, and Lilah drops her bouquet and runs out of the church, screaming Kiran's name. It is this voice that reaches Kiran, and a fantasy reunion is staged as the same butterfly flutters before Lilah's eyes. Thus *Sancharram* resorts to a break from realism in order to stage a resolution to the love story.

This formal turnaround, in order to enact a hopeful resolution to the problem the film poses, brings to the fore a clash of registers between the realist commitments of the film and its sudden slide into the realm of fantasy. The issue of lesbian suicides that the film is responding to and denouncing is rooted within the contemporary social field of Kerala. But

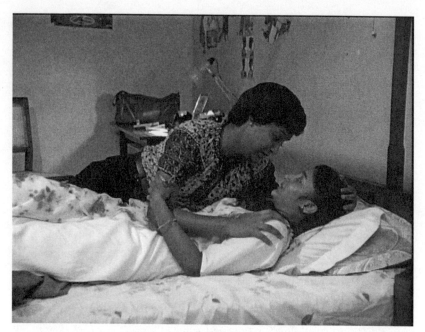

3.3 The final reunion between Sally and Nimmi: frame grab from *Deshadanakkili karayarilla* (1986), from the Surya-Sun TV Network.

the depiction of lesbian desire in this film as a romantic passion that can be realized only through an act of individual rebellion, reentrenches the privileges that structure the dominant imagination of a rebellious subject. The dreamlike quality of the ending of *Sancharram* is symptomatic of the split between the questions of sexuality within the social sphere of contemporary Kerala and the politics of sexuality that the film puts forward. This suggests a limited sexual politics, where rebellion is posited as an individual act of grand revolution and desire is set up as a radical force outside the realm of the social or the public. The opposition the film constructs between the "secret love" and a "land steeped in tradition" turns to a dream sequence as the necessary cinematic device through which a final act can be staged.

The final act of suicide in *DKK* is a difficult one to read, because the film makes a simple reading impossible. The film comes from a time period when lesbian suicides were not established in the public sphere as an object of public concern and political activism. So the suicide at the end of the film cannot directly be linked to the issue of lesbian suicide as we know it today. The film has an unexpected ending, when the morning after an intense night of reunion between Nimmi and Sally (figure 3.3) the viewer sees the inert bodies of the two girls in bed together. The euphoria and hope of their coming together the previous night does not in any way prepare the viewer for the rude shock of death in the next sequence. "To a faraway place, a safe faraway place," in white letters is the postscript to the ending of this film. The term "safe" is in English, echoing Nimmi's question to Sally about safe havens earlier in the film. The fact that the two girls have to commit suicide after they swear to be together forever points to the tenuous nature of their tactics of survival. It may signal the hopelessness of their search to find a livable space within existing social structures. But the sliding chain of referents within which the final shot of the entwined dead bodies of the two girls can be placed complicates the reading of the suicide simply as a statement about the impossibility of queer desires.

The suicide in *DKK* can be read within the conventions of denouements in Malayalam romantic films and literary plots. The resolution is reminiscent of endings in other celebrated heterosexual romances in Malayalam literature and film, where the ultimate triumph of love is to die together, especially in the face of social opposition.[39] By making two women stage this final act of togetherness, especially after a climactic scene of reunion in which they pledge to be with each other forever, the film once again mimes the conventions of heterosexual couplehood. Thus the suicide, instead of cementing and privileging a heterosexual matrix, functions as another trope through which the film troubles the normative sexual arrangements of society. In a culture of representations where the testimony to true love is to die together, Sally and Nimmi's couplehood becomes established beyond doubt through their suicide. Thus, one could argue, the film retains its ability to destabilize the social sphere even through this seemingly dark gesture of suicide. Even in the ending of the film, the two women are not brought back into the productive circuits of disciplining institutions such as the boarding school that plays an important role in fashioning femininity. They remain failed subjects who cannot be domesticated into the "straight time" of accumulation and progress.

My comparative reading of both these films posits the desire for cultural productions that capture a different language of queer politics in

Kerala, grounded in the specificities of the context. I show how some of the taken-for-granted assumptions of transnational queer politics, like the celebration of visible bodies, get radically thrown into question when we turn to regional sites of analysis. The location of Pullappally's film in the LGBT discourse in India and abroad makes it so enmeshed in setting up an established meaning for the term "queer" that the process of queering becomes one of stabilizing a chosen form of desire as the ideal one. This process of setting up a stable trajectory for queer desire freezes the spatial and social terrain of Kerala. The process of queering that *DKK* undertakes, in contrast, neither attempts to set up a particular subject position as the queer one nor does it plot a blueprint for the direction that same-sex desire should take. It sets out to trouble the naturalized construction of the heterosexual couple and injects a sense of instability into the social sphere itself.

Unlike *Sancharram*, which projects a picture-perfect Kerala disrupted by same-sex love, *DKK* puts a finger on the queerness within the nebulous terrain of sexuality in Kerala. This film gives a representational form to the destabilizing possibilities that are necessarily present in any social sphere but not always talked about. This might be why *DKK* can be more enabling or disturbing to a regional Malayali audience, while *Sancharram* can be accepted or dismissed easily as a quaint love story in an imagined Kerala. If the dominant sphere can be shown to be an unstable one, it is useful for a model of queer politics that is not always invested in the project of naming and solidifying identities but that can work within a terrain of the contingent. *DKK* puts forward a critical process of queering that is threatening to the formations of femininity and domesticity. The wanderings in this film push the viewers to traverse the risky terrain of hope and desire, disjuncture and failure; it makes us aware of the fragility and persistence of visions of another order.

In the next chapter I will continue the discussion on lesbian politics in post-1990s Kerala by focusing on an investigative project about lesbian suicides undertaken by Sahayatrika. Chapters 3 and 4 in this book complement each other. They work together to tell a contingent story of how multiple spatialities and temporalities get intertwined in the regional to trouble the very conception of *the* political subject. By drawing out the echoes, citations, and messy movements in and of vernacular texts and events, I underline the need for "wayward translations" (Arondekar and Patel 2016: 166). In the following chapter, I examine how the lesbian as a political subject in Kerala is a haunting presence that elides the language of identity politics and human rights. The lack of resolution of queer politics is a central concern in the next chapter, too.

CHAPTER 4

Living Together, Dying Together
The Politics of Lesbian Hauntings

IN 1947, NOTED BILINGUAL WRITER KAMALA SURAYYA (WRITING as Kamala), published the short story "Stree" (Woman) which was effaced from Malayalam literary history and returned only after the writer's death in 2009.[1] "Stree" is a bold declaration of lesbian love. "I might be a woman. But my friend, is there a rule that one woman cannot love another woman?" (Surayya 1947/2009: 35) is the resounding statement of the piece. This is a triangular love story that unfolds from the point of view of the male narrator, Ravi, whose love for Prasanna is thwarted by the presence of her college friend Ramani. The lesbian lover, Ramani, is repeatedly described as a "magical creation" (35) and an "extraordinary creature" (34) whose memory haunts Ravi throughout his life. The writer here uses the tropes of a *yakshi* story, in which the *yakshi* is a mythical figure that is the manifestation of uncontrolled, threatening female sexuality.[2] Ravi's disturbing encounters with Ramani are in the dead of the night. She appears as "a female figure whose head was covered in a white sari," "her eyes glow like embers," "she has a monstrous laugh," and "her face has an iridescent glow because of the full moon" (35). Her impact on the narrator is that of leaving him with a bone-chilling sense of fear: "I felt afraid not just of her, but of all women, an indescribable fear" (35). She is a figure of sexual excess that he cannot comprehend, and therefore she haunts his memory even after her death. An intimacy between two women that is perceived to be eccentric[3] is represented using the literary form of a ghost story that plays on the interstices between presence and absence, past and present, visibility and invisibility. Misplaced bodies, out of time and out of place, have the power to raise radical questions that disturb the social order.[4]

"Feeling backward" (Love 2007: 4),[5] carrying the traces of this ghostly story along, let me move to the present. Idam (Space) was one of the first public conventions on sexuality politics in Kerala, organized by the activist group Sahayatrika on September 20, 2008. The daytime was dedicated to political speeches, experience sharing, readings, and performances that focused on gay, lesbian, and transgender lives and politics. In the evening, a small group of about forty people marched through the traffic, shouting slogans and holding up posters and banners, finally gathering in front of Corporation Hall—the space for public protests in the heart of the town of Thrissur. The convention ended with a candlelight vigil in memory of lesbian couples who had committed suicide in Kerala. As I stood in the back of the group of demonstrators with a flickering candle in my hand, one of the resounding slogans I heard was "Lesbian suicides, down, down." In the public speeches that followed, speakers protested against the structures of violent exclusion in Kerala society that pushed individuals to commit suicide because of their sexual orientation. "Lesbian suicides," as they have come to be called, have a conjoined couple at the center of each instance, and these relatively unknown deaths are made public through activist intervention.[6]

Queer mobilization in Kerala is built on the political valences of remembering and grieving for lives that are no more. What does it mean to produce a discourse around lesbian sexuality that has at its center the event of suicide and the specters of women whose lives could have been saved? What are the narrative tropes through which the lesbian as a figure surfaces in the public sphere of post-1990s Kerala? How does the discourse on lesbian suicides in Kerala complicate dominant modes of thinking about sexuality, agency, and subjectivity? In the period from the early 1990s to 2010, the initial decades of the configuration of lesbian politics in Kerala, practices of memory and haunting have been crucial for mobilizing the lesbian as a political subject. A close reading and critical analysis of interviews conducted by activist groups in Kerala, in the wake of lesbian suicides, comprise a significant step toward engaging with ways of configuring the "lesbian" that disrupt the boundaries of the rights-bearing, cohesive political subject. The interviews I analyze are fact-finding reports produced and circulated in order to raise awareness about the marginalized position of women who love women in Kerala. The form and content of these oral narratives, as well as the practice of documenting and editing them, brings to the fore a political subject embedded in affective networks of loss and mourning, sentimentality and romance, and memory and relationality.

Reading practices attuned to the workings of spectrality that smudge the borders of well-ordered temporal and spatial edifices are central to recent studies on queerness in postcolonial contexts. These studies are attentive to the fraught formations of sexuality embedded in the structures of caste, class, and race (Patel 2016; Ramberg 2016; Maitra 2017). My analysis in this chapter is in conversation with these scholarly interventions that traverse the enmeshing between the spectral and the material. This chapter demonstrates that vernacular cultural practices are dense sites of imagining sexuality politics where the ghostly coexists with the fleshy contours of intimacy. I analyze how melodramatic and erotic literary forms commingle with narratives of loss and haunting in etching the lesbian. Deciphering the dynamics of "alternate modes of textuality and narrative like memory and performance" (Muñoz 1996: 10) enables us to create modes of knowledge production that are sensitive to the fleeting nature of experiences and the unpredictability of queer acts. Thus a close attention to the multilayered and shifting workings of language, cultural forms, and media is crucial in order to reflect on the formations of the political.

In my use of the term "lesbian," I refer to the categories through which certain lives are framed for public circulation in the media and through activist interventions. My attempt here is not to deploy experiences from nonmetropolitan contexts to stabilize the identity category of the lesbian; on the other hand, I trace the discursive processes through which the lesbian becomes a recognizable figure in a regional context. I listen to the gaps and silences and to the citations of existing narrative tropes that structure these activist interviews. I reflect on the fractured practices of conjuring a political subject in a context where the category of the lesbian is not the edifice through which the lives and deaths of the protagonists are plotted by the members of their community. Multiple slippages and excesses surface when acts and bodies that cannot be easily classified become the basis for claims for justice. My analysis tries to retain these tensions instead of consolidating a stable identity. There are conflicting impulses in this political project of using lesbian suicides as the basis of the sexuality rights movement. In the narratives I analyze, the language of melodramatic love and mourning on the one hand, and the claims of rationality and rights on the other, clash against and complicate models of political subjectivity. Sexuality politics in nonmetropolitan regions in South Asia, primarily staged through vernacular cultural practices, function as a "shadow archive of resistance" (Halberstam 2011: 129) imbued by affective workings of memory and spectrality.

One of the important questions that these interviews raise is, What and who can be the subject of politics? Eduardo Cadava puts forward a compelling argument for the conceptualization of what he terms a "politics of tears" (Cadava, Kelman, and Miller 2006: 7). He observes that conventionally, politics is based on the idea of clarity of vision and a contained, rational way of apprehending the world, but if you look at the world with tears, you are not looking at it clearly: "A politics based on the model of tears, therefore, would be a politics that takes its point of departure from the presupposition that we always act without seeing things clearly, that we always act with tears in our eyes. . . . The tear signals a kind of dissolution or melting of the self at the moment when one is trying to make this or that decision" (Cadava, Kelman, and Miller 2006: 7). Here the bodily secretion of tears assembles a political subject who deviates from the model of rational containment. Even at the point of action, the subject inhabits a zone of affective excess. Thus, there is a splintering of the subject in the scene of political action: action itself becomes a tenuous process, routed through this blurred vision. This model of politics radically reconceptualizes the punctual, self-knowing actor. My analysis shows how Sahayatrika's investigation of lesbian suicides foregrounds the imagination of politics that is not subsumed by a linear teleology of progress and coming into being.

I propose that the lesbian as a mobilizable figure haunts the public sphere of Kerala and that it is necessary to examine this process of haunting to understand the complexities of sexuality politics. I consciously stay away from verbs like "emerge" or "appear" and instead use the term "haunt," because the lesbian is a figure that inhabits the shadowy zones between visibility and invisibility and is constructed through multiple mediations. By "lesbian haunting" I refer to acts and practices that render vulnerable the regulatory norms of sexuality, as these practices are tentative and not solidified. I do not use the term "lesbian hauntings" only in a literal sense of women who are dead and whose memories fuel a movement and demands for justice, though this is definitely a significant part of the picture. But as Avery Gordon argues, ghosts are not merely dead or missing people, they are "social figures" produced at the dense site of violence and exclusion: "To write ghost stories implies that ghosts are real, that is to say, that they produce material effects" (1997: 17). Gordon's call to leverage the process of haunting to reach for a critical vocabulary in which the "phantoms" of the regulatory workings of modernity can be touched and recognized motivates my analysis in significant ways. The Malayalam word *bhootham* can refer both to the "past" and a "ghost"—gesturing toward the racking desire to grasp the past and incarnate what has ceased to be. The twin meanings of this word point to the recognition built into language about the lack of fixity of endings; it unties the linear plotting of space and time and populates the present with ghosts and scars. Practices of haunting, mourning, and memorializing enable us to traverse the disjointed terrains of the politics of sexuality.

The chapter initially focuses on how the category of lesbian suicides gathers attention and recognition in the public sphere of Kerala. It introduces a specific case of lesbian suicide documented by Sahayatrika and analyzes how the documentation of this suicide participates in the production of the lesbian as a political subject in post-1990s Kerala.[7] I go on to analyze in detail the textual codes and narrative forms deployed in the reconstruction of the lives and deaths of two women in a nonmetropolitan location. I investigate how the vernacular literary form of sentimental romance through which the relationship between the women is shaped disturbs the contours of the rational subject of politics. I argue that the language of haunting and spectrality, which surfaces both within these narratives and in the process of memory making that the Sahayatrika team initiates, reconfigures dominant conceptions of agency. The chapter concludes with an exploration of how the relational form of the interview foregrounds an active engagement with intersubjectivity. I focus on the centrality of location to imagine a politics of sexuality that does not erase the broken negotiations of lives at the margins.

"Lesbian Suicides, Down, Down"

In 2002–2003, Sahayatrika conducted a series of fact-finding investigations of select media reports on lesbian issues. These included an investigation of the expulsion of a group of seven girls from a government school in Trivandrum in 1992 after they formed a lesbian group called the Martina Navaratilova Club. They also conducted fact-finding reports of many cases of lesbian suicides and interviews with members of the MSM community in Kochi. Since the late 1990s, incidents of women who oppose their families' objections and assert their right to live together have created debates about lesbianism in Kerala.[8] But lesbian suicides became the core political issue in many of the initial campaigns on homosexuality in Kerala. In what follows, I focus on a compilation of investigative interviews with community members conducted by Sahayatrika after the suicide by two young women, Ammini and Meera, in 2001.[9] These interviews were published as the central part of the anthology *Mithyakalkappuram: Swawarga laingikata keralathil* (Beyond myths: Homosexuality in Kerala, 2004), one of the first anthologies on homosexuality to be published in Kerala.[10] The book is designed in such a way that the interviews can be read alongside theoretical essays on homosexuality in Kerala and India.[11] The glossary in the beginning of the book translates into Malayalam and gives brief definitions of terms such as "coming out," "homophobia," "queer," and "closet"—foundational terms in a global sexuality discourse. But the project is not a pedagogic one by which the "local" is enlightened by a liberated, transnational discourse. The core of this book is the investigative report on lesbian suicides, where dominant assumptions of global LGBT politics are questioned and reconfigured.

The published interviews reconstruct the lives and deaths of Meera and Ammini, who committed suicide by consuming poison in May 2001. They were both from an Adivasi (tribal) community in a rural part of central Kerala.[12] Ammini was a school student who was sixteen years old and Meera was twenty-two years old. Their families were related, and they lived in a close-knit community. Meera's family was less well-off than Ammini's, and she supported her single mother by doing a range of low-income jobs that included domestic work and manual labor in tapioca plantations. Meera and Ammini had expressed their desire to marry each other and faced much opposition, especially from Ammini's family. While both of them had basic education, it was difficult for them to find the resources to move out of their social network.[13]

The series of news reports about double suicides of women appeared at the same time when reports of the high rates of individual and family suicides in Kerala since the early 1990s became a cause of concern both within and outside the state. Many of these double suicides happen when two women face pressure to marry men or are separated coercively. From the late 1990s onward, the recurring reports of lesbian suicides in Kerala garnered attention from activist organizations in different parts of India.[14] Sahayatrika founder V. N. Deepa observes, "Newspaper reports of double suicides among women companions who were unwilling to be separated are probably the most visible indicator of the difficulties endured by women-loving-women in Kerala" (2005: 182). The juridical and governmental mechanisms through which sexual figures acquire meaning and legibility is limited in the case of the lesbian. Within the AIDS discourse, for example, the lesbian, "understood globally as a practically zero-risk demographic" (Dave 2006: 62), makes a limited appearance, unlike the figure of the sex worker or MSM who are hypervisible as "high-risk" categories in the AIDS discourse (Patton 2002b). The mobilization around lesbian suicides in Kerala deals with the relative absence of the lesbian as a juridical category, but complicates the assumption that visibility and open claiming of an identity is the only strategy through which an issue can be made political.

The interviews about Meera and Ammini's suicides were conducted in two rounds in February 2002 and May 2002. The interviewers were activists who supported Sahayatrika and have played an important role in discussions and mobilizations about sexuality in Kerala. My analysis is mainly of the interviews published in the book. But I sometimes draw on the unpublished fact-finding reports, too, because the field notes by the interviewers reveal the dynamics of the interview process more than the published material.[15] For all the interviews, the interviewers went as a team and talked to people in a group setting. For example, the interview with Ammini's parents took place "under the shade of an unfinished open thatch structure uphill from Manju's [Meera's] house" (Sahayatrika 2002). In the transcribed notes about this interview, it is mentioned that "several community and family members gathered around while we were conducting interviews; so they were not private interviews" (2002). The list of people they interview is quite exhaustive. This includes immediate family members of the women, their friends and neighbors, Meera's employer, for whom she did domestic work, a social worker in the area, the psychiatrist who treated them, the doctor who conducted the autopsy, and police officers who investigated the case. The police officers do not allow the recording of their interviews: "We could not include the comments by the police. They did not allow us to record it. They mainly spoke about the 'abnormality' of this relationship and the crucial need for treatment" (Sahayatrika 2004: 60). In the interview with Ammini's mother, the interviewer notes that "there was much silence between questions" (Sahayatrika 2002). They also reflect on the "tight and aloof demeanor" of Ammini's father, signaling the difficulties they faced in conducting these investigations (2002).[16]

I analyze interviews conducted by a group of activists in order to trace the public circulation of the lesbian through the event of lesbian suicides. These interviews come to me framed by both the introduction written by the Sahayatrika team and the preface to the anthology written by the editor, Reshma Bharadwaj; the oral narratives have been transcribed, edited, and arranged in a format that can speak to the reading public of Kerala. This allows me to examine not only the interview as a process but also the political stakes of why and how these acts of storytelling, ethnography, and history making produce this suicide as an event that is central to the queer movement in Kerala. One of the long-standing theoretical concerns of feminist scholarship and postcolonial theory has been the status of the voice of the marginalized within historical narratives. This question resonates in a different way in this series of interviews where the primary subjects are already dead.[17] There is no assumption of direct access to the concerned subject possible here. Meera and Ammini's lives and deaths are mediated through the memory of an array of people associated with them.

The interviews are part of a larger fact-finding project conducted by Sahayatrika that is in the framework of human rights activism.[18] In the current economy, nongovernmental organizations (NGOs) play an increasing role as the guardians of human rights, as "the increasingly swift movement of words, human beings, goods, and objects across boundaries of all kinds has contributed to a new currency of human rights discourse and its various implementations" (Balfour and Cadava 2004: 287). Political thinkers have cautioned that the globalization of rights can at times reinforce the discrimination and violence that such rights are meant to redress, the seamless knitting together of militarism and the language of women's rights as human rights in the US war rhetoric in Afghanistan being a case in point (Mahmood and Hirschkind 2002; Abu-Lughod 2002; Nguyen 2011). Matters of authority and political power play a crucial role in determining the contours of categories like "human" and "rights," which are in no way universal. These interviews are embedded in the human rights discourse but also pull against its conventions. They document narratives of violence for national and international attention but point to the complexities and challenges faced by sexual subjects in a specific location, where the protagonists do not see themselves as part of a political cause.

Since its inception, Sahayatrika's functioning has been different from other NGOs that work with specific identity-based populations, mainly on AIDS awareness issues. Sahayatrika does have national and transnational linkages in terms of funding and membership and also strategically deploys the political language of human rights. As Gopinath observes, this is an organization that takes on the task of using a universal language of human rights to bring into "national and international visibility the unmarked deaths of scores of young people due to the violence of heteronormativity" (2007: 346). But the reflective writings by V. N. Deepa, interventions, and public events organized by Sahayatrika testify to their productive struggle to find a language for sexuality politics that engages with the complexities of the Kerala public sphere. Deepa opens "Queering Kerala: Reflections on Sahayatrika" with comments on how this project "was problematic by almost every index of political correctness" (2005: 176) because of the international funding that the organization had in its first phase and her own status as a nonresident Indian whose prior political experiences were in Western gay/lesbian communities. But in this article, as well as in other writings, she emphasizes how a queer movement in Kerala has to take on the "specificities and conflicts of life in this region" (196) even as it is open to national and global influences. In its working, Sahayatrika engages with the intersections between caste, class, and sexuality; the paradoxes of visibility and identity; the centrality of families and local communities, and the connections between different sexual minority positions (177).[19]

Making available these interviews as a document for public circulation and interpretation—an insistence that these interviews should be read not for "facts" but for the multiplicity of "meaning-making"—marks their political project as different from that of setting up an attainable target with a well-laid out, enumerable plan of action (Sahayatrika 2004: 57). There is a dispersed network of voices in these interviews that enable the reader to access a complex field of how women lovers negotiate their day-to-day lives. Beyond a single voice of condemnation of same-sex love, what we see are different attempts to make sense of a friendship that is marked by what is perceived as an excessive and misplaced affection. It is by wading through these narratives, by questioning them and locating the cracks in them, that the interviewers document the story of Meera and Ammini's struggle to survive.

Practices of Naming

There are irresolvable tensions in the public recollection of Meera and Ammini's lives and deaths. In their attempt to make these lives enter the official archive of lesbian suicides, the Sahayatrika team frames this as a relationship between two women. But even though this series of interviews plays a central role in the production of the lesbian as a political subject in Kerala, one can see that the categories of both "lesbian" and "woman" are disrupted within these founding narratives. Gayatri Gopinath argues that Sahayatrika's use of a women-who-love-women framework to analyze suicides in which one of the protagonists is a non–gender normative partner may be because the organization "ultimately adhere[s] to a global LGBT and feminist rights-based discourse that fails to sufficiently trouble the category of 'woman'" (2007: 346). But replacing the frame of lesbian politics with that of transgender politics does not provide us with an exit strategy, because both these terms are equally entrenched in a global LGBT discourse.[20] The protagonists themselves do not directly enter into either of these discursive frameworks to structure their lives. Therefore, it is important to forge reading practices that retain the tensions and the incompleteness of practices of naming as they are played out in marginalized locations.[21]

In the introduction to the interviews collected in *Mithyakalkappuram*, the Sahayatrika team writes, "One of the anxieties that emerge in these narratives is about the relationship between Meera's external appearance and her biological sex. It seems that a large crowd gathered to see the dead bodies to resolve their doubt about whether Meera was a man or a woman" (2004: 60). Many of the interviewees dwell on Meera's "masculine" clothes, physical appearance, and behavior. The descriptions also focus on the way she occupies space nonchalantly with her loud voice and her whistling—all seen as markers of masculinity (65). There are repeated allusions to Meera's ability to do manual labor, including hard physical work such as splitting firewood, climbing trees, and cutting grass. The psychiatrist who treated Meera and Ammini refers to Meera as a boy. Though he is from the medical field, he does not enter into a discussion of the biomedical classification of Meera's body. Instead he focuses on appearances and acts and their links to gender: "The boy's gestures and actions do not make you feel that he is a woman" (98). These differing perceptions of whether Meera is a man or a woman, and the repercussions of that classification, repeatedly appear in the narratives. But except for the psychiatrist, most respondents perceive Meera as a woman who "thought of herself as a man" (65). In fact, it is the immediate community's perception of Meera and Ammini as women that circumscribes their mobility in multiple ways. Some of the respondents discuss how in the long-term it would have been difficult for two women to economically support each other because they would not be allowed to participate in certain forms of manual labor in spite of Meera's physical strengths and abilities.

Meera's mother, Shantha, counters the allegation about the intimacy between Meera and Ammini by asserting Meera's bodily femininity: "As if Meera has a man's thing hanging on her. Did Ammini see that and set off with Meera?" (Sahayatrika 2004: 76). Thus there is an insertion of the anatomical body marked by the absent penis in order to dismiss the possibility of a sexual relationship between the two of them. Shantha remembers how Meera, at times, worked within this framework and deployed it to assert a lack of risk in her relationship with Ammini: "It's not as if we are going to give birth to a child together—so what's the problem?" (74). Thus the body and conceptions of masculinity and femininity are deployed in differential ways within these narratives in relation to structures of labor, mobility, intimacy, and reproduction. While the relationship between Ammini and Meera is named as a "lesbian" relationship after their suicide, a close reading of these narratives draws attention to the instability of this naming. Thus, there are layered and contingent workings of language and narrative forms through which marginalized lives enter public discourse. Practices of naming are therefore open to contestation, and this instability should be retained for queer politics to retain its critical charge.

Sweat, Tears, and Blood: Forms of Romance

The language of romantic love, sexual intimacy, conjugality, and friendship gets entangled as the respondents describe the relationship between Meera and Ammini.[22] Some of the respondents close to Meera, like Shantha and Meera's friend and employer, Shailaja, stress the intense love these women had for each other and oppose any suggestion of sexual intimacy: "They never had the mindset to live like a husband and wife. Two girls who really love each other. That was the only kind of love here. Then it's true that the *attachment* [in English] was more than usual here. They wanted to be with each other all the time, a special kind of love like that" (Sahayatrika 2004: 70). Here Shailaja differentiates their intimacy from sexual desire; by stressing that the former was the "only kind of love," she tries to expel any suggestion of the sexual. She uses the English term "attachment" to mark the relationship as "special," unexpected, and in many ways difficult to describe in the familiar registers of the vernacular.

Many of the respondents move away from the realm of the linguistic and draw on bodily gestures of romantic love to describe their relationship. Shailaja uses an inscription on Meera's hand as a mark of the tight-knit relationship between the two of them, recalling, "Meera would inscribe the letter 'A' in her hand using henna. One day I saw it on her hand . . . and I asked her who that A stood for. It's by questioning her like this that I came to know that A stood for Ammini" (Sahayatrika 2004: 70). It is on her body that Meera inscribes Ammini's name, a gesture by which desire is exteriorized on to the surface. Prameela, Ammini's classmate, speaks about the *premam*, the term used to refer to sexualized romantic love in Malayalam, that Ammini had for Meera and her desire to marry Meera and live with her.

Taking a cue from the deployment of *premam*, I suggest that *painkili*, a vernacular sentimental and sensual romance, is a narrative form through which Ammini and Meera's love is retold. *Painkili* is a term used to denote a highly popular form of romantic writing, but through repeated usage it has come to mean a set of attitudes that is excessively sentimental. The term literally means a "singing bird" or "the babbling parrot," and some critics suggest that it entered into circulation in reference to the melodramatic aesthetics of the immensely popular love story *Paadatha painkili* (The beautiful bird that does not sing) by Muttathu Varkey, published in 1955. *Painkili* writings circulated widely in Kerala, often in the form of serialized novels that appeared in low-priced Malayalam weeklies since the mid-1950s. Ancy Bay observes that by the 1960s the category of *painkili* was used as a caricature "to represent an allegedly sensuous habitat of reading with formulaic long-tales, ordinary readers and non-serious writers" (2015: 98). This immensely popular literary form is delegitimized within high cultural circles because of its investment in the sentimental and the sensational.[23] Ammini and Meera's use of the conventions of romance draw our attention to the hierarchies within narrative forms created by the segmented divide between "high culture" and "low culture."

In fact, *painkili* is the term through which the first investigative reports on lesbian suicides frame the relationship between two women lovers. A pioneering journalistic report says, "Same-sex love exists among women in hostels in the cities. But it is rarely that these women become inseparable and go to the extent of ending their lives together. Most of these suicides happen in villages which are far away from cities. These women come from ordinary families and read *painkili* publications" (Sebastian 1999: 15). In spite of the effort to draw attention to these suicides, in this comment the journalist judges these women lovers as misguided. For an audience familiar with the registers of speech in Kerala, this is a description that triggers denigrating associations about the assumed consumer of *painkili* fiction. This is usually a young woman from the lower middle class to lower class with a basic level of education, for whom reading is an emotional exercise of indulging in titillation and sentimentality. *Painkili* fiction is often seen as misleading young women into the world of sensory pleasures: "This form of fiction is part of a process that pacifies the vision of reality and destroys a sense of practicality" (Raveendran 1986: 159). The readers of *painkili* fiction are characterized as overinvolved with these textual narratives, so much so that their life begins to imitate fiction. The journalist's comment about the women lovers as readers of *painkili* writing also shows how he does not think they are equipped to become political subjects. They may be literate, but their literary tastes are not evolved enough to mold them into individualized, agential subjects. Thus they are placed in the position of victims who need to be saved through outside intervention.

Reading is an important practice in the production of the Kerala woman as a progressive subject. As part of the state-endorsed literacy movement,[24] much energy was expended to mold the literary sensibilities of the public so that men and women would read forms of literature that would ameliorate them. As Jenny Rowena observes, the cultural establishment in Kerala, which includes literary critics, zealously guards the borders between aesthetic forms; the well-perpetuated literary presumptions about "the high/low divide is used to delegitimize the writings, culture and lives of people who are not in the upper strata of society (such as women, Dalits and many others)" (2005b: 60). In a culture that is heavily invested in print and visual aesthetic productions, there is an assumption that the performance of everyday living is complementary to practices of reading or viewing films. There is not a causal correlation such as reading about an act of suicide in a novel and then attempting suicide; it is more that the structures of the affective realm of the fictional world, its ways of dreaming, desiring, loving, and grieving, provide the reader with a mode of performing life itself. This is why a judgment on a literary form becomes a judgment on ways of living, too. The lesbian women in the suicide narratives lack political potential for Sebastian because they read the wrong kind of novels, and therefore their subjectivities are not shaped in a way that they can rebel in a "productive" fashion.

But a look back in history will tell us how it is that *painkili* indeed has provided the grammar for same-sex love, and that it is not surprising to encounter these tropes in the retellings of the Ammini and Meera relationship. *Randu penkuttikal* (Two girls; Nandakumar 1974), one of the earliest popular novels in Malayalam that weaves a scintillating tale of lesbian romance and sex, follows some of the conventions of *painkili* writing, pointing to the malleability of the form of the *painkili* novel. This is a tempestuous love story of two school friends, Kokila and Girija, that includes such moments as: "My golden beauty! Girija hugged Kokila's warm, naked body tightly. Her fingers slowly caressed Kokila's back. Then everything went upside down. . . . Both the young girls were drowned in the whirlpool of desire. In the end, they were soaked in sweat. They gasped, tightly clutching each other's bodies, luxuriating in the moist aftermath of their emotional outflow" (124).

The love story between Kokila and Girija unfolds through detailed descriptions of their externalized expressions of love, which includes their pleasure in dressing each other up and giving gifts to each other. The description of romance in the novel is highly dramatic, sentimental, and associated with bodily excess.[25] It is such surface-level sensory expressions of love that respondents focus on when they illustrate Ammini and Meera's relationship. Prameela describes Ammini's performance of being in love: "Ammini would write Meera's name in blood on a paper, she would cut her hand with a blade and write with that blood" (Sahayatrika 2004: 106). She later mentions how Ammini would write Meera's name on her hand with the sharp needle edge of a geometric compass. Their friends also mention the physical shows of affection between the two of them, how they would walk with their hands on each other's shoulders, and how Meera would give Ammini money to buy things she wanted. Tears and blood, markings on the body, physical intimacy, and consumption all become narrated as part of their love story. These gestures and expressions are of a markedly different order from the more interiorized, poetic configurations of romance associated with a reified romantic subject.

Scholars have argued that the interiorization and regulation of desire, a move away from "sensual gratification to self-restraint," is important in the ushering in of a new mode of individualized, agential subjectivity in modern Kerala (Kumar 2002: 134). The conception of the agential subject who enacts desire through interiority is contradicted in the sensory and bodily performance of love that we see in the narration of Ammini and Meera's relationship.

Naisargi Dave observes that the consolidation of the lesbian as a stabilized political subject in metropolitan India also involved a process of loss, that "one such loss was a circumscription of the affective space of politics such that sex, pleasure, and desire were gradually deemed less than fit for this emergent, newly politically aspiring, lesbian community" (2010: 608). The performances of *painkili* romance raise the political implications of retaining such affective excess, even when these markers make the protagonists deviate from the model of a suitable political subject. To arrive at a complex reading of their lives, there is a need for a conception of the subject that is not tied to interiorized desire and individual autonomy. The interviews conducted by the Sahayatrika team function as a rich archive that shows the limitations of a global gay/lesbian discourse that is invested in a rarefied conception of desire and action that will lead to self-empowerment. These narratives have the potential to rupture political frameworks that recognize only certain forms of living and loving and also point to the risks of what is lost and erased in the "normalizing imperative of identity" (598).

The Ghostly Lesbian

These interviews, instead of setting up the lesbian as a stable identity category, give us glimpses of the ways in which intimate relationships between women are viewed and how such a relationship is mapped onto what Raymond Williams termed as "structures of feeling"—a formative hypothesis that focuses on cultural processes to show how the social is not a finished product marked by the past tense but rather it is an alive, active, affective "forming and formative process" (1977: 129).[26] This makes possible the conception of the social as a trajectory or a force field where the present is shot through by residual and emergent feelings. Therefore, in a particular historical moment there can be queer performances that do not necessarily congeal as a rebellious stance, but they do have the potential to bring together the spectral and the corporeal to gesture toward an elsewhere.[27]

The tentative acts of sexual dissidence that I analyze in this chapter put into motion a set of relations between bodies and desires that exceed models of femininity fitted to the patterns of conjugal domesticity. Ammini and Meera's desire to live together and their resistance to plans of marriage place them in a vexed relation to existing social strictures. They push against the social contract of family and child rearing as they assert their desire to live together. In the shaky trajectory of Ammini and Meera's lives, there are incidents of direct conflict with institutions such as the family, the police, and the psychiatric system. While Meera's mother does not directly oppose her daughter, who is her main source of emotional and financial support, Ammini's family repeatedly controls their daughter's mobility and admonishes her for spending time with Meera. There are violent verbal and physical conflicts between Meera and Ammini's family. One of the most confrontational episodes involves Ammini going to Meera's house and staying the night. Ammini's father comes to the house, accompanied by a large group of men and women from the community, and forcefully demands that Ammini leave with them. Meera's mother's notes how Ammini remained silent that night: "One had to put a twig in Ammini's mouth and poke it if she had to speak" (Sahayatrika 2004: 80). She hugs Meera and cries and does not make a move to leave. The two women cling together and even hide under the bed in a desperate attempt to stay together. Ammini's father lodges a complaint at the police station when Ammini refuses to leave that night, and the next morning the two of them are taken to the police station and later to the psychiatric hospital.

When Ammini and Meera are taken to the police station, there is a confrontation with state institutions wherein the opposition to their relationship becomes more formalized and consolidated. The police function as arbitrators who speak on behalf of the heterosexual order that Ammini's father stands for. The grounds on which Ammini's father sought police intervention was that Ammini was a minor and therefore the parents were the legal guardians. Here we see how lesbian relationships are often governed through informal alliances between the institutions of the family and the judiciary, in which the women are placed as dependents needing guidance and protection, rather than through direct invocation of a legal prohibition of homosexual intimacy. In Meera's mother's evocative recollection of the traumatic time when they were being taken to the police station and the hospital, there is a complex play between action and passivity, resistance and despair: "Even in the police station the children were holding hands and sitting like that. They held hands when they got into the jeep, all the way to the station and inside the station too" (Sahayatrika 2004: 81). Meera's mother captures the intensity of the relationship by focusing on their immobile physical posture, the handholding that lasted for hours, stretching the perception of time. When the police advise the two of them to give up this relationship and get ready for marriage, Meera resolutely says that they only want to live with each other, that "we are only going this way sir, no marriage for us" (82). But Shantha tells us that a few moments before this, Meera had attempted to commit suicide by jumping in front of a bus. Thus there is a quick shuttling between angry words of resistance and her desperate act of attempted suicide.

From the police station they are both taken to the psychiatric hospital, and in Shantha's account of the hospitalization, there is again the juxtaposition of a powerful tirade against what is being done to her daughter and an overwhelming feeling of desperation. The transition between anger and despair is palpable in her recollections that "they gave her so many pills. She was sane, they made her insane. Then I remember I felt I just wanted to die. I didn't want to live" (Sahayatrika 2004: 82). The mother's death wish here cannot be read as a passive one, for it emanates from anger against a medical system that "makes her sane daughter insane" (82). She goes on to describe her daughter's frantic fight to get out of the hospital ward, reiterating that her daughter had no disease: "'I want to walk. I should not be locked up like this. Where have you locked me up?' She got up from the bed and started walking around and told me, 'Let's go, let's go' repeatedly" (83). This enactment of resistance is complicated, as the longing for self-annihilation cannot be pried apart from the dissatisfaction with social norms that make some "ways of living" not count as a life (Butler 1993: 16).[28] In the very articulation of this desire to end one's life, there is also a laying bare and drawing attention to the systemic ways in which certain ways of living are delegitimized.

Meera is not ghostly only after she dies; even when alive she does not fit into the mold of a recognizable subject. As Gordon observes, "To write stories concerning exclusions and invisibilities is to write ghost stories" (1997: 17). Meera's transgressions of gender norms and her "externalized" love for Ammini mark her as someone who cannot be contained within existing disciplinary structures. Even as Meera asserts her sanity and her ability to function and negotiate the everyday world—her need to get out, move, and occupy the world outside—she also holds on to the possibility of dying. Her mother, who feels akin to her daughter and intensely mourns her loss, says, "After Meera almost went under the bus my *uyiru* [life-force[29]] went up and was frantically running around there. My child's life-force was also shuttling around like that. Mine also. My soul is even now wandering around like that. Wherever my child's soul goes, my soul is just going there too" (Sahayatrika 2004: 83). Meera's mother is not just haunted by her dead daughter's spirit; she pictures herself as a ghost too. Her soul is unmoored from its physical habitation and frantically follows her daughter's soul. In her narrative of the hospital episode, she and her daughter both become ghostly presences. The body is wrenched away from the "life-force" that restlessly shuttles around. This excruciating experience of being torn apart body and soul, and the slippage into the language of spectrality and haunting, demonstrates how haunting here is a mode of narrating the painful disjuncture between subjects and the social structures that house them. The practice of mourning is here tied to the language of haunting where what ceases to be returns; the past seeps in and inhabits the crevices of the present.[30]

The mother's mourning points to the struggle to exit a violent system but also stake a claim on it and rage against it. Thus this "ghost-speech" that "defies the realist mapping of the social" becomes the mode of narrating splintered subjectivities that cannot be plotted within a developmentalist grid (Kumar 2010: 186). The interviews deal with the complexities of articulating a claim for justice when the bodies at the center of the discourse are marked as excessive, out of bounds in multiple ways. These figures occupy the gray areas between the inside and outside and disturb the alignment of their worlds in a tentative fashion.[31] Their life narratives are imbued with the threatening power of "ghosts and gaps, seething absences and muted presences" (Gordon 1997: 21). Ammini's tears and refusals to speak, the frozen handholding that lasts for hours, Meera's quick transitions from open rebellion to attempts of suicide—these shards of memories of their lives give us a complex narrative of disjointed acts that that cannot be classified easily as "agency" or "submission."[32]

Instead of a progression of rebellious acts that can be categorized as agential, we are caught in the orbit of stuttered movements—immobile gestures that still time, intense sensations that dilate it, and practices of mourning that wrench the spirit away from the body and push it into an uncanny realm of ceaseless shuttling. There is no suicide note left behind by Meera and Ammini, but there are multiple conflicting registers in which the act of suicide is placed in these interviews. This is a remembered conversation of Meera with one of her friends, Mini, that characterizes the act of suicide as destabilizing and threatening: "Meera would say she is not frightened of anyone anymore. I don't want anyone, I am strong by myself, she would say. And when I asked her why she said these things, she said 'simply, without a reason.' One day after drinking coffee in the morning Meera told me, 'maybe the earth will quake tomorrow.' She died the next day. She told me not to tell anyone anything. . . . I never told anyone. Now I am telling you" (Sahayatrika 2004: 91). Here, suicide is a final gesture of strength and refusal. It is a premonition of an earthquake, a death that will cause tremors in the life world that Meera occupies. But this is not the only register in which Meera refers to the act of suicide. Her mother describes her desperate words to the police officer after her foiled suicide attempt: "'I don't want tea, I don't want anything. Now our life is completely falling to pieces,' Meera said. She was the one who was talking. Ammini didn't say anything. She was crying. 'Why live now, sir. Everything is so complicated, sir'" (81). Here her decision to end her life is grounded more in her sense of being caught in a situation where movement is impossible.[33] The debilitating complications of life, the lack of options for living together, make her fall back on suicide as the only option.

These shades of desperation and confrontation intermingle in Meera's statement to Shailaja: "They won't let us live together, so we will die together" (Sahayatrika 2004: 64). Here the act of dying together is not only in defiance of people who will not let them live together but also a suggestion that there might not be any other way out for them. As for Ammini's reference to suicide, her classmate Prameela places it in a narrative of sentimental, romantic love: "She did say that she would die. . . . If we opposed her, she would tell us why does it matter to all of you. . . . She would write on her hand, right here, 'Meera' with a compass" (108). From rebellion to desperation to melodramatic love, there are multiple registers in which this suicide is plotted. There is a need to ward off the urge to name their deaths as martyrdom or murder, tragedy or rebellion. Instead of reallocating this act in familiar frameworks, we have to see their lives and deaths on their own terms as acts that are suspended between multiple, seemingly oppositional frameworks. My aim in this chapter is not in any way to recuperate Meera and Ammini as subjects for whom suicide becomes the only available act of agency. Such a claim would yet again fold them back into the model of the "knowing" sovereign subject of politics; rather, it is by retaining the tensions in their acts that we can reenvision dominant paradigms of the political.

The narratives about their suicide and their love for each other break down the conception of the subject as an intersecting vector of identities held together as a stable entity. Meera and Ammini are subjects who shuttle between different scripts that they not only inhabit but also exceed; their lives are marked by this never-ceasing movement as "bodies . . . that shuttle, always deficient, always in excess" (Tharu 1999: 203). Suspended between scripts of subjectification that they hold on to but also slip out of, they coalesce as eccentric, "melting" (Cadava, Kelman, and Miller 2006: 7) figures that inhabit the cracks between available modes of being. The suicide as an act should be read as part of these complex, broken negotiations—an act that demands a suspension of quick judgment and a willingness to hold together the threads of divergent scripts through which the subject is made and "annihilated."[34] Lesbian hauntings that do not follow the teleology of progress demand a revisioning of conventional models of politics.

Relational Politics

Sahayatrika's political mobilization through the interviews is part of a search for models of politics that engage with networks in a community and with a couple's rootedness in their immediate circle of friends and family. Ammini and Meera's lives could be recorded after their death only by relying on the memory of others associated with them. Thus this form of the interview produces a complex tapestry of voices that mediates their lives and deaths. Any interview is a relational activity produced in an intersubjective space. Here the interviews are not just an interaction between two people but are often staged in a larger community of speakers and listeners. The following is from the notes on the Fact Finding Report circulated by Sahayatrika (2002): "Interview with Pushpa, Manju's second sister. Present at interview: Jayasree, Reshma, Meena, Deepa [Sahayatrika members]. Pushpa's cousin Manju, Pushpa's three children and a neighbour (Shobana) and her daughter were also present. Villasini, her husband, and Madhavan were also present." The interview here is with Pushpa, but her extended family, acquaintances, and neighbors join her. The format of the interview encapsulates the overlapping and close-knit lives of the speakers.

The interviewers are sensitive to their positioning as outsiders to the community and attempt to address it. In the introduction, the interviewers draw attention to their position of privilege in relation to the members of the community with whom they interact: "As outsiders there were many limitations that we faced in this investigation. Concerns about us and the fears and anxieties we caused definitely influenced people's conversations" (Sahayathrika 2004: 59). Their political awareness about sexuality rights set them apart as much as their status as educated women from more urban contexts within Kerala. This is brought to the surface most clearly in the interview with the psychiatrist who uses English words quite often in the conversation to build a bond of solidarity with the interviewers: "Then there were tribals. But they didn't have the look of tribals at all. Did you see the *dead body* [in English]? Did you see the girls?" (97). The interviewers reply in the negative, a quick "no." The structure of the doctor's question draws on the dominant culture's assumptions about how a "tribal" should look. When he asks whether the interviewers have seen the dead body, he assumes that he and the interviewers would have in common the anthropological gaze of the "civilized" on the "native." This easy bonding that the doctor attempts motivates the interviewers to disrupt it toward the end of the interview by discussing the Sahayatrika project and their political investment in gay, lesbian, and transgender rights.

These interactive dynamics between the interviewers and interviewees come across most strongly in the interview with Meera's mother, who establishes a close bond with the interviewers as she says, "Only my daughter was there to help me. Now I have only two cats to help me . . . I don't have anyone to talk to—that's the saddest part. Now that all of you are sitting here at least I feel relieved I have someone to talk to" (Sahayatrika 2004: 74). She seeks support from the interviewers and shares with them her sense of isolation in the community. The interviews produce a document that troubles the binary divisions at work in the rights discourse of the unenlightened victim and the knowing savior. I am not claiming that there are "utopic" pockets of interventionist work that magically undo the power dynamics inherent in the human rights model of activism. These interviews are mired in these power structures, but the narratives that emerge from the memories of people point to the limits of the very discourse of human rights within which this project is partly housed.

Mini recounts how Meera came to her with an article in a popular Malayalam magazine, *Manorama Weekly*, about same-sex relationships in order to educate Mini about the fact that such relationships exist: "Women shouldn't go around together like that. But I have read about such things in *Manorama*. That between the same sexes such things happen in faraway places. Meera would read all these magazines and would show it to me and tell me, 'look at this, such things exist, then what's the problem with people here?'" (Sahayatrika 2004: 89). By using an article published in a non-elite magazine such as *Manorama Weekly*,[35] which also publishes *painkili* writings, Meera seeks to validate her desire for Ammini. The Sahayatrika team in their introduction to the interviews describe this incident as a heart-wrenching moment of resistance: "In the context of the absence of a community or movement we can see this as a moment where a woman single-handedly resists the rejection of her self-expression" (60).

Rather than characterizing this as a single-handed move of resistance, I would like to draw attention to how Meera uses the knowledge that she gains from the magazine, not to validate herself in her own eyes, but to negotiate with members of her community. Her process of etching herself as a subject is intricately tied to making herself recognizable in a web of people around her. There are intimate networks that both sustain and smother her: "Meera thought of her family, her neighbors, the people she knew around her . . . that small social network is the only thing she thought about. She never entered into the larger society. Her desires and lifestyle were so limited. She might have thought it was not too difficult for them to live together in that society" (Sahayatrika 2004: 71). This is Shailaja's understanding of Meera's attempt to find a space for herself and Ammini in the community she lived in. Sexuality politics, in regional contexts, struggles to address this messy and entangled fabric of marginalized lives. The model of an individual rights–based politics—with protagonists who can break out of the "home" and move ahead in search of a new horizon, such as Kiran in *Sancharram*, the film that I focus on in the previous chapter—does not map onto lives arranged in a different grid.[36]

By conducting and publishing these interviews, the Sahayatrika team underlines the need to examine the coercive fabric of femininity as tied to reproduction and domesticity in Kerala. People who were otherwise sympathetic to Meera and Ammini also opposed their intimate relationship. Ammini's father is the most direct in articulating his opposition: "Because it was between two women we were terribly opposed to it. How can we get a woman married off to another woman? So we opposed it. If it was a man, we could have considered marrying them off" (Sahayatrika 2004: 93). A social worker in the area, Saraswathy, says that the problem between two women living together would be that they would not have children. Meera's mother, who is usually more supportive of Meera's decisions, advises her against bringing Ammini home to stay for the night: "Both of you go around together in the day. But don't bring her here to stay overnight. They'll fight with us on that. Let her just sleep there. I just told her that it's fine to go around in the day. I never told her to bring Ammini home for the night" (79). On one level her advice stems from her concern about how Ammini's parents would respond, but on another she suggests that if Ammini and Meera went around in the daytime, it would be more public and therefore more easily described as a friendship. But their desire to share the night and also the domestic sphere of the home was more risky since it is associated with sexual intimacy and a crossing of the boundaries of friendship. As the interviewers attempt to track how the people in the area read lesbian relationships, what emerges is how a relationship like that of Meera and Ammini disturbs assumptions about the inevitability of both marriage and sexual attraction between a man and a woman. Their relationship in a tentative, fleeting way destabilizes the naturalization of heterosexuality, and in documenting it the Sahayatrika team makes these instances of dissonance more public and available.

The publication of these interviews is a crucial move in the politics of sexuality in Kerala because it etches this suicide into collective memory.[37] The documentation of oral narratives is an ethnographic and historical project that Sahayatrika believes is needed to record the present and the ruptures within it in order to engender new possibilities for the future.

The prolonged, everyday struggles and negotiations that formed the fabric of these women's lives are reconstructed through the interviews instead of marking their deaths as a point of culmination where all questions are silenced. Ammini and Meera's bodies become texts that are violently inserted into the public gaze at the scene of death. Shailaja, Meera's employer, speaks of the intrusive looks of the people who came to see the dead bodies of Meera and Ammini: "When the death happened a huge crowd came there. The reason why such a crowd gathered was mainly to find out if Meera was a man or a woman. That was the main reason they came" (Sahayatrika 2004: 71). In Shailaja's recreation of the scene of the suicide, at the time of death Meera's body is displayed before the public to be objectively measured. There is an attempt, once and for all, to settle the ambiguities of Meera's gender performances. These interviews delve back in time and produce a dense account of the relationship between Meera and Ammini and thus attempt to create a more complex framework in which to place their lives and deaths. The series of interviews counter the general media trend that reports a lesbian relationship as an isolated spectacle that "consume[s] itself in its own sensationalism and leave no traces of the life that was its context" (Sukthankar 1999: 15). The interviews foreground the power of narratives to sustain tensions and dissonances, instead of fixating on the spectacle of their deaths as an event with no history.

For Sahayatrika's political project, remembering the lesbian and channeling that ghostly presence exposes the heterosexual foundations of hegemonic social structures within which only some lives count as lives and only certain bodies matter. By undertaking this task of grieving, the interviewers push against the violent erasure of lives and bodies that do not adhere to the rigid molds of femininity. It is by holding on to the memory of lost struggles and tentative resistances that the early phase of the lesbian movement in Kerala forges a future that differs from the dominant models of LGBT politics, which relies on a stable conception of identity, inclusion, and representation. Lesbian hauntings not only are about death and loss but also underline the necessity to forge more grounded ways of doing sexuality politics. My suspended reading shows how these interviews provide us with a complex alchemy of struggle and anger, refusal and desperation, passionate questioning and melodramatic love, all of which blurs the monolithic positions of revolutionary lesbian lovers on the one hand, and passive, all-suffering victims on the other. I dwell on the immobility and sensory excess, spectrality and mourning, that produce backward and forward movements that queer the lineaments of time. The question that the ghostly lesbian raises for the present moment is whether "we can find ways to listen to all of these different forms of ghostliness, not only to put them to rest, but also to keep them alive" (Frosh 2013: 14). The interviews create a vernacular archive that signals the need to engage with queer acts that are marked by affect, fragility, and tenuousness and that cannot be quickly reclaimed for an identity-making project. The unruly figuration of the political subject created through the nonlinear workings of memory and relationality can be deciphered only if we are attentive to the specific formations of gender and sexuality in different regional contexts.

I place my analysis alongside the activist project of using these interviews for an immediate, political cause. While there are marked differences in the stakes and methods of these interventions, I suggest that such activist and academic endeavors are essential and can coexist to shape a grounded, regional politics of sexuality. In my reading of both the interviews and the strategies used by Sahayatrika, I have tried to be "wary of shorthands" (Gordon 1997: 19) and reflect on the political value of blurred ways of seeing the world. This chapter underlines the need to inhabit the itinerant political geographies of the regional and imagine a "politics of tears," so as to engage with the complexities of subjects who spill out of the liberal individualist mold. The regional does not function here as a space that can be bracketed away or contained within universal scripts; rather, it becomes a significant space of unruly acts and noncohesive subjectivities, a site that undoes the certainties of global and national paradigms of sexuality politics. The final chapter of this book focuses on the memorialization by artists and activists of the transgender activist Sweet Maria, who was brutally murdered in 2012, and engages with this affective web of cultural practices to reflect on the dynamics of doing sexuality politics in contemporary India.

CHAPTER 5

"What You Think Is Fire . . ."

Unspooled Movements and Suspended Readings

In a land where fire has not been discovered
in a desert where a flower has never bloomed
what you think is fire
what I think is a flower
—for that speck of red
we will keep searching till the light of dawn.

—ANITHA THAMPI, "KAZHINJU" (AFTER)

ARTIST AND ACTIVIST ARYAKRISHNAN'S CATALOG FOR HIS MAY
2014 art exhibition in Delhi, "Sweet Maria Monument: Doing and Undoing an Imaginary Archive,"[1] opens with the recollection of a dream in which his friend and transgender activist Sweet Maria comes back from the dead and asks him, "What are you doing about what we were doing?" (2014: 2). A dream then unfolds within this dream in which a congregation of people heed Maria's call and seek succor "under or outside" (2) Maria's ballooning skirt. As with most narratives of dreams, the contours of this recollection are both vivid and blurred. But what is communicated is a feverish set of questions about the dynamics of "doing" politics. Aryakrishnan puts both the verb "do" and the pronoun "we" in quotes—drawing attention to how these terms are not self-explanatory and need to be used with caution.

As I have mentioned earlier, there have been significant changes in the vocabulary and structure of sexuality politics from late 1990s, when the pattern of lesbian suicides in Kerala first garnered national attention, to the present.[2] This includes the organization of queer pride marches in Kerala since 2010, the formation of new LGBT organizations for Malayalis, such as Queerala, which started as a support group Facebook page and increased coverage by print and electronic media on gay, lesbian, and transgender lives.[3] The Kerala state also unveiled a transgender policy in 2015 to ensure nondiscriminatory treatment of transgender persons. In this chapter I draw on the memorialization of the murder of transgender activist Sweet Maria, whose given name was Anil Sadanandan, to explore how sexuality politics in Kerala continue to be imbued with a racking sense of irresolution. My method of reading this particular event traces how the modes of doing sexuality politics are suffused by the disjointed dynamics of memory and haunting. A careful engagement with the fraught terrains of sexuality politics is the running thread in all the chapters in this book. I reflect on how the expressive capacity of cultural practices that shape the volatile networks of the public make possible unruly figurations of sexual actors. The memorialization of Sweet Maria is a complex site to pause and dwell on the intricate links between vernacular cultural practices, figuration, and the political subject.

"Kazhinju" (After), the poem by Anitha Thampi (2010) with which I opened the book and to which I return now, evocatively captures the liminal movements that make possible unruly figures. The Malayalam word *kazhinju* is a conjunction that signifies past tense and refers to the chain of time—the grammatical imprint of the past on the present. Echoing the spirit of the opening poem, this conclusion, too, can be seen as yet another *deshadanam*, a wandering without a destination, as we search for that "speck of red" (Thampi 2010) whose meaning cannot be fixed. Projects on the contemporary formations of the political, which are constantly shifting, are difficult to conclude. In fact, even the desire to arrive at a conclusion undercuts the very premise that structures this book, as it explores the unsettling afterlives of the past in the present to trace a dense and multilayered language of doing politics. Therefore, what follows is a contingent conclusion woven with intractable questions rather than answers. My engagement with the memorialization of Sweet Maria becomes a way of looking back and looking ahead.

Moving Obituaries

"Harbor Worker's Neck Slit and Murdered at Kollam," "Man Found Dead at Tangasseri"—these are headlines from mainstream newspapers that report the murder of Sweet Maria.[4] The newspaper reports graphically describe the marks of extreme violence—the slit neck, mutilated stomach, deep wounds on the neck and the hands, the naked and prostrate body sprayed with chili powder to frustrate the dog squad. Multiple conjectures are offered about the motivations for the murder in the news reports, which also attempt to connect the murder to Maria/Anil's transgender identity.[5] The brutal murder of Sweet Maria on May 10, 2012, under circumstances that continue to be unclear, shocked activists and supporters of sexuality movements in different parts of India. Noted activist A. K. Jayasree, in her obituary for Sweet Maria, says, "The last days of Anil alias Maria's life was like walking on fire or rowing a boat in a tempest," and she goes on to observe that Anil's murder showed yet again how "torturous it is to lead a different kind of life in Kerala" (2012: 104). My analysis in this book suggests that it is this precariousness of acts of living that remains the undercurrent of sexuality politics in multiple contexts in India today.

In one of the few reflective pieces on this incident in a mainstream magazine, P. K. Sreekumar (2012: 98) observes that this murder of a transgender activist of a dark complexion did not make headlines nor did it get serious attention from the multiple 24/7 news channels at regional and national levels. K. K. Shahina articulates the blatant contradictions between Maria's practices of self-representation and the mainstream media coverage: "Sweet Maria had no hesitation in announcing her sexuality publicly but the media was reluctant to do so."[6] The sites and modes of memorializing Sweet Maria have been more at the margins of the mainstream news media, occurring mainly through online initiatives. The memorializations by activists and friends struggle to find a language and form with which to convey the risks she took and courage she showed in her life.

Historically, obituaries as a form serve the function of notifying the public about the death of an individual, especially through newspapers in contexts like Kerala where print culture occupies such a central location. The standard *charamakolam* (death notices) in Malayalam newspapers include a passport-sized photograph that is accompanied by the details of the deceased person; thus the photograph and printed words work together in a set schema to produce an account of a life that has now ended. A conventional obituary, at least temporarily, "fix[es] the subject's image in the public mind" (Couser 2004: 8). Like a memorial service, an obituary is a secular mode of mourning linked to colonial modernity, as private and intimate acts of grief are "oriented towards a public" (Chatterjee 2000: 38). Such commemorations translate grief into a manageable format—one in which the dead are relegated to the realm of the past and the living move on. The possibility of hauntings is quelled in this chronological ordering of worlds of the living and the dead. But in the case of the memorialization of Maria's death, there is an insistence on looking backward so as to touch the past in a palpable fashion.

The deceased is not laid to rest here; there is an intimate and tactile recalling of her gestures, appearance, and utterances. Jayasree argues that the lack of public outcry over this shocking occurrence is the sign of the tacit approval of a society to "annihilate" difference (2012: 104). In light of this, the responsibility to keep Maria's memories alive has been taken up primarily by activists from different parts of India. The personalized writings that circulate after Maria's death exceed and complicate the paradigms of a standard obituary. These are excerpts from obituaries written by activists Anil A and Gee Semmalar after Maria's murder:

> In the queer pride march and in every queer cultural event, her pleasure in dance and the joy s/he was filled with, still reverberates in those who knew her. It's still hard to absorb that we can't rock in laughter at the queer jokes that s/he laid out at every turn, and that we will not be able to see and hear from her any more. S/he will not be there in any more festivals . . . and the void is unbearable.[7]

> A juggler of identities. A gender queer performer. And what a performer she was! She would turn any situation into an assertion of her identity by making crude jokes that would shake others out of their heteronormativity. Sometimes, even making them feel ashamed for being heterosexual! . . . Someone so vibrant and full of life is no longer with us, to march and joke and struggle by our side.[8]

Rather than producing a frozen account of her life, these obituaries draw attention to her bodily performances that defied categorization. From dance to laughter to jokes, these modes of remembering dwell on sensual and sensory movements of the body that are disruptive and pleasurable. The spectacle of her moving body erupts into the present and challenges the practices of doing politics.

Gee Semmalar deploys the form of a letter as he titles his piece "For Maria, with Love and Pain." The direct address through the epistolary form acknowledges the ties that remain even after a person is no more. Thus through these modes of memorializing, an intense web of feelings is given a public form. The instances that are reconstructed in the quotes above involve a close interaction between bodies in public and private spaces—laughter that "rocks" the body, raunchy jokes that aim to "shake" others out of their heteronormativity. Even in the face of excruciating violence, these modes of memorialization push against the docile management of desires and feelings. They place us in touch with the "animating force of queerness" by opening up the terrain of "queer doing" rather than stabilizing the fact of a "queer identity" (Muñoz 2009: 84).[9]

These cultural practices of remembering retain an awareness of the threatening practices that Maria engaged in as she performed her "coming out" in a hostile social world and thus function as a searing reflection on modes of doing politics in a blatantly asymmetrical present. Rumi Harish, in "'I Am Coming Out': What Awaits Me? Life or Death," writes about how Sweet Maria had come out as being transgender and her life had brutally ended: "What we need to look at is also how this 'coming out' costs us the lives of sexual and gender minorities who like anyone else have dreams, desires, likes and dislikes, rights and assertions."[10] Jayasree observes that when people who take the initiative to come out and speak about their rights are killed, it creates "a situation of emergency" (2012: 105). Semmalar recalls Maria's unbridled openness, writing that she was "dangerously open. Most of us around her have, at times, felt unsafe and disturbed by how fearlessly open she was in everyday life."[11] In retrospect, these writings bring to the fore complex questions about strategies of queer politics in contexts where an overt claim over public spaces and an unguarded expression of sexual and gendered identities is met with intense violence and even annihilation of the transgressing subject. The recurring question that reverberates in the cultural expressions that proliferate after Maria's death is, How does one continue to imagine the political?[12] Instead of setting out any blueprints for action or models of being, how can we engage with the more tentative, fragile, and fractured terrains of doing politics?

"Stitching Your Own Costumes"

The art exhibition by Aryakrishnan in May 2014 that I referred to in the beginning of this concluding chapter was envisaged as a multimedia monument for Maria and curated the work of multiple artists who engage with concerns about body and sexuality. Aryakrishnan observes in the catalog that there is no given language at any point of time for politics and aesthetics. Therefore the process of monumentalizing Maria is a fragmented exercise that is bound to fail. He writes, "Monumentalizing something which is moving and changing, which cannot be housed or entombed, is an impossible task and there is failure of complete access and communication written into this process" (Aryakrishnan 2014: 2). He is well aware that the archive he assembles in this exhibition undercuts the documentary impulse of state and humanitarian projects because it does not commit itself to the project of knowledge production in which the subject is measured, mapped, and rendered legible (2). Monumentalizing and archiving could be read as practices that give solidity and permanence to the past and produce a record that can classify bodies, events, or acts. But rather than order, solidity, and stasis, here the emphasis is on movement and change. Not only is the archive "imaginary," but it is also tied to a perpetual cycle of "doing and undoing" in which the various "traces" of Maria's body are gathered and dispersed in the space of the exhibition.

Analyzing the aesthetic practices in this exhibition is beyond the scope of this concluding chapter. Therefore, I narrow the focus and examine how the exhibition catalog and the short film that was part of it work through the irresolvable complexities of doing queer politics in India today. *Azhinajattam* (Loose dance; "In and as Directed by Maria," says the title card), a short film that consists primarily of footage from the first queer pride march in Kerala, organized in Thrissur in 2010, ran on a loop in this interactive art space. In a conversation with me, Aryakrishnan said that he did not envisage a life for this short film outside of the multidimensional space of the exhibition, so I want to emphasize that I analyze this film as a partial and fragmentary text. This is not a self-contained artifact but a recording that retrospectively throws light and shadow on the interactive art and activist space that it was part of.

The short film consists of shots of organizers preparing for the first queer pride march in Kerala on July 2, 2010, one year after the Delhi High Court judgment that was hailed as effectively decriminalizing homosexuality, and of people who gather around and linger to see this sight on the streets of Thrissur. The recording is not event driven; the camera meanders and does not hierarchize between the consequential and the inconsequential. The camera is often handheld and marked by sudden jerks, blurred images, and quick pans. It shows us trees, shop fronts, grass, and stones on the ground; the gathering of activists and supporters putting up the banner, distributing masks, and tying up the rainbow flag; and the actions of onlookers around them. The sound recording is muffled and not in sync. We hear traffic sounds and snatches of conversations. The dominant perception of queer pride marches is in terms of breaking the silence, asserting identity, coming out, and embracing visibility; in fact, the banner of this march says "From Silence to Celebrations."

There are documentary films whose aesthetic practices uphold this framework of visibility as agency. For example, *Out and Proud* by transgender activist Kalki Subramaniam focuses on the 2010 queer pride march in Kerala and fits more neatly into the more obvious paradigms of documenting a queer pride march.[13] *Out and Proud* has a voiceover that names this event as the first queer pride march in Kerala. It consists of footage of the march itself, with slogans such as "377 Gone, Gone" and images of people dancing and celebrating. It also includes declarations and comments by activists. Maria is one of the speakers, and she says, "This is a declaration of our freedom, an event where we throw away our masks and proclaim our identity in front of society."[14] In contrast to this, into the frameworks of visibility and identity that is central to the conception of the queer pride march itself, *Azhinjattam* injects a seething sense of uncertainty. It captures how queer pride marches in Kerala consisted of a coalition of diverse sets of people and their tentative attempts to forge new practices to claim the public. As in my analysis of the regional contours of the global AIDS discourse in chapter 2, this points to how even a paradigmatic event in the global LGBT movement, such as the queer pride march, does not travel seamlessly to all parts of the world; there are multiple fissures in its enactment in different contexts.

There are certain familiar symbols of LGBT politics in the film: the rainbow colors of the flag and the balloons bob in and out of the frames many times. But rather than stabilizing a universal language of LGBT politics, these markers take on new meanings in this context as they meet the gaze of a public who watches with bewilderment and curiosity, rather than easy recognition. One of the snatches of conversation in the recording goes as follows:

"Are you not recording them?"
  "Yes, I am. Those people who are standing there gaping at us with their mouths wide open [*vaayanokki*], right?"
  "Yes, we have spectators [*kaanikal*]."

Some of the people who gather around and watch the pride march preparations are described using the term *vaayanokki*—commonly used to derogatorily refer to men who stand on the roadside, near shops or junctions, and spend their time loitering, gaping, and directing comments toward those who pass by, especially women. The second term used is *kaanikal*, which refers to spectators who gather to watch events ranging from a film to a football match. These references make us aware how an organized political act, such as a queer pride march, is staged in a particular formation of the public shaped by historical practices of looking and engendering bodies. Through the term *vayanokki*, what is conveyed is the organization of the public in which women's bodies are sexually charged spectacles triggering fantasies and anxieties, while the masculine position carries the power to look. Public demonstrations such as the queer pride march—in which all actors are marked as sexual subjects and the neat binary between the masculine and the feminine is troubled through acts of dressing up and fashioning the body—engage with and possibly interrupt existing scopic regimes in contingent ways.

The everyday acts of looking that shape public encounters in small towns in Kerala are activated here, but they acquire another layer because of the technological intervention of the camera, as in the case of the night vigil in March 2008 that I analyzed in the introduction to this book. There is a plethora of cameras in the space, ranging from mobile phone cameras to video cameras. Apart from the camera that is recording the footage that becomes part of the film, we see shots of others recording the activities and also watching the recording on their own camera screen. The onlookers, who are mainly men, whip out mobile phones and record the participants in the march. Aryakrishnan, in our conversation, observed that since the onlookers were aggressively staring at them and even recording them head to toe with mobile phones, the only option for the organizers and participants to garner a degree of safety was to record the onlookers as well. This comment refers to the risk and fragility of these acts of claiming the public sphere. The organizers recording these public encounters rely on the witnessing and evidentiary power of the camera and a hope that the presence of a recording device might prevent direct acts of affront or violation. But even this looking back entails a careful negotiation between visibility and invisibility. For example, the particular camera that records the footage that we see tends to be located inside a vehicle; we see the preparation for the march through the frame of the car window. The spots and black specks on the window cast a pattern on the happenings that unfold outside. Thus there is a thin line between safety and visibility, anonymity and publicity, the event and the ordinary, that play out in this short recording of that day, troubling the paradigms of a linear movement from inside to outside, to unfettered openness as liberation.

As in the case of the 2008 night vigil and its repercussions, and the narratives about the initial functioning of Sahayatrika that I discussed earlier in the book, the contradictions of strategies of visibility in volatile and mediated publics are made available for analysis in the memorialization of Maria. There is much concern about how Maria's claiming of public space through her bodily practices, clothing, and opinions expressed in TV talk shows might have played a part in her murder (Jayasree 2012: 104). Photographs of her dressed up for queer pride parades in flowing gowns of pulsating colors and glimmering fabric, rainbow and red, accompany almost all the obituaries written after Maria's death. She stands out prominently in the recorded images of queer pride marches in 2010 and 2011. Her spectacular performances exceed the registers of the representation of transgender bodies that we encounter in popular visual media such as Malayalam cinema, TV reality shows, comedy shows and dance shows. An eye-catching profusion of red fabric, a voluminous skirt that dangled like a ballooning tent from the ceiling to the ground in the exhibition space by Aryakrishnan,[15] pays tribute to this desire on Maria's part to invent a corporeal language for doing politics that flagrantly pushes against the visual regimes of gendered bodies and sartoriality in Kerala:

> There is a difference in raising a question in an existing "political," humanitarian language, and stitching your own costumes which don't represent Kerala, or queer, or anything in particular.
>
> It is a making. You are inventing something which doesn't represent any essential content to it, so when somebody is enacting that kind of a politics, what is happening? (Aryakrishnan 2014: 2)[16]

Like the swirling movements of the vibrant red fabric of Maria's gown that takes center stage in the exhibition space, we enter here into the realm of figurations that are not the means to an end; rather, the uncontained movements themselves have an expressive power—an intense yet fleeting potential to disrupt the edifices of the present. The narratives about her life and death reflect on the disjointed gestures of a subject who put her body on the line and did not follow existing scripts. In the quote from Aryakrishnan reproduced above, terms such as "stitching," "making," and "inventing" capture the expressive and performative potential of everyday political acts that do not reproduce pregiven templates. In the oral narratives on lesbian suicides and the stuttered autobiographical practices by Nalini Jameela, questions are raised about how the contours of the political are destabilized when marginalized bodies that do not fit into the mold of the cohesive subject make claims for justice. The same question reverberates in a different fashion in the remembering of Sweet Maria's life and politics.

Azhinjattam, the title of the short film, literally refers to a "loose dance"—unchoreographed movements like that of a thread that is left free, unspooled, directionless. This term captures in a telling fashion the expressive dynamics of the figures in this book. The term *attam* means both "dance" and "movement"; it can be used to refer to both movements of the body and ways of inhabiting space. The term *azhinjattam* is gendered and sexual in its connotations; it is often used negatively to refer to the actions of women who do not discipline themselves to stay within the limits of ideal femininity. A disorderly femininity is marked by the sensual exhibition of the body and unruly movements in space. Aryakrishnan writes about how Maria used her body to challenge and rewrite dominant conceptions of masculinity and femininity. She accessed and provocatively deployed the prototype of the "loose woman" who is available for a sexualized gaze: "Kadappuram Maria (a flamboyant persona at times dressed up for performance) comes from a cinematic lineage of stereotypes of a whore, a loose woman. Sweet Maria took this popular image everywhere—to C-class movie theatres, markets, the beach, protest marches, the football ground, media discussions/TV shows, and many other places" (Aryakrishnan 2014: 2). Thus *Azhinjattam* consciously invokes practices of viewing sexually explicit films and remembers the figurations of women performers, such as the spectacle of Raji's body in *Avalude ravukal*.

It underlines the fissures in the fabric of the social in Kerala, where film-viewing practices and low-budget theaters function as a site of sexual excess. There are multiple ways in which cinematic practices are brought into the space of the exhibition. A drawing of Maria wearing a red brassiere with A (adults only) written on her pink skirt is the image that accompanies the catalog (figure 5.1). This image was also placed like a film poster, with the announcement "coming soon" written on it, in the entrance of the exhibition space.

The title *Azhinjattam* is written in big block red letters on a splash of yellow, reminiscent of the title cards of low-budget soft-porn cinema. By bringing in the aesthetic codes and modes of circulation of soft-porn cinema, which I analyzed in the first chapter, "Tracing the Prostitute: Between Excess and Containment," into the space of the art exhibition, there is an attempt to keep alive the multiple layers through which a bodily performance acquires meaning. It shows how in "re-imagining our everyday practices" (Aryakrishnan 2014: 2) for a political purpose, there is a composition of the subject by reiterating the tropes of femininity that are available within a particular cultural context.

It is important to note here that the mood of *Azhinjattam* is not celebratory; it is cut by a deep sense of loss and uncertainty. It is as if the recorded footage of the march insists on the ephemerality of queer acts as an undeniable reality that demands reckoning in sexuality politics in India. As the footage is edited for its exhibition screening, there are

5.1 "Sweet Maria Monument" art exhibition 2014. The poster in the exhibition that refers to soft-porn cinema. Photograph by Aryakrishnan Ramakrishnan. Reproduced with permission.

certain insertions that accentuate this sense of loss and looking backward. Taking footage of the pride march and intercutting it with short interludes produce a text that is haunted by absent yet present voices and bodies. The film's title card says, "*Azhinjattam*: In and as Directed by Maria," granting authorship to Maria even as she was absent in the assembling of the film after her death. But like the dream sequence that I refer to in the opening of the paper, which Aryakrishnan (2014: 2) cites as the *monere* that drives this art exhibition,[17] *Azhinjattam* is haunted by Maria's presence.

One sequence that is repeated twice, both times in slow motion, is Maria's flamboyant entry into the 2010 queer pride march in her satin rainbow-colored gown that unfurls around her. The purple hat, pink earrings, and layers of satin in vibrant colors catch the viewer's eyes as she enters the scene and swirls around. It marks her entry as a moment worthy of returning to as the film ends with the same sequence. This theatrical entry is intercut with a grainy recording of Maria performing a popular Malayalam song from the 1970s, "Innenikku pottukuttaan" (Today, to adorn myself with a *pottu*),[18] noted for its expression of sensual feminine desire and erotic rendering of the woman's body. The gendered markers of Maria's body are different in both the clips. The gown, earrings, and bodily marker of breasts, which are part of her gendered performance in the first clip, are absent in the second one. Dressed in a blue-checkered shirt and loose black pants, Maria/Anil lip-synchs and performs the sensual moves of an iconic Malayalam heroine in the latter clip. There are indications of an audience who watches this performance and claps in the end. Then, for a second, the screen goes pitch black while the recorded song continues to play on, unanchored by the image. After this gaping blackness, the film cuts back to the scene of the pride march. There are discordant layers of time and space and differential expressions of gender and sexuality spliced into this footage.

The other insertion in the film is a recording of a song by transgender activist Deepu from Kerala, who committed suicide in July 2012.[19] In the memorialization of Deepu after his death, through newspaper reports and writings and videos that circulated on the internet and social media, many remember his powerful and moving voice.[20] In the film, from a shot of rainbow-colored balloons bobbing in a clouded sky, there is an abrupt cut to a silhouette of Deepu that appears on the screen. "Prit kee lath mohe aisee lagee, ho gayee mai matwalee" (I have become intoxicated because of my addiction to my love),[21] a popular rendering of a Sufi song of being broken and decimated by the madness of love, washes over the viewer. The edges of his fingers glimmer in white, the whole body in darkness. There is a sharp aural cut, like that of the swish of a knife, when this sequence moves back to the pride march preparations. The "celebrations" of the queer pride marches are pervaded by the reverberating voice—the painful memory of a life rendered unlivable within given social structures. Through replaying these performative renderings of desire in the interactive space of the art exhibition, questions about "doing" queer politics suffuses the march as we look at it retrospectively. The traces of lives and bodies that met with brutal ends bleed into the footage of the queer pride march and raise pertinent questions about the structures of violence in the present and how to imagine possibilities for the future.

Looking Back, Looking Ahead

My interlinked reading of the nonlinear traffic of cultural practices within the history of Kerala gestures toward the centrality of practices of memory in the domain of sexuality. The persistence of the impressions of the past in the present fuels political movements. The trajectories of Sweet Maria, Kunjeebi, and Ammini and Meera are quite different from each other. Yet the interviews on lesbian suicides, the afterlives of Kunjeebi, and memorialization of Maria create vernacular archives that show the tenuous and affective terrain of sexuality politics, which cannot be quickly reclaimed for an identity-making project. This must not be seen as an impediment that needs to be overcome or erased; on the other hand, this irresolution marks the potential for sexuality politics that is not curtailed by a linear trajectory of identity and recognition. The intense and blurred gestures within *Azhinjattam*, journeys without a set destination in *Deshadanakkili karayarilla*, and the writing and rewriting of Nalini Jameela's life narratives—the unruly figurations in this book question the certainties of politics that are tied to an empowered subject.

This book tracks subjectivities-in-process as they are formed through cultural practices. This is reflected quite literally in the grammar of my chapter titles, which use terms such as "tracing the prostitute," "searching till the light of dawn," and the "politics of lesbian hauntings." As the imperative to render sexual identity categories legible and recognizable to the state and multinational structures of governance has gained greater prominence in the last decade in India, the stutterings, wanderings, and hauntings that I dwell upon in this book remind us to pause and ask questions about the erasures of bodies and acts essential to forge a universal and pan-Indian model of sexuality politics. My analysis foregrounds the significance and necessity of organized sexuality movements in Kerala in order to counter the violent policing and regulation of sexual acts and identities. At the same time, I point to how the unified subject at the center of identity politics and rights-based discourses comes undone when we take into account the struggles by marginalized sexual actors. I analyze the fraught mediations by sexual subjects who demonstrate the need for models of politics that are not rigid and foreclosed.

The acts and actors one encounters in this book cannot be contained within neat paradigms of liberation as they shuttle between multiple scripts of being. The *azhinjattam* through which they exceed these scripts and spill out of them point to the ruptures of identity categories and gestures toward the potentiality of queer politics. Muñoz argues that queerness is an ideality, a horizon imbued with potentiality: "Queerness is essentially about the rejection of a here and now and an insistence on potentiality or concrete possibility for another world" (Muñoz 2009: 1). My central conception of unruly figurations points to political acts that do not form a traceable arc but appear as flickering movements that cannot be reified.

This book captures the need to revise politics in favor not of a set path but of one that holds within it different possibilities. Mourning and loss, failure, and rewriting are integral to such itinerant political topographies. From the photographs of Kunjeebi's murder to the memorialization of lesbian suicides and Maria's murder, my analysis shows how in the terrain of queer political acts in Kerala, the horizons for the future are carved through the shards of the past that can both cut and realign structures of thinking and feeling. My aim in this book has also been to bring to the surface the knotted processes of "working in and on time" (Ramberg 2016: 226) that interrupts the teleology of progress. A central axis of this project is the nexus between the AIDS network, sexuality movements, and discussions about the new, unprecedented sexual boldness of post-1990s globalized India. My discomfort with this neat narrative of progress—where all pockets of the world can learn to be sexually liberated in the right way—has fueled this project. I demonstrate how the cultural realm becomes the unsettling site where the fractures of the universal human rights language and the politics of visibility surface. For example, in my analysis of oral narratives of lesbian suicides, I demonstrate how the political is reenvisioned when acts and bodies that do not fit into the liberal-humanist paradigm make claims for justice. I ward off the temptation to fix these protagonists as either heroic naysayers or tragic victims and argue for the importance of retaining unresolvable tensions between agency and victimhood.

The trajectories of gay and lesbian politics and sex workers' movements from the 1990s to the present have been markedly different. The sex workers' mobilizations have seen a staggered growth, while LGBT politics has acquired a more streamlined format ensconced primarily in the frameworks of privacy, legality, individual freedom, and choice. The key structural questions in sex workers' mobilizations about forms of labor and employment, equal access to resources, and public cultures of eroticism seem to have lesser resonance within national debates in India today. The distance between sex workers' activism and the more mainstream face of gay and lesbian politics has only grown in the last decade. In this context the interventions of this book that bring the sex worker and the lesbian into the same frame gains greater pertinence.

The intersections of the discourse on sexuality and gender in multiple sites in this book function as constant reminders of the need for feminist scholarship to tactically reinvent categories of analysis so that we can engage with the unstable horizons of the political. In light of the unprecedented public outrage and protests against the December 16, 2012, Delhi gang rape, the "Indian woman" has gained a newfound visibility in national and international circuits. But these seething protests run the danger of being quickly contained through legislative and surveillance measures (Kapur 2012). For we are yet again confronted with the limitations of a feminist and sexuality politics anchored upon visible bodies in the rational public sphere. This is not to impute homogeneity to the current configurations of feminism in India as a discourse within which the public/private and rational/emotional binaries remain unquestioned. From the late nineteenth- and twentieth-century nationalist and reform movements and the emergence of women's organizations in the early twentieth century, to the shifting articulations of the gender question in post-independence India, feminism has been a contested and heterogeneous field.[22]

Scholars have posed significant questions about the sexualization of Dalit women's bodies in the public and the spectacular ways in which women's bodies are subjected to public humiliation and violence in order to maintain hierarchies of caste within rural and urban economies (Rao 2009; Patil 2014). There are significant feminist writings on the body and on strategies of dissent in the light of the public protest in Manipur, a state in northeastern India, in 2004 to oppose the rape and custodial murder of a young Meitei woman. During the protest, several women appeared nude holding a banner: "Indian army rape us" (Bora 2010; Misri 2014).[23] But in spite of a large range of political articulations that rework the conception of the rights-bearing political actor, the desire for an autonomous subject who can occupy the public sphere continues to dominate discussions on gender and sexuality in India. Scholars observe that in the contemporary social and political landscape, the representative woman is molded through the paradigms of freedom, autonomy, and choice and becomes the site to stage the aspirations and anxieties of a globalizing nation (Sreekumar 2017: 61).[24] In this context, the question that Susie Tharu raises still remains critical: "To what extent has the embodied and agential self—or a very similar one—also been the body-self unwittingly affirmed and renewed by historical feminism? What does that norming cost the feminist movement?" (1999: 195). If the transformative potential of the contestations in the present has to be tapped, it is essential to imagine an unruly subject of feminism. Recognizing the affective organization of publics makes possible the imagination of a political terrain in which the individualized, rights-bearing subject is not taken for granted. Sexual actors who cannot be contained within the framework of visibility raise pertinent questions about the formations of the political—and these are questions we need to pay heed to in order to imagine the future of feminist politics.

The archive I assemble and the traffic between different time periods that I trace in this book shows that the links between post-1990s and pre-1990s is a complex, interpenetrated one. In my analysis of the state processes of the disciplining of sexuality, I point to the continuities between the post-1990s and pre-1990s period. I show how the developmental discourse of model Kerala since the early period of state formation regulated women's sexuality and how the iconic figure of the "Kerala woman" shapes the present, too. The regulatory mechanisms of the state that exerts control over women's bodies, especially through the institution of the police, is an area of continuing concern for sexual minorities even as they are now repositioned as targets of governmentality. I also examine how institutions of modernity such as the psychiatric hospital, in addition to schools and colleges, function as sites for the disciplining of sexuality. But in spite of these regulatory processes, unruly figures cast disruptive shadows on the edifice of the domestic woman through the volatile workings of cultural practices. The domestic woman in this book is continually disturbed and reconfigured by her "others."

The fourth chapter, on lesbian suicides, is focused specifically on the process of haunting that disturbs the domestic ordering of the social, but the workings of memory and the afterlives of cultural texts and events are a recurring concern in all the chapters. I examine the intermedia and intertextual connections that cut across time periods and that play a formative role in disrupting the foundational narratives of Kerala and its privileging of the reproductive heterosexual family. Acts of remembering and reiteration are crucial to the composition of sexual subjects in the post-1990s period. My research also participates in this process of recreating the ruptured network of cultural memory. I examine the charged trajectories within *Avalude ravukal*, particularly that of the prostitute figure reading a controversial novel from the 1940s and the dispersed reception of heterogeneous elements of the film. These shifting public networks provide a complex mapping of how disruptive cultural practices can rock the "scenography of reason" (Butler 1993: 52). The shuttling movements in this book between the pre-1990s and post-1990s embody a dense, enmeshed connection between the past, the present, and the future. The nonlinear trajectories of cultural circuits play an important role in creating a discourse of sexuality that has possibilities of unrest built into it, and this is crucially linked to my argument about the region as a dense, layered, and complex space. In order to substantiate this argument, I also draw on scholarship on other linguistic contexts in India.

My process of writing this book was very different from how a traditional literary scholar would work, mainly because my object was to see how cultural representations spill over and become interwoven with day-to-day political performances of sexuality and subjectivity. My attempt has been to track the process of citation and reiteration, the live, shifting, everyday circuits of cultural representation. The ethnographic aspect of my project was necessary for this purpose; I attended political meetings, visited sexuality-based NGOs, went to public health events organized by KSACS, and also tracked the sedimentation of sexual figures through multiple mass mediums such as cinema and print culture. Some of the cultural texts I focused on were obvious choices; for example, Nalini

Jameela's books had created such a plethora of discussions that I had to include it in my archive. But I moved toward other cultural sites in a different fashion. For example, one reason I focused on the controversial Malayalam film *Avalude ravukal*, which was initially labeled as pornographic and later revised as a realist text in the post-1990s period, was the multiple ways in which I encountered the songs from this film during my research. A queer activist from Kerala mentioned how the title song about the restless dreams and sleepless nights of a prostitute was one of his all-time favorites. At a Christmas party in 2007, as friends and family members sat chatting after dinner, a friend started singing this song to entertain all of us. A friend's mother mentioned how "Unni ara-ariro" (Child, sleep peacefully), another popular song from this film, was the lullaby she had sung routinely to put her children to sleep. Even four decades after the release of this film, when I do presentations on *Avalude ravukal* in academic contexts in India, the poster of the film produces titters of recognition. It is the dispersed aura of this film and the range of emotional responses it produces even today that made me reconsider its afterlives.

I push against the autonomous status given to cultural texts. Rather, I look at the practice of circulation. It is through the intertextual and intermedial traffic in the public sphere that representations acquire meaning and significance. My focus is not on externalized global flows but specifically on how the contingencies of a region determine the imagination of sexuality and subjectivity. My work provides a thick description of the regional public sphere and pays close attention to the tensions within it. I demonstrate how vernacular expressions of sexuality interrupt global paradigms of knowledge formation that seek to render local differences intelligible by translating them into universally understandable frameworks. Working on a regional public sphere that is dynamic is a challenging task, because one is perpetually negotiating multiple languages, rhetorical tropes, and theoretical registers. But this shuttling is part of the critical task of this book because I argue that it is important to inhabit unsettling terrains, where political options are not foreclosed. My focus on the detailed analysis of the recent past through a vernacular archive also questions the nostalgia for an organic, fluid, precolonial past and the quick celebration of post-globalization representations of sexuality. One of my contributions to the field of sexuality studies in South Asia is the cautionary note that a yearning for a precolonial past runs the risk of erasing the complexities and tensions of the post-independence period.[25] While this book is aware of the political and theoretical need to keep alive memories of the past, it also argues for a critical awareness of our relationships to the past and the ways in which we mobilize it.

The labor of this book has been to forge reading practices that retain the tensions and the incompleteness of technologies of subjectification. I insist on the need to be wary of the longing for closure and for worked-out strategies of political action. I select sites of analysis and methods of interpretation that enable me to navigate the shifting zones in which unresolved struggles are not reappropriated and transformed into heroic tales of agency. Such suspended readings are necessary to create a politics of sexuality grounded in the fragments of regional life worlds. Pushing against the rush for enumeration and the quick consolidation of identities, this study on the politics of sexuality in Kerala is a call for an intellectual practice that pays close attention to the details of mobile networks within a region. The journey that I ask the reader to undertake with me is one that values the confusing, painstaking process of movement itself. What the book traces are the making of unruly figures through stutters, hauntings, *deshadanam*, and *azhinjattam*—that beckon us to touch and feel an elsewhere. These are blurred visions of unrest rather than a reaching for clarity. This is a book that has faith in the power of unresolved questions and interstitial spaces and that sketches the stuttered movements of sexual subjects. Investigations at the edges of the social and the global cannot risk neat endings, for they point to the very need for suspended readings and situated knowledges.

Notes

Introduction: Sexual Figures of Kerala

1 This state came into existence as a political entity in 1956 with the passing of the States Reorganization Act that brought together areas where Malayalam was the dominant language. Most of the texts I analyze in this book are in Malayalam. All the translations from Malayalam in the book are mine, unless otherwise mentioned.

2 Urbanization in Kerala is quite widespread, and this has produced a network of well-connected towns with modern amenities. But this region does not have large-scale metropolitan centers such as Delhi, Mumbai, or Chennai.

3 This is not to construct a neat divide between the national and the regional. Sexuality politics in different contexts in India, including metropolitan spaces, are fractured and contested formations. I am critiquing a prominent strand of LGBT politics that is embedded in the discourse of stabilizing identity categories and claiming legal recognition.

4 The National Family Health Survey, conducted in 2005–2006, ranked Kerala as the state with the most media exposure in India. International Institute of Population Studies, *National Family Health Survey (NFHS-3), India, 2005–06: Kerala* (Mumbai, December 2008), http://rchiips.org/nfhs /NFHS-3%20Data/ke_state_report_for_website.pdf.

5 The government-owned national television service, Doordarshan, expanded its services in the 1980s, and terrestrial broadcasts were available to 70 percent of the population in India by 1983–1984 (Rajad-hyaksha 2009: 237). It was the only television provider in the country till the 1990s, when private channels came into the Indian market after economic liberalization in 1991. Asianet, the first Malayalam satellite channel launched in Kerala in the early 1990s, is one of the first satellite television channels in India (Joseph 2016). Currently in addition to the government-run TV channel Doordarshan Malayalam, there are more than thirty commercial satellite television channels in Malayalam.

6   S. V. Srinivas, 2000, "Is There a Public in the Cinema Hall?" *Framework:
    The Journal of Cinema and Media* 42, http://docs.wixstatic.com/ugd/32cb69
    _95584ff57df547febafo4c3e0bafa3fc.pdf.

7   The linkages between cinema and literature are also strong because of the
    development of the Malayalam film industry in close contact with
    literature. There are many film directors in Kerala who are also writers,
    and literary fiction is often adapted to films. The screenplay of most films
    are brought out and sold in book shops across the state and thus claim the
    label of "literature."

8   The Communist Party of India was founded in the 1920s and its Kerala
    committee was formed in the 1930s. The first serious rupture in the
    Communist movement took place in 1964, following India's war with
    China (Nossiter 1982). The CPI (M) was formed soon after the split in
    the Communist Party. CPI and CPI (M) continue to play a crucial role in
    electoral politics in Kerala.

9   In 1975, the United Nations published a case study with reference to
    Kerala (United Nations 1975), and since then there has been a significant
    amount of debate about the Kerala model, which is presented as an
    exceptional phenomenon of human development without the correspond-
    ing economic advancement or industrialization.

10 Sangari and Vaid (1990); Chatterjee (1993); Sarkar (2001); Basu and
    Ramberg (2015).

11 For a discussion of matriliny, see Jeffrey (1975, 1992), Arunima (2000,
    2003b), Kodoth (1998, 2001), and Nair (1996).

12 There are multiple developmental indices used to measure Kerala
    women's "empowered" status: this is the only state in India where women
    outnumber men in terms of the population ratio. The rural female literacy
    rate in Kerala is 90.8 percent, according to the 2011 census, while that of
    India is 58 percent. "Census Information India 2011: Final Population
    Totals," www.dataforall.org/dashboard/censusinfoindia_pca.

13 Statistics with the State Crime Record Bureau point to multiple reports of
    rape, molestation, domestic violence, dowry harassment, and sexual
    harassment. M. Suchitra, "In the Grip of Depression," December 2002,
    questfeatures.org/articles/depn.html.

14 Dalit as a political category emerges from radical struggles against caste
    discrimination in India since the early twentieth century. In descriptions
    of mobilization for dignity and against caste inequality, the term "Dalit"
    is today widely used to describe India's former untouchables. Ramna-
    rayan Rawat and K. Satyanarayana observe that "beginning with the
    Dalit Panthers' movement in the 1970s, the term acquired a radical new
    meaning of self-identification and signified a new oppositional conscious-
    ness" (2016: 2) in different regions in India.

15 For a historical analysis of colonial modernity and the trajectories of
    Dalit consciousness in nineteenth- and twentieth-century Kerala, see

Mohan 2015. For an introduction to the history of Dalit movements and struggles against the violence of the caste structure in contemporary Kerala, see Satyanarayana and Tharu (2011), Rowena (2005a), and Raj (2013, 2016).

16 Prabha Kotiswaran (2011a: 214) observes that the political rallies, pamphlets, and events of the National Network of Sex Workers (NNSW) suggest that sex workers' groups in India have supported the rights of sexual minorities.

17 Sex workers' collectivization and LGBT politics take shape in the post-liberalization period in the backdrop of the growth of NGOs and the establishment of the HIV/AIDS awareness and prevention machinery. Since the 1990s, sex workers in different parts of India have formed collectives to combat the moral stigma of sex work and fight for better working and living conditions.

18 Section 377 of the Indian Penal Code that came into force in 1862, during the colonial period, has been a highly contentious issue in India since the 1990s. The penal provision says, "Whoever voluntarily has carnal intercourse against the order of nature with any man, woman or animal, shall be punished with imprisonment for life, or with imprisonment of either description for a term which may extend to ten years, and shall also be liable to fine" ("The Indian Penal Code," https://indiankanoon.org /doc/1569253/). The 2009 Delhi High Court judgment in the matter of *Naz Foundation v. NCT of Delhi and Others* read down Section 377, effectively allowing for same-sex sexual acts between consenting adults in private. The reversal of this judgment in 2013 by the Supreme Court led to protests and agitations. In spite of this reversal, there has been a greater visibility for LGBT issues in India since 2009 in terms of increased media coverage, advertisements that feature gay and lesbian characters, and public events such as queer pride marches. On September 6, 2018, the five-judge Constitution Bench of the Supreme Court restored the Delhi High Court judgment. They partially struck down Section 377 underlining how "the sexual autonomy of an individual to choose his/her sexual partner is an important pillar and an insegregable facet of individual liberty" (Supreme Court of India Judgment, "Navtej Singh Johar and Others versus Union of India," September 6, 2018, www .thehindu.com/news/national/article24880700.ece/binary /Sec377judgment.pdf). This has been hailed as a landmark judgement in the struggle for LGBT rights in India.

19 Laura Ann Stoler (1995) argues that by short-circuiting empire, Foucault's history of European sexuality misses key sites in the production of that discourse.

20 The fragment has been an important concept in subaltern historiography because it has the power to reimagine the whole and challenge the grand narrative of the nation (Pandey 1992: 28).

21 *Merriam-Webster Online*, www.merriam-webster.com/dictionary /figuration.

22 She published *Oru laingikathozhilaliyude aathmakatha* (The autobiography of a sex worker; Jameela 2005b) as told to the activist I. Gopinath and then in the span of six months produced another autobiography in collaboration with a different group of activists and intellectuals.

23 Here one can find echoes of the "figural" in Lyotard's conception of the term as moments of intensity that resist and escape all regulating power, be it linguistic discourse or the order of the conscious or political constraints (Ionescu 2013). But this is not the singular mode in which I deploy the concept of figuration.

24 The valuable remarks from the anonymous reviewer helped me to augment and foster the rhetorical dimensions of the notion of figuration in this book. I am grateful to the reviewer for conceptually pushing me further in this direction.

25 Butler (2004: 41) observes that a norm operates within social practices as the implicit standard of *normalization* and can govern the field of intelligibility. I draw on her conception of the norm not as a timeless and unchanging ideal but only as it persists "to the extent that it is acted out in social practice and reidealized and reinstituted in and through the daily rituals of bodily life" (48). Susie Tharu (2007) draws on citation and reiteration as a cluster of terms linked to the life of the norm and pointing to the durability of the workings of power. She argues that disciplined and decorous as well as unruly citation can be a key to understanding political practice in the domain of representation (18).

26 The caste structure in Kerala consists of Nambudiris, who are placed at the peak of ritual hierarchy, and the Nairs belong to the next rung. Their access to land and other economic resources enabled them to become a dominant caste group in modern Kerala. The Ezhava community has struggled against practices of stigmatization since the late nineteenth and early twentieth centuries, and their search for upward social mobility has been well documented (Osella and Osella 2000). Dalits, a large number of landless caste groups, were slaves of the upper caste landlords and denied access to public spaces such as roads and markets till the mid-nineteenth century (Mohan 2016: 42). Dalit mobilizations against discrimination and exclusion have a long history in contemporary Kerala.

27 In May 2015 a matrimonial advertisement, labeled as the "first gay matrimonial ad" in India, was published in *Mid Day* newspaper, in which an upper caste mother sought a groom for her gay son, expressing preference for a vegetarian Iyer man. This lead to a public debate on how caste boundaries are maintained even as homosexuality is publicly recognized. See "Mother Seeks Groom for Son in First Gay Matrimonial Advertisement," *Times of India*, May 21, 2015, http://timesofindia

.indiatimes.com/city/mumbai/Mother-seeks-groom-for-son-in-first-gay
-matrimonial-advertisement/articleshow/47363670.cms.

28 Rekha Raj observes that a different representation of the family emerges
in Dalit feminist articulations in Kerala in the 1990s that is not present in
mainstream feminist debates: "Dalit women activists in this period see in
the family a means to attain social status and an institution which
provides scope for gaining both economic and social capital" (2013: 59).

29 Founded in 2001, Sahayatrika is the first organization in Kerala that
focuses mainly on the issues faced by lesbian and bisexual women. They
have played an important role in making lesbian sexuality—and, more
broadly, women's sexuality—a matter of political concern.

30 In a sustained and powerful agitation that started in 2007 and continued
for more than five years and was opposed by all the major political parties
in the state, about five thousand landless families occupied the privately
owned Harrison Malayalam rubber plantation at Chengara, demanding
ownership of cultivatable land. The Chengara land struggle exposed the
adverse living conditions among Dalits and Adivasis, who did not benefit
from Kerala's model of social development (Sreerekha 2012).

31 The title video for this news program has the image of a wide-open eye
looking at the world. This is a news program that offers satirical commentary on political issues in Kerala.

32 Masala films refer to films that are racy and sensational and aim to
titillate the audience.

33 This ritual of *adichuthali* is an act embedded in practices of caste hierarchies, a purity/pollution ritual. Kerala has a history of an extremely rigid
caste structure, with pollution rituals such as "distance" regulations
between different castes. Former slave castes were not only regarded as
untouchable, "but they were even supposed to make themselves 'invisible'
as the mere sight of them were considered polluting to higher castes"
(Lindberg 2005: 21).

34 For a more detailed analysis of the night vigil, modes of protest, and the
politics of visibility, see Mokkil 2018b.

35 C. S. Venkiteswaran observes that a set language of political protests has
emerged over the years in Kerala. Specific formats such as hunger strikes,
stone pelting, sit-ins, and *bandhs* "are graded, calibrated and performed"
according to the demands of particular situations. He argues that the
night vigil was attacked because it deviated from this accepted "grammar
of protest." C. S. Venkiteswaran, "The Grammar of Protest," *Infochange*,
April 23, 2008, www.infochangeindia.org/human-rights/42-human-rights
/analysis/7005-the-grammar-of-protest.

36 Namita Malhotra, 2010, *Porn: Law, Video and Technology*, Centre for
Internet & Society, http://cis-india.org/raw/histories-of-the-internet
/blogs/law-video-technology/law-video-and-technology-old.

37 Reshma Radhakrishnan in conversation with author, May 10, 2008.

38 Here, it is useful to turn to theorists like Wendy Brown (2000) who have pointed to the problem of the conceptualization of pornography as a mirror of heterosexual violence. She rather sees it is a symptom of the cultural crisis around the erosion of gender subordination in the late twentieth century in the United States and an attempt to shore up or stabilize eroding gender dominance.

39 Jenny Rowena. "The 'Dirt' in the Dirty Picture: Caste, Gender and Silk Smitha," June 17, 2012, www.dalitweb.org/?p=736.

40 M. Swathy Margaret, "Dalit Feminism," June 3, 2005, https://www .countercurrents.org/feminism-margaret030605.htm.

41 Here, it is useful to note the etymology of the term "pornography" from the Greek term *pornographos*, "writing about prostitutes." "Pornography and Censorship," *Stanford Encyclopedia of Philosophy*, October 1, 2012, http://plato.stanford.edu/entries/pornography-censorship.

42 Vanita (2005a); Gopinath (2005); Majumdar (2009); Katyal (2016); Keshavamurthy (2016).

43 Kamala Surayya (1934–2009) is one of the most significant bilingual writers from Kerala. She has written in English as Kamala Das and in Malayalam as Kamala and Madhavikutty. After her conversion to Islam in 1999, she named herself Kamala Surayya. In this book I refer to her as Kamala Surayya, and the references indicate the name she used in specific publications.

44 Halberstam (2005) conceptualizes "queer time"—models of temporality that disturb incremental and calibrated temporal frames—and connects it to place-making practices that push against the accumulative logic of capital.

45 Vanita (2002); Bhan and Narrain (2005); Menon (2007); Bose and Bhat- tacharya (2007).

46 Ding (2000); Tellis (2003); Kotiswaran (2011a); Dave (2012); Sukthankar (2012).

47 Geeta Patel defines "proprietary heterosexuality" as "heterosexuality that accumulates and is bolstered by access to property, personhood, and social/political and financial capital" (2016: 268). Thus, Patel's call is to parse out the specificities of what buttresses formations of heterosexuality.

48 Massad (2002); Tellis and Bala (2015); Arondekar and Patel (2016); Bakshi, Jivraj, and Posocco (2016). In a global gay identity discourse, developments within the Global South are often seen as derivative. For example, Yasmin Nair criticizes how the Delhi High Court landmark judgment (which was later reversed by the Supreme Court in 2013 and restored in 2018) reading down the Section 377 of the Indian Penal Code, thus decriminalizing private same-sex relations between consenting adults, was described in the media as "India's Stonewall." "Why India's S. 377 Ruling Is Not Stonewall," July 8, 2009, windycitymediagroup.com

/gay/lesbian/news/ARTICLE.php?AID=21779. See chapter 3 for further discussions about how this book intervenes in the scholarship on queer politics in India.

49　See chapter 2 for a detailed account of the debates on sex work and its links to the terrains of the law, the public health machinery, and NGO-ization in India.

50　Lucinda Ramberg (2016) addresses the conundrum of bringing into conversation Dalit studies and queer studies because it is often perceived that sexual respectability is naturalized in caste critiques and put to shame in queer theory. She dislodges this separation by paying attention to how *devadasis* and Dalit converts "are out of joint" with "straight time" (226) and put forward asynchronous ways of acting in and on time. The critical frameworks she offers on caste, queerness, and temporality speaks to my analysis in the last two chapters in this book.

51　See Jenny Rowena, "The 'Dirt' in the *Dirty Picture*: Caste, Gender and Silk Smitha," June 17, 2012, http://roundtableindia.co.in/index.php?option =com_content&view=article&id=5283:the-dirt-in-the-dirty-picture -caste-gender-and-silk-smitha&catid=119&Itemid=132.

52　Rekha Raj, "Nammude rashtriyam athava nammudeyokke rashtriyangal" (Our singular or our plural politics), December 15, 2013. This was pub-lished as a note on Rekha Raj's Facebook page in which she reflects on an incident at IFFK (International Film Festival of Kerala) 2013. Accessed December 20, 2013.

53　In April 2014, the Supreme Court of India passed the NALSA (National Legal Services Authority) judgment that grants constitutional rights to transgender people. In 2015 Kerala became the first state in India to introduce a state policy for transgender persons. Within the articula-tions of trans experiences, questions of caste, labor, and livelihood acquire greater traction. "(Trans)gender and Caste Lived Experience— Transphobia as a Form of Brahminism: An Interview of Living Smile Vidya," *Sanhati*, January 26, 2003, http://sanhati.com/excerpted/6051. I signal toward these shifting formations of sexuality politics in the conclusion of this book, but my primary focus is on an earlier phase of activism.

54　Donna Haraway argues for a feminist theory of situated knowledges, which insists "that the object of knowledge be pictured as an actor and agent, not a screen or a ground or a resource, never finally as slave to the master that closes off the dialectic in his unique agency and authorship of 'objective' knowledge" (2004: 95). This recognition is necessary for a feminist epistemology.

55　Jamaica Kincaid's *A Small Place* (1988) is a powerful indictment of unequal geopolitical dynamics. I draw on her usage of the small place to pull together the multiple ways in which a region might get frozen even as it circulates in the global economy. The tourism industry plays a crucial role in freezing Kerala as a beautified location: "God's Own Country" is the tagline for Kerala tourism. I look for discourses in which the region is not appropriated as just another "local/e" that fits into the global umbrella.

56 www.imdb.com/title/tt0470913/mediaviewer/rm2641428992.

57 "To make a claim on behalf of the fragment is also, not surprisingly, to produce a discourse that is itself fragmentary. It is redundant to make apologies for this" (Chatterjee 1993: 13).

Chapter 1: Tracing the Prostitute

1 See Slaughter for a study on how in an era of globalization, literary forms such as the coming-of-age novel "disseminate and legitimate the norms of human rights" by making "each other's common sense legible and compelling" (2007: 3).

2 E. V. Sreedharan mentions how the established heroines in Malayalam were not ready to take up this controversial role (1999: 6). So it became the launch vehicle for a new heroine, and Seema went on to become one of the most successful heroines of Malayalam cinema. Her entry through a film like *Avalude ravukal* did not restrict her acting career. From action films to family drama, Seema was noted for her versatility and range.

3 *Avalude ravukal* is still seen by many noted film critics as responsible for unleashing a series of soft-porn films in Malayalam. In an article on the female body and Malayalam cinema, C. S. Venkiteswaran writes, "The watershed film that turned the tide was I. V. Sasi's *Avalude Ravukal*, which virtually opened the floodgates of a soft porn genre that went on to capture a national market for a brief period of time" (2010: 46). The notoriety of this film because of its national circulation coexists with recent attempts to recuperate it.

4 The first conference of the All India Progressive Writers Association took place in 1936 in Lucknow. Participating in the radical currents of the Progressive Writers Movement and its call to create new standards of beauty by focusing on the common man (Coppola 1986: 27), Jeeval Sahitya Sangham was founded in Kerala in 1937. Political leaders and thinkers from the Communist Party were some of the earliest leaders of this group. The Sangham changed its name to Purogamana Sahitya Sanghatana (Progressive Writers Association) in 1944 with more prominent writers joining the group. In the time period of 1947–1949, many heated debates were conducted between literary critics and political leaders about the mandate, meaning, and purpose of this literary movement (Chandrasekharan 1999: 61). In these contestations we see the attempt to deploy Marxist criteria to evaluate art. Within this literary movement in Kerala, there was a desire to engender an aesthetic sensibility that would shock the reader's consciousness and force one to

confront the ugly realities of the world (see Ramakrishnan 2011; Chandrasekharan 1999).

5   The first Malayalam color film came out in 1961, and by 1978 many films were being produced in color. Hence making this film in black and white contributes to its realist aesthetic. Black and white is perceived to be stark and less glossy and therefore more capable of capturing "real life." It is closer to the aesthetics of newsreels and documentary footage.

6   The music of this film, especially the background song and the lullaby sung by Raji's mother, "Unni arariro" (My child, let me sing you to sleep), are significant elements in the sustained popularity of the film. "Sleepless are Her Nights" received nostalgic praise on YouTube, where the song sequence was available for viewing until it was removed owing to a copyright issue: "Sweet voice of S. Janaki from the picture *Avalude Ravukal*. How can we forget this song"; "One of the best songs . . . evergreen . . . everlasting."

7   Darshana Sreedhar Mini suggests that in terms of narrative structures, thematic content, stylistic markers, and industrial aspects, it would be useful to study soft-porn in Malayalam as a genre in itself (2016: 129) even though it is not a predetermined category.

8   Babu Jayakumar, "It All Started with . . . Her Nights," July 6, 2006, www .canadiandesi.com/read.php?TID=13853.

9   One of the methodological questions raised by this chapter is, What are the possible sources and methods to track the ways in which a film lives on in popular memory? The internet, where film viewers interact with each other and actively distribute and comment on film clips and song sequences, has made possible new debates on films from earlier periods of time. This is a medium that gives us access to a virtual world of popular memory, albeit a limited one that needs to be complemented with ethnographic methods.

10 Lotte Hoek observes how film posters on city walls "speaks to the omnipresence of the film image in South Asia far beyond the discrete audience and particular viewers of a film" (2016: 74). This dispersed presence of cinema in the field of mass publicity and its ability to touch the sensorium of disparate viewers, beyond the audience who see the film on screen, animates the afterlives of a film such as *Avalude ravukal*.

11 The link between literature and cinema is made within the diegesis of the film through Raji's love for literature. Her intellectual capability and depth of thinking is demonstrated when she refers to her reading practices in a conversation with Babu. Babu is awed by her insights and says that though he is a student of English literature, he does not have the ability to think like her. The film posits a reading prostitute to demonstrate that she deserved to be far above the situation that the audience finds her in. This trope is repeated in a more recent film, *Susanna* (2000), which received public attention as an iconoclastic representation

of the prostitute figure and was lauded by the sex workers' organizations in the state. In this film the protagonist asks, "Can't a veshya (prostitute) read Kazantzakis?" thus deploying her reading practices as a marker of her emancipated status.

12 In the autonomous women's movement in India, in the 1980s, protests against obscenity and the commodification of women's bodies were staged by tearing down offensive film posters or pouring tar on them. Here again it is the publicness of film posters and their openness to multiple gazes that made them a target of protest. See Ghosh (1999) for a critical account of this mode of feminist protest.

13 Vaikom Muhammad Basheer (1908–1994) is one of the most vibrant and iconoclastic writers of modern Malayalam literature. His immensely popular writing has been praised for its experiments in themes, form, and language.

14 In the well-known introduction to a novel by Basheer, *Balyakalasakhi* (Childhood companion, 1944), M. P. Paul described it as a "page torn out of life. There is blood on the edges" (Paul 1944/2008: 2605). It is these powerful realist labels attributed to Basheer's writings that the film deploys.

15 Literary critic Kesari Balakrishna Pillai (1947) predicted that *Shabdangal* would raise a storm in critical circles. Basheer's writing of *Shabdangal* is compared to Thakazhi Sivasankara Pillai's (1947) writing of *Thottiyude makan* (*The son of a scavenger*) about a profession considered too unclean for literary representation. Here we see how the boundaries of literary representation are enmeshed in the vectors of caste and sexuality.

16 We can see parallels to the publication of the Urdu text *Angarey* (Live coals) in 1932 (Zaheer 1932/1990). This book was the cause of much furor, and the United Provinces government banned the book in 1933 (Coppola and Zubair 1987; Jalil 2012). This is marked as a key event that led to the formation of the Progressive Writers Association. The violent attack against this collection and its characterization as "filthy," "foul," and "shameless" (Coppola and Zubair 1987: 170) is tied to its proposition that sexuality is a domain that needs to be the subject of literary works committed to social transformation.

17 Caste hierarchies in Kerala have been maintained through the division of spaces, forms of labor, and bodies as clean or unclean. The ritual cleansing conducted by the AIDWA members at the night vigil in 2008, which I discuss in the introduction, points to how pollution and purity rituals are deployed to sanitize public spaces at present.

18 The five writers who contributed to the anthology are Basheer, Thakazhi Shivasankara Pillai, S. K. Pottekkad, P. Kesavadev, and Ponkunnam Varkey. In S. K. Pottekkad's "Kallapashu" (The mischievous cow), a male domestic servant recounts his sexual escapades with the wife of his employer; Basheer's "Bharyayude kamukan" (Wife's lover) is an ironic

commentary about a husband's anxiety that his ownership over his wife's body has been challenged because she had a lover before her marriage; Kesavadev's "Pativrata" (The virtuous wife) stages the internal battles of an aging widow who lives a life of chastity only to be shocked by the sexual desire she feels for her grown-up son; and "Nattumporathe veshya" (The countryside prostitute) by Thakazhi depicts an aging prostitute's struggle to survive in a system in which she is valued only for her transient good looks. Thus the anthology focuses primarily on women's sexual desires and the fraught terrains of structures of domesticity.

19 Accounts of the controversy surrounding the publication of *Angarey* (1932) show that Rashid Jahan, the sole Muslim woman who contributed to this anthology, was the most vilified specifically because of her gender (Coppola and Zubair 1987).

20 Inaugurated in 1973 by Prime Minister Indira Gandhi, this police station in Calicut is hailed as the first all-woman police station in India. Kunjeebi's custodial murder points to the brutality of systems of policing and the callous treatment of street sex workers even in the face of the construction of full-fledged women's police stations.

21 Interview with Ajitha that I conducted on December 13, 2008.

22 The political alliance between feminists and sex workers in India has been complex and shifting. This is also linked to the changing positioning of the sex worker in regional, national, and global discourses of law, governance, and public health from the colonial period to the present. The reform model through which feminists such as Ajitha operated in the 1980s later led to differences with political articulations by sex workers in the post-1990s context. Rajeswari Sunder Rajan maps the debates in Indian feminism on the "prostitution question" that complicates the binary of coercion/consent and revises the conception of female "agency" (2003: 117). These questions will be explored in more detail in the next chapter.

23 Drawing attention to the Mathura case and the Rameeza Bee case—custodial rape cases in police stations in Maharashtra and Andhra Pradesh—which were central to the feminist movement in India in the 1970s, Mary John and Janaki Nair observe how the legal judgment on a case of rape is predicated on the social positioning of the woman: "The class and/or ethnic status of the woman more or less automatically places her in the category of inviting rape while consistently denying the status of 'victim' to women with a sexual past" (1998: 25).

24 I spoke to her in February 2009. She asked me not to use her name in my writing because she did not want any form of publicity.

25 Foucault in "Governmentality" argues how "we need to see things not in terms of the replacement of a society of sovereignty by a disciplinary society and the subsequent replacement of a disciplinary society by a

society of government; in reality one has a triangle, sovereignty-discipline-government, which has as its primary target the population and as its essential mechanism the apparatuses of security" (1994a: 243).

26 C. Choyikutty is a news photographer who has worked in the print media field since the 1960s. He is noted for his photographs on marginalized lives, and he did a photographic exhibition, "Memories from the Street," in 2004. In an interview with me he said that his aim as a photographer has been to record and draw attention to unknown and neglected issues.

27 Susan Sontag observes that even in this era of electronic media and nonstop imagery, "When it comes to remembering, the photograph has the deeper bite. Memory freeze-frames; its basic unit is the single image" (2003: 22).

28 Choyikutty mentioned how he was able to get access to this sensitive crime scene because he was mistaken as a police photographer: "There were no advanced technical tools then, like mobile camera phones, only flash photography, and my camera could not be concealed."

29 Walter Benjamin (1969) discusses the origins of the photographic medium and its links to recording crime scenes. Forensics has relied on the evidentiary power of photography to capture traces that are not visible to the naked eye. See Jean Comaroff and John Comaroff's discussion on the colonial history of photography and forensics techniques and the sensational occurrences in legal history that render the "hard facts" of forensics as subject to conflicting interpretation (2016: 121).

Chapter 2: To Claim the Day

1 This move toward self-representation can be read alongside the use of autobiographies and testimonials as a political form in mobilizations by different marginalized groups in India, significantly the publication of Dalit autobiographies in multiple regional languages in India. See Ramakrishnan (2012) for further discussion on the publication of experiential narratives from the margins in Kerala since the latter half of the 1990s.

2 From the blurb on the back cover of the first autobiography.

3 This includes reports in Malayalam magazines and newspapers and all major English language national magazines in India such as *Tehelka*, *Outlook*, and *India Today*. National television news channels such CNN-IBN and NDTV also covered this story. The international media also picked up on this literary event. "Indian Prostitute Mum Sparks Storm with Book" was a December 20, 2005, *China Daily* article (www.chinadaily .com.cn/english/doc/2005-12/20/content_504790.htm). A July 6, 2010, report in the *New York Times* on life narratives by marginalized women from India also focuses on Nalini Jameela (Roy 2010). The book has been

translated to a number of regional languages in India including Tamil, Hindi, Telugu, and Kannada and foreign languages such as French and Spanish.

4   Kamala Surayya also wrote two versions of her life story in two languages. Her autobiography in Malayalam, *Ente katha* (My story, 1973), was followed by *My Story*, in English, in 1976. Both these books garnered instant national attention primarily on account of her unabashed portrayal of women's sexual experiences outside the sanctioned bounds of the heterosexual monogamous family. The two versions addressed different reading publics and therefore there are significant differences between them. For a comparative reading of the politics of gender and the production and reception of Jameela and Suyayya's autobiographical writings, see Devika 2006.

5   AIDS as a pandemic has produced an "epidemiological mapping of the world" (Patton 2002a: ix), and Asia in a space-time framework is positioned as Pattern Three, where "AIDS arrived late" in distinction to North America and Europe (Pattern One) and Africa (Pattern Two) (Patton 2002a: ix). The first cases of HIV in India were diagnosed among sex workers in Chennai, Tamil Nadu, in 1986 (Godbole and Mehendale 2005). Because of funding from international agencies such as WHO and UNICEF, philanthropic organizations such as the Bill and Melinda Gates Foundation, and multination organizations such as USAID, the AIDS awareness and prevention program is one of the most well-supported public health endeavors in India today (Kotiswaran 2011b; Shah 2014).

6   The AIDS control programs positions MSM (men who have sex with men) as a high-risk category, and male sex workers are placed in this grouping. The official website of the Kerala State AIDS Control Society mentions that the route to HIV transmission is 82 percent heterosexual and 2 percent homosexual. KSACS, "Facts and Figures: HIV/AIDS in Kerala," http://ksacs.kerala.gov.in/index.php/2014-02-13-06-12-21/ksacs-and-you /fact-and-figures.

7   An NGO in Kerala that has been working since 1995 to provide legal and economic support and counseling to marginalized communities, Federation for Integrated Research in Mental Health (FIRM) facilitated the formation of Sex Workers' Forum Kerala (SWFK), and in May 2006, SWFK was registered as a charitable society with legal status. The sex worker's organization Durbar Mahila Samanwaya Committee (DMSC), which is based in Kolkata, and SWFK were part of the National Network of Sex Workers (NNSW). Discussion for the formation of the NNSW started in November 1997 at the first National Conference of Sex Workers in India. Over the years, NNSW and its member organizations have conducted several campaigns to raise issues at both the national and regional levels. The organization is now formally registered as All India Network of Sex Workers (AINSW).

8   See Christy 2017 for an analysis of Nalini Jameela's autobiographies that foregrounds how her sociocultural positioning of being a lower-caste woman sex worker is central to the analytical reading of the context of her becoming "public." Christy explores the notion of in-between spaces and the permeated relation between the public and the private that shapes the figure of the sex worker (97) and complicates the paradigms of feminist politics in India.

9   Excerpts from the first document are given as an appendix to *Oru*. See Kotiswaran 2011b for English translations of these documents.

10 *Suraksha* centers are projects run under KSACS , which funds and gives guidelines to NGOs and community-based organizations (CBOs) in different parts of the state to work with high-risk groups such as sex workers and injective drug users.

11 In many cities in India, like Mumbai and Kolkata, there are specific areas where sex workers work in brothels. These areas are often known as red-light areas, referring back to the colonial history of the formation of these streets as areas where British soldiers had access to sex and to the institutionalization of prostitution in India under the colonial medical and juridical regimes (Shah 2014: 151).

12 In a UNAIDS report, peer education is described as "a popular concept that implies an approach, a communication channel, a methodology, a philosophy, and a strategy" (1999: 5). This report explains how peer education draws on behavioral theory and participatory education models that believe that equals talking among themselves will elicit behavioral change and empowerment (6).

13 NACO, "National AIDS Control Programme IV," http://naco.gov.in/nacp.

14 Since 2007 the global anti-AIDS effort has changed track, moving away from the focus on using sex workers as peer educators (Center for Development Studies 2008: 153). Currently, there is concern that excessive focus on sex workers might have ignored the vulnerability of married women to AIDS. This also points to the problem that the sex worker and the married women are often perceived as mutually exclusive categories. But the KSACS website still states that one of their main objectives is to prevent new infections in high-risk groups through targeted interventions. KSACS, "Goals & Objectives," http://ksacs.kerala.gov.in/index.php/messages/goals-objectives.

15 Indian manufacturers of generic antiretroviral medicines facilitated the rapid scale up of HIV/AIDS treatment in developing countries though the provision of low-priced, quality-assured medicines (Waning, Diedrichsen, and Moon 2010).

16 According to the information given by KSACS, with an estimated fifty-five thousand HIV-positive people, Kerala's average is less than the national figure, at about 0.26 percent. This is in spite of the fact that it is surrounded by four high prevalent states. KSACS, "Facts and Figures."

17 *Painkili* is a term used to denote a highly popular form of romantic writing in Malayalam since the 1950s, but through repeated usage it has come to mean a set of attitudes that is excessively sentimental.

18 There is also a positioning of sex workers as childlike by presuming that they have the leisure and inclination to sit around in NGO-supported office spaces to play board games. One of the employees at Sangamitra, a community-based organization in Thrissur, Kerala, mentioned that sex workers rarely sit down to play this game, which they perceive as a "juvenile" activity. Thus there are many slippages and "backtalk" (Pigg and Adams 2005: 3) by various social actors as these campaign materials circulate in translocal institutions.

19 Scholars note how "gendered notions of governmental self-regulation" (Rankin 2001: 23) become well entrenched with the growth of profession-alized NGOs in the global south that work within an economically defined development agenda (Mukhopadhyay 2007, 2016). Scholars have critiqued "NGO-ization" as a "process through which issues of collec-tive concern are transformed into projects in isolation from the general context in which they are applied" (Jad 2007: 177). They argue that radical and redistributive movements run the risk of being contained and reframed to service rather than resist neoliberal globalization (Alvarez 1999; Amar 2013). Mimi Nguyen (2011: 374), in her analysis of develop-ment projects in Afghanistan, observes that globally there is an emphasis on entrepreneurial individualism and financial responsibility as the path toward grooming the subaltern third-world woman as an agent of her own transformation.

20 For this particular instruction, the addressee is male. Many of these materials are produced not just for female sex workers. Other high-risk categories, such as MSMs, are also included in this rubric. Office spaces and drop-in centers run by the state-supported NGOs cater to these different target groups of AIDS interventions.

21 UNICEF, "Red Ribbon Express: HIV/AIDS Awareness on Wheels," http://unicef.in/Story/236/Red-Ribbon-Express-HIV-AIDS-awareness-on -wheels.

22 This appearance of the family and the clothing of the woman are not typical of Kerala. Since the Red Ribbon Express was a national campaign, most of the materials were produced for a pan-Indian audience. But the language was changed as the train moved from one state to another to communicate better in every region.

23 See the introduction for debates on the "Kerala woman."

24 Krupa Shandilya (2017) argues that repetition, duality, and interrelation-ality are significant moves in the fashioning of the courtesan in Urdu literature in the nineteenth century. She bases her analysis on two interlinked novels by Muhammed Hadi Ruswa, both published in 1899; the first is a fictionalized biography of the courtesan Umrao Jaan, as

narrated to the interlocutor Mirza Ruswa, and the second is staged as Umrao Jaan taking revenge against Ruswa's disclosure of her memoirs by revealing the intimate details of Ruswa's private life (80).

25 Tambe (2009) argues that the positioning of the sex worker as a medicalized body who has to be policed and sanitized to protect male clients and the social body has continuities with the regulatory mechanisms of the Contagious Diseases Act (CDA) in the colonial era. The CDA was enacted in India under British rule in 1868 to prevent the spread of venereal diseases to British soldiers, and the body of the prostitute was severely monitored under the workings of this act through mandatory medical heath examinations and lock hospitals for treatment and retention. See Levine 2003 and Arnold 1993.

26 Interview by author with Sreela, coordinator of the KSACS *suraksha* center in Calicut, January 10, 2008.

27 Chatterjee (2004: 74), in his use of the framework of governmentality, moves toward the conceptualization of the political society as a population group that seeks and finds recognition through the moral attributes of community. He distinguishes this tenuous logic of strategic politics as different from the sanitized rights claims within civil society. My focus is on the political claims of the sex worker as a subject through the form of the autobiography, and so I do not enter into a discussion of this frame of the "political society."

28 Ration cards have been an important part of the Public Distribution System in India. On the basis of their economic status, people can buy goods like food grains, sugar, kerosene, etc. at varying prices with the help of their ration cards. A ration card functions as an important tool of identification for Indian citizens.

29 "The Emergency" was a tumultuous period in Indian history that extended from June 26, 1975 to March 21, 1977, when the Indian president, upon request by Prime Minister Indira Gandhi, declared a state of internal emergency under Article 352 of the Constitution of India, effectively bestowing on her the power to rule by decree, suspending elections and civil liberties.

30 See Sunder Rajan's (1993) cautionary note against the tendency in political interventions to fetishize the body in pain as stasis.

31 A. K. Jayasree draws on accounts from sex workers from 1995 to 2001 to provide factual evidence to support Jameela's claims: "Street sex workers are arrested in Kerala 3–4 times a month, according to oral histories by the women, and an average of 1–2 incidents of violence are reported every day to one drop-in center" (Jayasree 2004: 61). Data shows how 90 percent of those arrested under the Immoral Traffic Prevention Act are women sex workers. The other 10 percent are brothel keepers, pimps and clients (62).

32 See Raj 2005 for debates in Kerala about sex work as a feminist issue.

33 Jameela (2008), in the article "Round and Round the Town," which is a short, personalized introduction to Thrissur town and forms part of the travel-writing anthology *Cities of Kerala: Actually Small Towns*, provides a layered account of women's access to public spaces and their precarious negotiations within it. She observes how to negotiate spaces in the town that are less accessible to women: "Many women who work odd hours rely on sex workers to accompany them. They include flower vendors, construction workers, home nurses, servants, sweepers and other women travelling at night. In this context, sex workers are recognized and appreciated as a powerful group" (111). Thus she places the sex worker in the company of many other working-class women in the informal labor sector for whom negotiating urban spaces and the risks that come with it is an unavoidable part of their everyday lives.

34 In 2000, Jwalamukhi conducted a public meeting to felicitate the director and main actress of the film *Susanna* (2000). This was the first time sex workers claimed the public sphere not as victims but as spectators responding to a cinematic representation of the prostitute figure. This move shows how cultural practices are crucial to sexuality politics in Kerala. The sex worker's reception of *Susanna* is a critical gesture that invents a new position for the sex worker in the public sphere (Menon 2005; Mokkil 2003).

35 In the section about naming, Jameela also tells us about her relationship with different religious practices. Even as a young girl, her relationship with organized religion was ambivalent. After her separation from her husband, Shahul, she seeks refuge in mosques and the Muslim community offers her sustenance during this period of serious illness. She mentions that she started calling herself Nalini Jameela, which is a mixture of Hindu and Muslim naming practices, much after she started living together with Shahul and converted to Islam (Jameela 2005a: 111)

36 Vijayalakshmi Vadlapati (1960–1996), known by her screen name Silk Smitha, starred in over four hundred Tamil, Malayalam, Telugu, Kannada, and Hindi films. Her raunchy dance numbers and provocative performances made her *the* glamorous sex symbol of South Indian cinema. Her stardom raises questions about the caste and class location of actresses, their casting in sexually explicit "vamp" roles, and their positioning in the film industry. Her suicide at the age of thirty-five gives a tragic aura to the public memorialization of this hugely popular and controversial film star. The mobile circuits and instabilities of the star persona of Silk Smitha can be tracked through varied attempts to memorialize her—ranging from the Malayalam poetry anthology *Visudha Smithakku* (For Saint Smitha; Kankol 1998) to the popular Hindi film *The Dirty Picture* (2011).

Chapter 3: Wandering in the Vernacular

1   Lesbian suicide is one of the issues around which sexuality has become a political issue in the Kerala public sphere in the last three decades. Since the early 1990s, there have been multiple newspaper reports in Kerala about women who die together. Initially these were unspecified reports tucked away in a corner of the newspaper, but as the pattern repeated, it drew the attention of some concerned individuals and groups. Today, as the category of the "lesbian" is well circulated in public discourses, even mainstream newspapers name such suicides "lesbian suicides." The public discourse on lesbian suicides and its role in positing the lesbian as a political subject will be the focus of the next chapter.

2   Public discussions on gay and lesbian sexuality, in print and visual media, emerged in the late 1980s and early 1990s in India, running parallel to the establishment of NGOs, support networks, and collectives that focus on issues of sexuality and marginalization. Reports and resource books such as "Less Than Gay: A Citizens' Report on the Status of Homosexuality in India" by AIDS Bhedbhav Vidrohi Andolan (ABVA) in 1991, *Khamosh: Emergency jari hai!* (Lesbian emergence: A citizen's report) by Campaign for Lesbian Rights (CALERI) in 1999, and *Humjinsi: A Resource Book on Lesbian, Gay and Bisexual Rights in India* (Fernandez 2002) were central to the early phase of LGBT politics in India.

3   There is a large body of scholarship that analyzes the complex intersections between the state, the legal domain, and LGBT politics, especially in the light of the mobilizations for the repeal of Section 377 of the Indian Penal Code (Bhaskaran 2004; Bhan 2005; Kapur 2005; Puri 2016).

4   See Ratti 1993; Sukthankar 1999; Merchant 1999; Vanita and Kidwai 2000; Vanita 2002; and Bhan and Narrain 2005.

5   Pandey Bechan Sharma, who wrote under the name Ugra (meaning fierce or forceful), published the anthology *Chaklet* in 1927 that lead to an uproar because of its "mis-en-scène of debauchery" (Katyal 2016: 82), primarily the candid exposure of male-male desire. Akhil Katyal draws attention to the copresence of a sensationalizing intent and a sober pedagogic one in the framing of this anthology (82). This book was catapulted into the nationalist discourse with interventions by public figures such as Mahatma Gandhi. See Vanita and Kidwai 2000; Katyal 2016.

6   Ismat Chughtai's *Terhi lakeer* (The crooked line, 1945/1995) recasts the gendered contours of the public and the private, the nation and the home, through experiments with the autobiographical form.

7   I thank the anonymous reviewers for urging me to place the discourse of sexuality in Kerala in conversation with other regional contexts in India.

8   "The obscenity law prohibited the use of four letter words," said Chughtai in an interview about the trial: "'Lihaaf' does not contain any such words.

In those days the word 'lesbianism' was not in use. I did not know exactly what it was. The story is a child's description of something she cannot fully understand. It was based on my own experience as a child. I knew no more at that time than the child knew. My lawyer argued that the story could be understood only by those who already had some knowledge. I won the case" (Kishwar and Vanita 1983: 5).

9   I would suggest here that literary texts such as "Lihaaf" and *Shabdangal* also partake in this realm of the cinematic by activating the multisensory potential of acts of reading.

10 There are certain common tropes that this film shares with other representations of erotic relationships between women in Malayalam literature, the most noted one being V. T. Nandakumar's *Randu penkutti-kal* (Two girls, 1974) and other narratives in women's magazines. One of these tropes is the concern around the possible intimacies between women in sex-segregated spaces like women's hostels and educational institutions. Muraleedharan (2010) provides a detailed discussion of the history of the representation of women's friendship and solidarity in Malayalam cinema from the 1970s onward. He argues that in many of these films, women's friendships are sidelined as the resolution privileges the heterosexual bond.

11 Writer and filmmaker Padmarajan (1946–1991) made films from 1979 to 1991. He continues to be a prominent cultural icon in Kerala. In a short span of twelve years, he made twenty films and wrote screenplays for another twenty. At the time of release and in the decades after that, his films have enjoyed both popular appeal and critical appreciation.

12 Ligy J. Pullappally was born in Kerala and grew up in Chicago. She is a trial lawyer by profession who has worked specifically on women's issues. *Sancharram* is Pullappally's first foray into full-length feature films.

13 Arvind Narrain, "Moving beyond the Limits of *Fire*: *Sancharram* as a Queer Exploration," *Sancharram* website, 2004, accessed January 2, 2008. The Sancharram official website (no longer online) provided information about the film, including the director's note on its making, film stills, list of film festival screenings and awards, and links to film reviews.

14 Scholars have analyzed the shifting idioms of romance and intimacy in Indian cinema, its links to structures of the feudal family, aspirations for modernity, and the ambivalent status of the couple as a closed and insular unit in the Indian context. Madhava Prasad (1998) and Moinak Biswas (2000) have analyzed the complex codes of representation of desire in Indian film, where a public gaze often disrupts the private space of the formation of the heterosexual couple. Biswas (2000), in his study of the highly popular Bengali film *Hurano Sur* (1957), observes that the journey from the familial to the conjugal remains largely unfulfilled in popular Bengali cinema in this period. In fact, he suggests that the

lasting popularity of *Hurano Sur* is because it finds a way to recognize and articulate the absent space of the couple.

15 The Nairs are a dominant Hindu caste group from Kerala. They were part of the civil, administrative, and military elite of the princely kingdoms and British-administered areas that later merged to become the state of Kerala. This is one of the communities in Kerala that followed matrilineal forms of family arrangement and inheritance until the early twentieth century.

16 T. Muraleedharan (2002, 2005) has argued that the absence of a recognizable gay/lesbian cinema need not undermine the relevance of queer mass culture studies in India. His articles carved a new direction for the study of representations of sexuality in popular Malayalam cinema by teasing out the implications of same-sex attraction deployed in the narrative construction of masculinity. In the last five years there have been popular Malayalam films such as *Mumbai Police* (2013), *Odum raja aadum rani* (2014), *My Life Partner* (2014), and *Ka Bodyscapes* (2016) that openly represent gay characters and are positioned as films that deal with questions of masculinity and homosexuality. These shifts in practices of representation need further analysis that is beyond the scope of this chapter.

17 Shohini Ghosh argues that the representational practices of *Fire* and the raging debate that this film ignited is linked to how in this film "everyday spaces get inhabited by queer desires" (2010: 88). She focuses on the choreography of the bodies of the two women, Sita and Radha, that activates the space of the middle-class home. From the exchange of spices in the kitchen and hopscotch on the terrace to the kiss in the bedroom, homoerotic expressions are woven into the hallowed sphere of domesticity. See Patel on how the circulation of erotic transactions between women who inhabit the structures of conjugality—"the homely housewife who runs amok" (2004: 153)—destabilizes the ideologies of domesticity and homeliness as intimacy.

18 From love letters to lyric poetry, sensational fiction to devotional poetry, scholars have examined the vast field of literary and other artistic productions in South Asia that produce a "conceptual and aesthetic vocabulary for talking about love" (Orsini 2006: 23). Studies from different fields such as visual anthropology, visual culture, and film studies point to the formative role of cinema and photography in the organization of romance and conjugality. This includes the significance of couples photographs, family albums, and the role of marriage videos in the shaping of rituals of love and conjugality (Abraham 2010).

19 Since the 1950s, *painkili* is a term used to denote a popular form of romantic writing that stages intense scenes of sensuality and sentimentality. This genre of writing, which is available cheaply and is consumed widely, is looked down on in the Kerala public sphere because it is seen as

sensational and therefore not of high literary value. The links between *painkili* writing and economies of desire are discussed further in the next chapter.

20 This question of class, taste, and the divide between aesthetic forms of romance is central to my analysis in the next chapter. This is also significant because one of the well-known lesbian novels in Malayalam, *Randu penkuttikal* (Two girls, 1974) is in the tradition of sentimental pulp fiction.

21 *Sancharram* website, director's note on events in Kerala that inspired her to make this film, accessed July 15, 2012 (no longer online).

22 Alternative Law Forum, Bangalore, "Annexure D: Table of Lesbian Suicides," http://lib.ohchr.org/HRBodies/UPR/Documents/Session1/IN /PLD_IND_UPR_S1_2008anx_LesbianSuicides.pdf, accessed September 10, 2015.

23 This is the pseudonym used by V. N. Deepa, the founder of Sahayatrika, in the early phase of her activist career.

24 V. N. Deepa (writing as Devaki Menon), "Lessons from Sahayatrika," January 23, 2006, www.suedasien.info/analysen/1676, accessed March 1, 2013.

25 Gayatri Gopinath (2007) cautions the reader of the risks of reifying and romanticizing the matrilineal Nair past. But she goes on to argue that the redeeming power of *Sancharram* as a regional text is in its ability to resuscitate the matrilineal Nair past that stubbornly refuses to die in spite of nationalist judicial interventions that abolished matriliny. This is a risky claim on which to validate the film, especially when we read it in relation to the fact that most reported lesbian suicides, including the one that motivated the film, were committed by women from an underprivileged, non-dominant caste background.

26 The etymology of the word can be traced to the pre-independent practice of dividing a princely kingdom into smaller land units called *desham*. The current usage of *desham* refers to a regional district within the Kerala state. One of the examples of the use of the term *desham* in this way is the well-known Malayalam novel by S. K. Pottekkad, *Oru deshathinte katha* (The tale of a *desham*, 1971/2015), which records the life world of one particular location within Calicut district in Kerala and shows the layers of movement unfolding within this small place.

27 This is the conventional architectural structure that was the housing and property unit of affluent Nair families. Wealthy *taravads* encompassed a spacious house built in a specific architectural style, and a freshwater pond (*kulam*). These *taravads* have become a symbol of Nair privilege in contemporary Kerala, and though structures like this are relatively few today, they are repeatedly invoked in Malayalam films and writing as part of the process of constructing an essentialized Nair identity.

28 "Chronotope" literally means "time-space" and comes from Mikhail Bakhtin's influential theorization that chronotope is a formally

constitutive category of literature. There is a fusion of temporal and spatial indicators in this term: "Time, as it were, thickens, takes on flesh, becomes artistically visible; likewise, space becomes charged and responsive to the movements of time, plot and history" (Bakhtin 1981: 84).

29 Raja Ravi Varma (1848–1906) was a painter who is seen as one of the founding figures of modern Indian art (Arunima 2003a; Kapur 2000). His depictions of Indian women, especially Nair women, and scenes from Hindu epics are mass produced and well circulated in Kerala even today.

30 "Film Review by Vikram," *Gay Bombay*, 2004, accessed May 2, 2008. Sancharram official website (no longer online).

31 Cochin is a port city in Kerala and has been the center of tourism and urbanization. It is also at present depicted in popular Malayalam cinema as the city where you can see the darker sides of urban life. It is here that gang wars and smuggling are often staged. We can see the traces of this imagination of Cochin in *DKK* with multiple references to signs of urbanity and criminality.

32 In addition to speaking English and behaving like tourists, the women capitalize on their class privilege as convent-educated girls in order to ward off harassment on the streets.

33 *Sancharram* official website, accessed June 1, 2008 (no longer online).

34 *Fire* tells the story of two sisters-in-law in a joint family who break the stifling bonds of duty and tradition to enter into a sexually and emotionally sustaining relationship with one another. The film premiered in 1996 at the Toronto Film Festival and it was distributed in India in 1998. The protests against the film targeted the Indo-Canadian filmmaker's depiction of lesbianism in the heart of the Hindu family.

35 The public "event" of *Fire* is primarily staged in the metropolitan spaces of Mumbai, Delhi, and Kolkata. Many commentators mention that the film did release widely in different states in India and in many theaters the tickets were sold out. In some cities, women-only screenings were organized (Ghosh 2010: 59). The film's exhibition history and its modes of reception in small towns and other cities need further investigation.

36 Organizers of CALERI also address the need for coalition building and the importance of working with vernacular languages in order to reach out to a diverse range of people (Basu 2006: 25).

37 John and Niranjana's (1999) discussion on *Fire* points to how the sexual "choice" of the two women is valorized in the film through the vilification of the sexuality of the servant, Mundu, and his consumption of pornography. They argue, "The expressive and emergent feminist self becomes thus coded in the film as upper caste and middle class, defined against subjectivities that are neither" (583).

38 Middle cinema is the name given to a segment of films within the Malayalam film industry that self-consciously carved out an aesthetics of

its own. In accounts of Malayalam film history, middle cinema is seen as occupying an intermediary space between "art" cinema and "commercial" cinema. The exponents of middle cinema in the 1980s and 1990s were seen as producing films that appealed to a broader audience than the niche audience of the 1970s art cinema. For more discussion on the ambiguities and significance of these categorizations within Malayalam cinema, see Menon 2008.

39 One of the classical examples of this is Kumaran Asan's poetic work *Leela* (1914/1975), an epic of romantic love in which the heightened moment of union between the hero and heroine is the moment of death, with the hero ending his life in the river and the heroine following the same course. *Chemmeen* (Shrimp, 1965), an internationally acclaimed Malayalam film based on a cult love story by noted novelist Thakazhi Shivashankara Pillai that was published in 1956, also tells the story of a couple whose desire transgresses social norms. They finally have to die together in order to stage their eternal union.

Chapter 4: Living Together, Dying Together

1 "Stree" was published when the writer was only fifteen years old in *Mathrubhumi Weekly*, but it was not included in her first anthology of short stories which came out in 1955. The story was republished in 2009 in the literary journal *Bashaposhini* under the title "The first lesbian story in Malayalam." A write-up on the history of this story speculates on how notions of respectability might have been one of the reasons why this story was excised from her oeuvre (Premkumar 2009). More explicit depictions of lesbianism by Kamala Surayya in *Chandanamarangal* (The sandal trees, 1988/2007) and *My Story* (1976) have received critical attention by scholars such as Rosemary Marangoly George (2000, 2002). The liminal presence of this story in Kamala Surayya's body of work might also be linked to how it deploys the conventions of "low" cultural forms such as sentimental romance, horror, and ghost stories.

2 Tapati Guha-Thakurta (2002) describes the *yakshi* as a primordial goddess associated with wealth, abundance and fertility (Guha-Thakurta 2002). The common imagination of the *yakshi* today as bloodthirsty feminine creatures who prey on men is a product of a wide array of popular cultural representations in modern Kerala. The representation of the woman who bears markers of undomesticated sexuality as a mythical figure is a trope that is often used in Malayalam literature and cinema. Malayattoor Ramakrishnan's novel *Yakshi* (1967/1995) reinvents the form of a *yakshi* story to explore the crisis of masculinity and the fear and fantasy linked to feminine sexuality. S. Sanjeev (1995) analyzes the popular Malayalam film *Manichithrathazhu* (The ornate lock, 1993), in which a dancer from the past possesses the body of the heroine and is projected as the negative,

disorderly aspects of her femininity. See Mokkil 2018a for my analysis of *Yakshi* and its cinematic adaptations.

3   Teresa de Lauretis positions the lesbian as an "eccentric subject," by which she refers to a critical, epistemological position "attained through practices of political and personal dis-placement across boundaries between sociosexual identities and communities" (1990: 145). I examine how this position of "displacement" shapes the trajectories of lesbian lives and its documentation in the public sphere.

4   My analysis in this chapter is in conversation with critical interventions on temporality in queer studies that allow us to question the reliance on visual metaphors and linear mappings in the study of lesbian representability (Jagose 2002). These studies reflect on how "working on time— cutting, splicing, looping, and knotting time" (Ramberg 2016: 224) is crucial for the collective imagination of transformative futures.

5   Heather Love observes that "over the last century, queers have embraced backwardness in many forms: in celebrations of perversion, in defiant refusals to grow up, in explorations of haunting and memory, and in stubborn attachments to lost objects" (2007: 7). Critical reading practices that parse out the intimate links between haunting and queer politics are significant to my analysis.

6   Kerala has drawn attention in the late 1990s and early 2000s because of its high rates of suicides; it was even labeled as the suicide capital of India in this period (Chua 2014). According to state statistics and news reports in 2008, Kerala's suicide rates were triple the national average. *The Hindu*, "Suicide Rates Remain High in Kerala," September 10, 2008, www .thehindu.com/todays-paper/tp-national/tp-kerala/Suicide-rate-remains -high-in-Kerala/article15300426.ece. Jocelyn Lim Chua's (2014) work deploys suicides in Kerala as a complex lens to understand the experiential dynamics of development and global change in India.

7   Sahayatrika initially worked by providing a helpline and a postbox number so that women could seek guidance and support through mail or phone. It played in important role in making lesbian sexuality and, more broadly, women's sexuality a matter of political concern by conducting investigations, organizing public events, publishing reports, and providing support to negotiate with institutions such as the family, the police, and the judiciary. Deepa (2005: 176) locates the formation of Sahayatrika in the social and political churning of the late 1990s—the growing attention to reports of same-sex suicides, the handful of "renegade" voices emerging from the feminist movement of people ready to support sexual minority groups, and the impact of the increased visibility of LGBT groups in urban centers in India.

8   Sheela and Sree Nandu's decision to live together in 2003 was the first incident of a highly visible "lesbian" relationship in the public sphere of Kerala. This was a controversial event in which the intrusive and

sensational media coverage raised questions about the "advantages and pitfalls of visibility" (Deepa 2005: 175). Nandu's later assertion of his transgender identity showed up the slippages in the public naming of this relationship as lesbian.

9   In order to protect the identity of the people they interviewed, the Sahayatrika team does not give details of the location or actual names of people involved in the published interviews. This information is given in Malayalam newspaper reports on the event. See *Mathrubhumi* (2001) and *Kerala Kaumudi* (2001). Since I analyze the published interviews, I use the names Ammini and Meera, which are used by the Sahayatrika team.

10   See Sridevi Nair's (2011) analysis of *Facing the Mirror: Lesbian Writing from India* that showcases multiple voices without editorial devices to distinguish real names from pseudonyms. Nair reflects on the significance of the form of the anthology and the strategy of anonymity for the emergence of lesbian writing in India.

11   The book also has translations of articles written by activists and theorists who are prominent voices within a metropolitan gay/lesbian movement. This includes writers such as Ruth Vanita, Nivedita Menon, and Arvind Narrain. This is in addition to articles in Malayalam on queer sexuality in Kerala by activists and scholars such as Reshma Bharadwaj, Dileep Raj, S. Sanjeev, Deepa Vasudevan, and A. K. Jayasree.

12   "Adivasi" literally translates as "the original dwellers." This is a term that refers to the tribal communities in Kerala. Adivasis have been highly critical of the Kerala model of development and form a group that has been heavily marginalized. The last two decades in Kerala has witnessed large-scale land rights struggles by Adivasis.

13   Maya Sharma, in *Loving Women*, a collection of oral narratives of working-class women in same-sex relationships, observes how in India "women who came into the public gaze as a result of the sexuality issue were mostly women from the working class" (2006: 15).

14   A select list of lesbian suicides, reported in the print media in India from the 1980s to 2002 and compiled by the Alternate Law Forum, an organization that works for the legal rights of sexual minorities, has thirteen cases and ten out of the thirteen are from Kerala. "Annexure—D: Table of Lesbian Suicides," http://lib.ohchr.org/HRBodies/UPR/Documents /Session1/IN/PLD_IND_UPR_S1_2008anx_LesbianSuicides.pdf, accessed April 10, 2012.

15   The "Fact Finding Report" compiled by the Sahayatrika team in February and May 2002 was circulated in English and Malayalam. The Sahayatrika members gave me access to the full draft of the transcribed interviews that were part of the report. The interviews that are published in the book, which I analyze, have been translated into English by me.

16   They were talking to immediate family and friends who were reeling under a deep sense of loss and were also suspicious of outside

interventions. As A. K. Jayasree observes in the introduction to Sebastian's book of journalistic reports on lesbian suicides, "In a society which sees suicide and homosexuality as humiliating, the plight of families that experience both is quite tragic. In the midst of the flurry of media output that approach these issues without any comprehension or sensitivity, it is difficult to conduct direct investigations" (quoted in Sebastian 2003: 11).

17 The fabrication of subjectivities that appear in the public eye at the site of death has raised significant questions about gender, agency, and representation in different contexts in South Asia. In Neloufer De Mel's critical study of militarization in Sri Lanka, she argues that the "LTTE suicide bomber makes her subjectivity available to the public only at the precise moment in which she is silenced, and silences herself through her final act of violence" (De Mel 2007: 192–93). In tracking the figurations of the female suicide bomber, De Mel argues that the important issues for inquiry are of "how her agency is framed, when is it foregrounded and retracted, and on what affective registers is it introduced" (200).

18 Such investigations play a critical role in determining what issues get to be known in an international network of human rights and are in the tradition of a mode of political mobilization used by civil liberties groups in India, like People's Union for Civil Liberty (PUCL), which publishes fact-finding reports on acts of violence against minority groups in different parts of India. These reports are appeals to a larger international and national body to put pressure on local governments to take the necessary steps to put an end to the violence. For example, PUCL Karnataka's report, *Human Rights Violations against the Transgender Community: A Study of Kothi and Hijra Sex Workers in Bangalore, India*, September 2003, http://ai.eecs.umich.edu/people/conway/TS/PUCL/PUCL%20Report.html, is an influential document in the sexuality rights movement in India.

19 Many of the struggles of Sahayatrika have resonances with issues faced by other LGBT organizations that have emerged since the mid-1990s in different parts of India. Some of these organizations mark their distance from the more dominant formations of gay identity politics and foreground questions of location, access, and the need for coalition building. They also focus primarily on issues faced by lesbian, bisexual and transgender persons. See Basu (2006); Shah (2005); and Shannon Mathew, "Understanding Trans and Queer Issues in Women's Movements: An Interview with Chayanika Shah," April 4, 2017, www.the ypfoundation.org/news-2/2017/3/31/interviewing-chayanika-shah.

20 Aniruddha Dutta undertakes a critique of the institutionalization of transgender identity in India by examining how an alliance between transnational activist networks and development industry, primarily linked to the AIDS discourse, reify "gender/sexually variant communities into fixed cartographies of marginality" (2013: 497). Nithin Manayath (2015: 255) also examines the mechanics through which a developmental

discourse, firmly embedded in the sexuality/identity framework, reorder the terrain of erotic sociality in India as the hijra is subsumed into the global language of LGBT rights.

21 In this chapter, I use the pronouns "she" and "her" to refer to Meera because these are the terms used in the public discourse produced both by the Sahayatrika team and the community members through which Meera and Ammini's lives become available for analysis.

22 Ruth Vanita calls these joint suicides by same-sex couples in different parts of India "a type of marriage—a public statement of intent to be united forever" (2005b: 124). She focuses on the rituals related to death and on documents such as love letters and suicide notes in order to examine how acts of dying inscribe same-sex couples into patterns of love and marriage in the subcontinent. Rather than creating a capacious definition of love and marriage, my argument is that the memory of these lives and deaths create a dissonance within naturalized formations of heterosexual marriage and domesticity as the primary sexual, economic, and emotional fulcrum of women's lives.

23 The novelists who played a significant role in making reading a popular activity in the fifties and sixties later become sidelined and labeled as "cheap" literature. The devaluation of Muttathu Varkey's *painkili* novels is a prime example of the stigmatization of popular forms of romantic fiction. In a spirited protest against the erasure of Varkey from Malayalam literary history, acclaimed writer Punathil Kunjabdulla says, "I will say without doubt that if anyone writes a history of the reading practices of Malayalis the position that Muttathu Varkey and *Paadatha Painkili* has in it is unparalleled" (2002: 50).

24 According to official state history, adult and nonformal education activities in Kerala started in an organized manner in the early decades of the twentieth century. The Travancore Grandhasala Sangham (Travancore Library Association) was set up in 1945 as the apex body of forty-seven rural libraries. The state was declared a totally literate one on April 8, 1991. "Total Literacy," *Official Web Portal, Government of Kerala*, https://kerala.gov.in/total-literacy.

25 T. Muraleedharan translated an extract from *Randu penkuttikal* (Nandakumar 2000) for *Same Sex Love in India* (Vanita and Kidwai 2000), a pioneering anthology on queer representations in India. Before the novel was repositioned in this fashion, one could safely assume that its networks of circulation were mainly as a *painkili* novel. It was first published as a serialized novel in a magazine, *Chitra Karthika*, and the novelist mentions that his readers were mainly women and students (Nandakumar 1974: 2). A Malayalam film based on this novel titled *Randu penkuttikal*, directed by Mohan, was released in 1978. In spite of multiple attempts, I have not been able to locate a copy of this film in formal or informal repositories of Malayalam cinema.

26 Raymond Williams defines "structures of feeling" as meanings and values in a particular time and space that are actively lived and felt, "specifically affective elements of consciousness and relationships: not feeling against thought, but thought as felt and feeling as thought: practical conscious-ness of a present kind, in a living and inter-relating continuity" (1977: 132).

27 Raymond Williams's dynamic conceptualization of the social has been used by queer scholars to "tarry with the emergent in their description of radically anticipatory stances or gestures that have not yet congealed into dominant cultural forms like identity, community, or market niche" (Freeman 2007: 163).

28 Butler draws attention to the ways in which hierarchies of grief operate in the global arena: "How do our cultural frames for thinking the human set limits on the kind of losses we can avow as loss? After all, if someone is lost and that person is not someone, then what and where is the loss and how does mourning take place?" (2004: 32).

29 The literal translation of *uyiru* is "life." The term assumes a division of the bodily and the spiritual, and *uyiru* refers to core or essence of life. So I have translated it as "life-force."

30 As Geeta Patel observes, mourning is an intense experience of embodied recall, suffused with an overwhelming tendency to turn back time: "Mourning demands returns" (2016: 247).

31 The lesbian that emerges in these interviews is not a figure of abjection, as suggested by Devika, who argues that the "abjects of development" are those bodies on to which sexuality is projected (Devika 2009: 31). According to her, prostitutes, sexual minorities, and AIDS patients are all pushed into this realm of abjection, which is beyond the pale of reform. When we look closely at the mediated life stories of Meera and Ammini and their interactions with the community, the category of abjection is not quite apt. They have a tentative power to impinge upon and disturb the formations of the social.

32 Dave examines queer archives from India on family and death "to show that both are constituted through a continuous play of presence *and* absence; moreover, that neither condition has any clear value on its own" and underlines the significance of readings that take into account "the space between" (2014: 162).

33 This resonates with Spivak's definition of the subaltern as "those removed from lines of social mobility" (2004: 531). Rekha Raj, in her analysis of the positioning of Dalit women as political agents, observes that "whether in political or new social movements, we find that the dalit participants failed to gain mobility precisely because they lacked the economic, social and symbolic capital to survive the different kinds of repression or backlashes that each of these movements came to face" (2013: 56).

34 Susie Tharu (1999), in her reading of Baburao Bagul's short story about a Dalit widow, argues that this drama of life and death in the scene of the

family brings into being a world where nothing can be taken for granted. Here there is no occasion for "con-solid-ation for reader or story teller" and the subject is "impossible because it is continuously annihilated" (198). By introducing caste into the scene of desire, she points to the necessity to rework classical categories of political theory—personhood and agency.

35 Publications such as *Manorama Weekly*, *Mangalam Weekly*, and *Manorajyam Weekly*—commonly referred to as "Ma" publications—play an important role in popularizing *painkili* writing.

36 Organizations such as Sangama in Bangalore, Karnataka, have played a significant role in providing a supportive space for sexual minorities who migrate out of Kerala. This has been a life-sustaining exit point, but activism within Kerala points to the need to engage with local communities to make any change possible. In my conversation on July 3, 2008, with a member of Sahayatrika who had to leave home at a young age because of her relationship with another woman, she mentioned her reasons for staying on in Kerala and not leaving to Bangalore or other urban centers. She explained that she would feel out of place and uprooted in Bangalore; everything, including the language, would be alien to her. She has opted to live in a small city in Kerala and negotiate the boundary lines between visibility and invisibility at an everyday level. She stressed how this was a difficult option, but there were no easy exit strategies.

37 These questions of relationality and the violence of being unclaimed resonate in the documentary film *Ebang bewarish* (And the unclaimed, 2013) on a lesbian suicide in 2011 in Nandigram, West Bengal. See Chatterjee (2018) for an in-depth engagement with the politics of queerness, subalternity, and subjectivity in which this suicide in 2011 functions as a site of "melancholy, uncertainty and responsibility" (Chatterjee 2018: 119). For details on lesbian politics in West Bengal, also see Roy (2014).

Chapter 5: "What You Think Is Fire . . ."

1 This exhibition was part of the two-day public display of installations, video art, and paintings by visual art students at Ambedkar University Delhi, May 3–4, 2014, titled "None the Less Art."

2 As discussed in the introduction, the 2009 Delhi High Court judgment read down Section 377 of the Indian Penal Code. But this was later reversed in 2013. In September 2018 the five-judge Constitutional Bench of the Supreme Court reinstated the 2009 judgment, effectively allowing for same-sex relations between consenting adults in private. This judgment guarantees fundamental rights to members of the LGBT community and dismantles the indefensible labeling of consensual sexual

acts as "unnatural" and "abnormal." Since 2009 there have been multiple debates on the activism against Section 377 and its links to right to privacy, choice, and autonomy.

3   Chayanika Shah and Shals Mahajan, activists who are part of LABIA, a queer feminist collective in Mumbai, in their presentation "What's a *Morcha* Doing in My Parade?" (October 15, 2015, at Jawaharlal Nehru University, Delhi), discussed the shifting terrain of queer organizing since 2009 and asked how and why issues of caste, religion, and class are sidelined in its highly visible formations at present, such as the queer pride marches.

4   *Mathrubhumi*, "Harbor Worker's Neck Slit and Murdered at Kollam," May 11, 2012, a report on the *Mathrubhumi* online edition that provides regional, national, and international news coverage, no longer online; *The Hindu*, "Man Found Dead at Tangasseri," May 11, 2012, www.thehindu .com/todays-paper/tp-national/tp-kerala/article3406945.ece.

5   From media reports and online discussions, it emerges that the investigation of the murder has been unsatisfactory and inconclusive so far. Reports show how the preconceptions of the police about transgender people as criminals and carriers of HIV/AIDS color this investigation, leading to further victimization and persecution of sexual minorities (Gee Imaan Semmalar, "For Maria, with Love and Pain," June 10, 2012, www.dnaindia.com/lifestyle/report-for-maria-with-love-and-pain -1700448; Sreekumar 2012).

6   K. K. Shahina, "The Obit of a Transgender Activist," May 26, 2012, www .openthemagazine.com/smallworld/obit-of-a-transgender-activist.

7   Anil A., "Obituary: Sweet Maria," May 14, 2012, http://feministsindia.com /obituary-sweet-maria.

8   Semmalar, "For Maria."

9   Ann Cvetkovitch writes about how cultural artifacts that bear the traces of collective losses, built around intangible feelings, "remain alert to forms of affective life that have not solidified into institutions, organizations, or identities" (2003: 9).

10 Rumi Harish, "'I Am Coming Out': What Awaits Me? Life or Death," May 15, 2012, www.socialism.in/index.php/i-am-coming-out-what-awaits -me-life-or-death.

11 Semmalar, "For Maria."

12 Muñoz asks the significant question about utopian political imaginations in a world where the violent fate of queer youths of color point to how they have no guarantee of a future (Muñoz 2009: 95). This resonates in the Indian context today as we are faced with the institutional murders of subaltern youths, especially Dalit students in colleges and universities, raising questions about how transformative politics can be shaped in the face of death.

13 YouTube, www.youtube.com/watch?v=IwU3ieFUJ9o, accessed May 10, 2015.

14 Maria was an extremely active organizer and participant of the queer pride marches in 2010 and 2011, and her murder happened when she was in the midst of organizing the pride march in 2012.

15 In the first, more small-scale version of this exhibition, all the things on display were arranged under the cover of the skirt that ballooned like a big tent. In the second exhibition, which is the one I focus on, the red skirt dangled in the room, and other paintings, installations, and performances were organized around it (conversation with Aryakrishnan, May 5, 2015, Delhi).

16 Art critics Santhosh S. and Vidya Shivadas conducted a conversation with the artists who participated in this exhibition about their distinct artistic concerns. Extracts of this conversation are included in the "None the Less Art" catalog (MA Visual Art Students 2014).

17 The term "monument" literally means "something that reminds" and is etymologically linked to the Latin word *monere*, "to remind, warn." *Online Etymology Dictionary*, www.etymonline.com/index.php?term=monument, accessed May 5, 2015.

18 This is a popular song from the film *Guruvayur kesavan* (1977) featuring Jayabharati and Soman. Shot in the backdrop of the temple, a decked-up and ornate Jayabharati seduces the hero, and the song ends in a climactic scene of sexual union. The lyrics of the song are by P. Bhaskaran and celebrate the plenitude of nature that participates in beautifying the heroine, "Innenikku pottukuttan sandhyakal chalichu sindoorum" (Today the twilight dissolves into *sindoor* for me to adorn myself). There is an affinity between the visual codes of this song sequence and the depiction of the heroine's body in other films noted for the eroticization of the woman's body, such as *Avalude ravukal*.

19 Divya Trivedi, "Troubled Trans-lives," *The Hindu*, July 31, 2012, www .thehindu.com/todays-paper/tp-national/troubled-translives /article3705504.ece.

20 Deepu was part of the LesBiT (a support group for lesbian, bisexual, and transgender individuals in Bangalore) theatre group that performed at Chennai's queer pride cultural festival in 2010. He was brought to the screen in Gee Imaan Semmalar film *Kalvettukal* (Sculpture, 2012) a docu-fiction film on transgender men in Southern India. *Orinam*, "R.I.P. Deepu," July 30, 2012, http://orinam.net/r-i-p-deepu. *Breaking the Binary*, a study by LABIA: A Queer Feminist LBT Collective that analyzes the negotiations and struggles of queer PAGFB (persons assigned gender female at birth), is dedicated to Deepu (1988–2012). The dedication dwells on the "ardor and luminosity" of his voice that still echoes poignantly and "also rages loudly as it demands to be heard, and not trivialized, dis-missed, or forgotten so that others who travel beyond the boundaries are not compelled to break their hearts or smash their bodies against the walls of narrow minds" (Shah et al. 2013). The other recent study that

explores the life worlds of female born gender and sexual minorities of South India is *Towards Gender Inclusivity*, published by Alternate Law Forum and LesBiT (Mohan 2013).

21   This is the first stanza of the Kailash Kher's popular song "Teri deewani," which was released as part of his album *Kailasa* in 2006.

22   Tharu and Niranjana (1996) reflect on the conjuncture that feminism in India finds itself at in the late 1980s and 1990s that necessitates a re-examination of the category of gender and the normative subject of feminism—that is, the "woman" unmarked by any other social location.

23   This protest was a powerful statement against the Armed Forces Special Powers Act (AFSPA).

24   Lata Mani argues that Indian feminism needs to take a critical distance from the "neo-liberal paradigm and its notion of freedom" (Mani 2014: 26). She points to the dangers of opposing violence against women in public spaces by anchoring it in a "notion of untrammeled freedom, an unrealistic presumption with little historical precedent" (29).

25   Anjali Arondekar (2009) observes that the coupling of archive with minoritized knowledge formations has led to some simplistic and triumphant forms of empiricism. She argues for the need to be aware of the "*politics* of the archive . . . because it is rarely a simple matter of revealing secrets waiting to be found" (20).

References

Books, Articles, Manuscripts, Reports, and Presentations

Abraham, Janaki. 2010. "Wedding Videos in North Kerala: Technologies, Rituals, and Ideas about Love and Conjugality." *Visual Anthropology Review* 26 (2): 116–27.

Abu-Lughod, Lila. 2002. "Do Muslim Women Really Need Saving? Anthropological Reflections on Cultural Relativism and Its Others." *American Anthropologist* 104 (3): 783–90.

Agnes, Flavia. 2007. "State Control and Sexual Morality: The Case of the Bar Dancers of Mumbai." In *Enculturing Law: New Agenda for Legal Pedagogy*, edited by Mathew John and Sitharamam Kakarala, 158–75. New Delhi: Tulika Books.

AIDS Bhedbhav Vidrohi Andolan (ABVA). 1991. *Less Than Gay: A Citizens' Report on the Status of Homosexuality in India*. New Delhi: AIDS Bhedbhav Vidrohi Andolan.

Ajitha. 1987. "Kunjibiyude lock-up maranavum athuyarthiya prashnangalum" (Kunjibi's lock-up death and the problems that raised). *Kalakaumudi* 632:13–17.

Alvarez, Sonia E. 1999. "Advocating Feminism: The Latin American Feminist NGO 'Boom.'" *International Feminist Journal of Politics* 1 (2): 181–209.

Amar, Paul. 2013. *The Security Archipelago: Human-Security States, Sexuality Politics, and the End of Neoliberalism*. Durham, NC: Duke University Press.

Amin, Shahid. 1995. *Event, Metaphor, Memory: Chauri Chaura, 1922–1992*. Berkeley: University of California Press.

Anandhi, S. 1991. "Representing Devadasis: 'Dasigal Mosavalai' as a Radical Text." *Economic and Political Weekly* 26 (11/12): 739–41, 743, 745–46.

Anju cheetha kathakal (Five bad stories). 1946/1996. Kollam: Imprint Books.

Antharjanam, Lalithambika. 1966. "Prathikara devatha" (Goddess of revenge). In *Thiranjedutha kathakal*. Kottayam: Sahitya Pravarthaka Sahakarana Sangham.

Appadurai, Arjun. 1996. *Modernity at Large: Cultural Dimensions of Globalization*. Minneapolis: University of Minnesota Press.

Arnold, David. 1993. *Colonizing the Body: State Medicine and Epidemic Disease in Nineteenth Century India*. Berkeley: University of California Press.

Arondekar, Anjali R. 2009. *For the Record: On Sexuality and the Colonial Archive in India*. Durham, NC: Duke University Press.

———. 2012. "Subject to Sex: A Small History of the Gomantak Maratha Samaj." In *South Asian Feminisms*, edited by Ania Loomba and Ritty A. Lukose, 244–66. Durham, NC: Duke University Press.

Arondekar, Anjali, and Geeta Patel. 2016. "Area Impossible: Notes toward an Introduction." *GLQ: A Journal of Lesbian and Gay Studies* 22 (2): 151–71.

Arunima, G. 2000. "A Vindication of the Rights of Women: Families and Legal Change in Nineteenth Century Malabar." In *Changing Concepts of Rights and Justice in South Asia*, edited by Michael R. Anderson and Sumit Guha, 114–39. New Delhi: Oxford University Press.

———. 2003a. "Face Value: Ravi Varma's Portraiture and the Project of Colonial Modernity." *Indian Economic and Social History Review* 40 (1): 57–79.

———. 2003b. *There Comes Papa: Colonialism and the Transformation of Matriliny in Kerala, Malabar, c. 1850–1940*. Hyderabad: Orient Longman.

———. 2006. "Imagining Communities—Differently: Print, Language and the 'Public Sphere' in Colonial Kerala." *Indian Economic and Social History Review* 43 (1): 63–76.

Aryakrishnan. 2014. "Sweet Maria Monument: Doing and Undoing an Imaginary Archive." In MA Visual Art Students 2014.

Asan, Kumaran. 1914/1975. "Leela." In *Selected Poems of Kumaran Asan*. Thiruvananthapuram: University of Kerala.

Bairy, Ramesh. 2010. *Being Brahmin, Being Modern: Exploring the Lives of Caste Today*. New Delhi: Routledge.

Bakhtin, Mikhail. 1981. *The Dialogic Imagination: Four Essays*. Edited by Michael Holquist, translated by Caryl Emerson and Michael Holquist. Austin: University of Texas Press.

Bakshi, Sandeep, Suhraiya Jivraj, and Silvia Posocco, eds. 2016. *Decolonizing Sexualities: Transnational Perspectives, Critical Interventions*. Oxford: Counterpress.

Bal, Mieke. 2004. "Figuration." *PMLA* 119 (5): 1289–92.

Balfour, Ian, and Eduardo Cadava. 2004. "The Claims of Human Rights: An Introduction." *South Atlantic Quarterly* 103 (2/3): 277–96.

Banerjee, Sumanta. 1998. *Dangerous Outcast: The Prostitute in Nineteenth Century Bengal*. Calcutta: Seagull Books.

Barthes, Roland. 1981. *Camera Lucida: Reflections on Photography*. Translated by Richard Howard. New York: Farrar, Straus and Giroux.

Basheer, Vaikom Mohammed. 1947/2007. *Shabdangal* (Voices). Thrissur: Mangalodayam Limited.

———. 1952/2008. "Pavappettavarude veshya" (Prostitute of the poor). In *Pavappettavarude Veshya*, 30–34. Kottayam: D. C. Books.

Basu, Ranjan Amit. 2006. *Lesbianism in Kolkata*. Kolkata: Sappho for Equality.

Basu, Srimati, and Lucinda Ramberg, eds. 2015. *Conjugality Unbound: Sexual Economies, State Regulation and the Marital Form in India*. New Delhi: Women Unlimited.

Bay, Ancy. 2015. "At the End of the Story: Popular-Fiction, Readership and Modernity in Literary Malayalam." In *Kerala Modernity: Ideas, Spaces and Practices in Transition*, edited by Satheese Chandra Bose and Shiju Sam Varughese, 92–108. Hyderabad: Orient Black Swan.

Benjamin, Walter. 1969. "The Work of Art in the Age of Mechanical Reproduction." In *Illuminations*, edited by Hannah Arendt, 217–52. New York: Schocken Books.

Berlant, Lauren, ed. 2004. *Compassion: The Culture and Politics of an Emotion*. New York: Routledge.

Berlant, Lauren, and Michael Warner. 1998. "Sex in Public." *Critical Inquiry* 24 (2): 547–66.

Bhan, Gautam. 2005. "Challenging the Limits of Law: Queer Politics and Legal Reform in India." In Bhan and Narrain 2005, 40–48.

Bhan, Gautam, and Arvind Narrain, eds. 2005. *Because I Have a Voice: Queer Politics in India*. New Delhi: Yoda Press.

Bhaskaran, Suparna. 2004. *Made in India: Decolonizations, Queer Sexualities, Trans/National Projects*. New York: Palgrave Macmillan.

Biswas, Moinak. 2000. "The Couple and Their Spaces: *Hurano Sur* as Melodrama Now." In *Making Meaning in Indian Cinema*, edited by Ravi Vasudevan, 122–42. New Delhi: Oxford University Press.

Bora, Papori. 2010. "Between the Human, the Citizen and the Tribal: Reading Feminist Politics in India's Northeast." *International Feminist Journal of Politics* 12 (3–4): 341–60.

Bose, Brinda, and Shubhabrada Bhattacharya, eds. 2007. *The Phobic and the Erotic: The Politics of Sexualities in Contemporary India*. Calcutta: Seagull Books.

Bose, Satheese Chandra, and Shiju Sam Varughese. 2015. "Situating an Unbound Region: Reflections on Kerala Modernity." In *Kerala Modernity: Ideas, Spaces and Practices in Transition*, edited by Satheese Chandra Bose and Shiju Sam Varughese, 1–25. Hyderabad: Orient Black Swan.

Brown, Wendy. 2000. "The Mirror of Pornography." In *Feminism and Pornography*, edited by Drucilla Cornell, 198–217. Oxford: Oxford University Press.

———. 2005. *Edgework: Critical Essays on Knowledge and Politics*. Princeton: Princeton University Press.

Butler, Judith. 1993. *Bodies That Matter: On the Discursive Limits of "Sex."* New York: Routledge.

———. 2001. "Giving an Account of Oneself." *Diacritics* 31 (4): 22–40.

———. 2003. "Value of Difficulty." In *Just Being Difficult? Academic Writing in the Public Arena*, edited by Jonathan D. Culler and Kevin Lamb, 199–216. Stanford: Stanford University Press.

———. 2004. *Precarious Life: The Powers of Mourning and Violence*. New York: Verso.

———. 2005. *Giving an Account of Oneself*. New York: Fordham University Press.

Cadava, Eduardo. 1997. *Words of Light: Theses on the Photography of History*. Princeton: Princeton University Press.

Cadava, Eduardo, David Kelman, and Ben Miller. 2006. "Irresistible Dicta-tions: A Conversation with Eduardo Cadava Featuring David Kelman and Ben Miller: October 21, 2001." *Reading On* 1 (1): 1–17.

Campaign for Lesbian Rights (CALERI). 1999. *Khamosh: Emergency jari hai!* (Lesbian emergence: A citizen's report). Delhi: CALERI.

Center for Development Studies (CDS). 2008. *Gendering Governance or Govern-ing Women? Politics, Patriarchy, and Democratic Decentralization in Kerala State, India*. Research Report Submitted to IDRC, Canada, Mimeo. Thiruva-nanthapuram: Center for Development Studies.

Chandra, Shefali. 2012. *The Sexual Life of English: Languages of Caste and Desire in Colonial India*. Durham, NC: Duke University Press.

Chandrasekharan, M. R. 1999. *Keralathile purogamana sahithya prasthanathinte charithram* (History of the progressive literary movement in India). Kozhikode: Olive Publications.

———. 2008. "Statement in Solidarity to Participants in the Night Vigil." Unpublished manuscript.

Chatterjee, Partha. 1993. *The Nation and Its Fragments: Colonial and Postcolonial Histories*. Princeton: Princeton University Press.

———. 2000. "Two Poets and Death: On Civil Society and Political Society in the Non-Christian World." In *Questions of Modernity*, edited by Timothy Mitchell, 35–48. Minneapolis: University of Minnesota Press.

———. 2004. *The Politics of the Governed: Reflections on Popular Politics in Most of the World*. New Delhi: Permanent Black.

Chatterjee, Shraddha. 2018. *Queer Politics in India: Towards Sexual Subaltern Subjects*. London: Routledge.

Cheerath-Rajagopalan, Bhawani. 2005. "Why Fear Being Yourself." *Deccan Herald*, January 2, 2005.

Chopin, Kate. 1899. *The Awakening*. Chicago: Herbert S. Stone & Co.

Christy, Carmel K. J. 2015. "The Politics of Sexuality and Caste: Looking through Kerala's Public Space." In *Kerala Modernity: Ideas, Spaces and Practices in Transition*, edited by Satheese Chandra Bose and Shiju Sam Varughese, 126–45. Hyderabad: Orient Black Swan.

———. 2017. *Sexuality and Public Space in India: Reading the Visible*. New York: Routledge.

Chua, Jocelyn Lim. 2014. *In Pursuit of the Good Life: Aspiration and Suicide in Globalizing South India*. Berkeley: University of California Press.

Chughtai, Ismat. 1941/1994. "Lihaaf" (The quilt). In *The Quilt and Other Stories*, translated by Tahira Naqvi and Syeda Hameed, 5–12. New York: Sheep Meadow Press.

———. 1945/1995. *Terhi lakir* (The crooked line). Translated by Tahira Naqvi. London: Heinemann.

Cohen, Lawrence. 2005. "The Kothi Wars: AIDS Cosmopolitanism and the Morality of Classification." In *Sex in Development: Science, Sexuality, and Morality in Global Perspective*, edited by Stacy Leigh Pigg and Vincanne Adams, 269–304. Durham, NC: Duke University Press.

Comaroff, Jean, and John L. Comaroff. 2016. *The Truth about Crime: Sovereignty, Knowledge, Social Order.* Chicago: Chicago University Press.

Coppola, Carlo. 1986. "Premchand's Address to the First All-India Progressive Writers' Association: Some Speculations." *Journal of South Asian Literature* 21 (2): 21–39.

Coppola, Carlo, and Sajida Zubair. 1987. "Rashid Jahan: Urdu Literature's First Angry Young Woman." *Journal of South Asian Literature* 21 (2): 166–83.

Couser, Thomas G. 2004. "The Obituary of a Face: Lucy Grealy, Death Writing and Posthumous Harm." *Auto/Biography* 12:1–15.

Cruz-Malavé, Arnaldo, and Martin F. Manalansan, eds. 2002. *Queer Globalizations: Citizenship and the Afterlife of Colonialism*. New York: New York University Press.

Cvetkovitch, Ann. 2003. *An Archive of Feelings*. Durham, NC: Duke University Press.

Dave, Naisargi. 2006. "Between Queer Ethics and Sexual Morality: Lesbian and Gay Activism in New Delhi, India." PhD diss, University of Michigan.

———. 2010. "To Render Real the Imagined: An Ethnographic History of Lesbian Community in India." *Signs: Journal of Women in Culture and Society* 35 (3): 595–619.

———. 2012. *Queer Activism in India: A Story in the Anthropology of Ethics.* Durham, NC: Duke University Press.

———. 2014. "Death and Family: Queer Archives of the Space Between." In *Routledge Handbook of Gender in South Asia*, edited by Leela Fernandes, 160–72. New York: Routledge.

De Certeau, Michel. 1984. *The Practice of Everyday Life.* Berkeley: University of California Press.

Deepa, V. N. 2005. "Queering Kerala: Reflections on Sahayatrika." In Bhan and Narrain 2005, 175–96.

de Lauretis, Teresa. 1990. "Eccentric Subjects: Feminist Theory and Historical Consciousness." *Feminist Studies* 16 (1): 115–50.

De Mel, Neloufer. 2007. *Militarizing Srilanka: Popular Culture, Memory and Narrative in the Armed Conflict.* New Delhi: Sage Publications.

———. 2017. "A Grammar of Emergence: Culture and the State in the Post-tsunami Resettlement of Burgher Women of Batticaloa, Sri Lanka." *Critical Asian Studies* 49 (1): 73–91.

Desai, Manisha. 2002. "Transnational Solidarity: Women's Agency, Structural Adjustment, and Globalization." In *Women's Activism and Globalization:*

Linking Local Struggles and Transnational Politics, edited by Nancy A. Naples and Manisha Desai, 15–33. New York: Routledge.

Deshabhimani. 2008. "Rathrisamaram masalamayam" (The masala-filled night vigil). March 9, 2008.

Devika, J. 2006. "Housewife, Sex Worker and Reformer Controversies over Women Writing Their Lives in Kerala." *Economic and Political Weekly* 41 (17): 1675–83.

———. 2007a. *En-gendering Individuals: The Language of Re-form in Early Twentieth Century Keralam*. Hyderabad: Orient Longman Limited.

———. 2007b. "'Memory, Alive and Clear': An Interview with Nalini Jameela." In Jameela 2007, 134–43.

———. 2007c. "Translator's Foreword: Nalini Jameela Writes Her Story." In Jameela 2007, vi–xv.

———. 2008a. "Chuuline veendedutha adichuthelikkar" (The ritual purifiers who reclaimed the broom). *Mathrubhumi Weekly*, May 18–24, 2008, 52–55.

———. 2008b. "Idangalil athiridumbol" (When spaces get bounded). *Mathrubhumi Weekly*, April 20–26, 2008, 36–40.

———. 2008c. *Individuals, Householders, Citizens: Malayalis and Family Planning, 1930–1970*. New Delhi: Zubaan.

———. 2009. "Bodies Gone Awry: The Abjection of Sexuality in Development Discourse in Contemporary Kerala." *Indian Journal of Gender Studies* 16 (1): 21–46.

———. 2012. "Migration, Transnationalism, and Modernity: Thinking of Kerala's Many Transnationalisms." *Cultural Dynamics* 24 (2–3): 127–42.

Devika, J., and Mini Sukumar. 2006. "Making Space for Feminist Critique in Contemporary Kerala." *Economic and Political Weekly* 41 (42): 4469–75.

Ding, Naifei. 2000. "Prostitutes, Parasites and the House of State Feminism." *Inter-Asia Cultural Studies* 1 (2): 305–18.

Dreze, Jean, and Amartya Sen. 1995. *India Economic Development and Social Opportunity*. New Delhi: Oxford University Press.

———. 1996. *India: Development and Participation*. New Delhi: Oxford University Press.

Dutta, Aniruddha. 2013. "Legible Identities and Legitimate Citizens." *International Feminist Journal of Politics* 15 (4): 494–514.

Eng, David, J. Jack (Judith) Halberstam, and Jose Esteban Muñoz. 2005. "Introduction: What Is Queer about Queer Studies Now?" *Social Text* 23 (3–4): 1–17.

Eyben, Rosalind. 2007. "Battles over Booklets: Gender Myths in the British Aid Programme." In *Feminisms in Development: Contradictions, Contestations and Challenges*, edited by Andrea Cornwall, Elizabeth Harrison, and Ann Whitehead, 65–78. London: Zed Books.

Fernandez, Bina, ed. 2002. *Humjinsi: A Resource Book on Lesbian, Gay and Bisexual Rights in India*. Mumbai: India Centre for Human Rights and Law.

Filmfare. 1978. "Show All, Tell All." September 16–30, 1978, 10.

Foucault, Michel. 1978. *The History of Sexuality: Volume I.* New York: Vintage Books.

———. 1980. *Power/Knowledge: Selected Interviews and other Writings 1972–1977.* New York: Pantheon.

———. 1985. *The Use of Pleasure: The History of Sexuality: Vol 2.* New York: Vintage Books.

———. 1994. *The Essential Foucault.* Edited by Paul Rabinow and Nikolas Rose. New York: New Press.

Freeman, Elizabeth. 2007. "Introduction." *GLQ: A Journal of Lesbian and Gay Studies* 13 (2–3): 159–76.

Frosh, Stephen. 2013. *Hauntings: Psychoanalysis and Ghostly Transmissions.* New York: Palgrave Macmillan.

Gadihoke, Sabeena. 2011. "Sensational Love Scandals and Their Afterlives: The Epic Tale of Nanavati." *BioScope: South Asian Screen Studies* 2 (2): 103–218.

Gargi and Hasan. 2008. "Love in the Time of Chengara." Paper presented at the Estate, State, Fourth Estate conference, Thiruvananthapuram, April 12.

Geedha. 2013. "Olinjunottakarude kumbasarangal" (Confessions of the voyeurs). *Chandrika Weekly*, June 6–14, 2013, 8–17.

George, Rosemary Marangoly. 2000. "Calling Kamala Das Queer: Rereading *My Story.*" Feminist Studies 26 (3): 731–63.

———. 2002. "'Queernesses All Mine': Same-Sex Desire in Kamala Das' Poetry and Fiction." In Vanita 2002, 111–26.

Ghosh, Shohini. 1999. "The Troubled Existence of Sex and Sexuality: Feminists Engage with Censorship." In *Image Journeys: Audio-Visual Media and Cultural Change in India*, edited by Christiane Brosius and Melissa Butcher, 233–60. New Delhi: Sage Publications.

———. 2010. *Fire: A Queer Film Classic.* Vancouver: Arsenal Pulp Press.

Ghosh, Swati. 2005. "Surveillance in Decolonized Social Space: The Case of Sex Workers in Bengal." *Social Text* 23 (2): 55–69.

Godbole, Sheela, and Sanjay Mehendale. 2005. "HIV/AIDS Epidemic in India: Risk Factors, Risk Behaviour and Strategies for Prevention and Control." *Indian Journal for Medical Research* 121:356–68.

Gopal, Meena. 2012. "Caste, Sexuality and Labor: The Troubled Connection." *Current Sociology* 60 (2): 222–38.

Gopal, Priyamvada. 2005. *Literary Radicalism in India: Gender, Nation and the Transition to Independence.* London: Routledge.

Gopinath, Gayatri. 2005. *Impossible Desires: Queer Diasporas and South Asian Public Cultures.* Durham, NC: Duke University Press.

———. 2007. "Queer Regions: Locating Lesbians in *Sancharram.*" In *A Companion to Lesbian, Gay, Bisexual, Transgender, and Queer Studies*, edited by George E. Haggerty and Molly McGarry, 341–54. Malden: Blackwell.

Gopinath, I. 2005. "Preface." In Jameela 2005, 5–6.

Gordon, Avery. 1997. *Ghostly Matters: Haunting and the Sociological Imagination.* Minneapolis: University of Minnesota Press.

Guha-Thakurta, Tapati. 2002. "The Endangered Yakshi: Careers of an Ancient Art Object in Modern India." In *History and the Present*, edited by Partha Chatterjee and Anjan Ghosh, 71–107. New Delhi: Permanent Black.

Gupta, Charu. 2001. *Sexuality, Obscenity, Community: Women, Muslims, and the Hindu Public in Colonial India.* New York: Palgrave Press.

Guru, Gopal, ed. 2009. *Humiliation: Claims and Context.* New Delhi: Oxford University Press.

Halberstam, Jack (Judith). 2005. *In a Queer Time and Place: Transgender Bodies, Subcultural Lives.* New York: New York University Press.

———. 2011. *The Queer Art of Failure.* Durham, NC: Duke University Press.

Hall, Stuart. 1997. "The Local and the Global: Globalization and Ethnicity." In *Dangerous Liaisons: Gender, Nation, and Postcolonial Perspectives*, edited by Anne McClintock, Aamir Mufti, and Ella Shohat, 173–87. Minneapolis: University of Minnesota Press.

Haraway, Donna Jeanne. 2004. "Situated Knowledges: The Science Question in Feminism and the Privilege of Partial Perspective." In *The Feminist Standpoint Theory Reader: Intellectual and Political Controversies*, edited by Sandra G. Harding, 81–102. New York: Routledge.

Hareesh, V. C. 2005. "Pathinetaandu kazhinjittum kunjibiyude nillakaatha thengal" (Even after eighteen years Kunjeebi's sobs do not cease). *Kerala Kaumudi*, March 2, 2005, 10.

Hayes, Patricia. 2005. "Introduction: Visual Genders." *Gender and History* 17 (3): 519–37.

Hoek, Lotte. 2010. "Unstable Celluloid: Film Projection and the Cinema Audience in Bangladesh." *BioScope: South Asian Screen Studies* 1 (1): 49–66.

———. 2013. *Cut-Pieces: Celluloid Obscenity and Popular Cinema in Bangladesh.* New York: Columbia University Press.

———. 2016. "Urban Wallpaper: Film Posters, City Walls and the Cinematic Public in South Asia." *South Asia: Journal of South Asian Studies* 39 (1): 73–92.

Ionescu, Vlad. 2013. "Figural Aesthetics: Lyotard, Valéry, Deleuze." *Cultural Politics* 9 (2): 144–57.

Ittyipe, Minu. 2005. "The Life of the Silenced." *Tehelka*, July 30, 2005, 22.

Jad, Islah. 2007. "The NGO-ization of Arab Women's Movements." In *Feminisms in Development: Contradictions, Contestations and Challenges*, edited by Andrea Cornwall, Elizabeth Harrison, and Ann Whitehead, 177–90. London: Zed Books.

Jagose, Annamarie. 2002. *Inconsequence: Lesbian Representation and the Logic of Sexual Sequence.* Ithaca: Cornell University Press.

Jalil, Rakshanda. 2012. *A Rebel and Her Cause: The Life and Work of Rashid Jahan.* New Delhi: Women Unlimited.

Jameela, Nalini. 2005a. *Njan laingika thozhilali: Nalini Jameelayude aathmakatha* (Me, sex worker: The autobiography of Nalini Jameela). Kottayam: D. C. Books.

———. 2005b. *Oru laingikathozhilaliyude aathmakatha* (The autobiography of a sex worker). Retold by I. Gopinath. Kottayam: D. C. Books.

———. 2007. *The Autobiography of a Sex Worker*. Translated by J Devika. Chennai: Westland Books.

———. 2008. "Round and Round the Town." Translated by Suresh Thomas. In *Cities of Kerala: Actually Small Towns*, edited by Baiju Natarajan, 104–15. Mumbai: Marg Publications.

———. 2018. *Romantic Encounters of a Sex Worker*. Translated by Reshma Bharadwaj. Noida: Om Books.

Jameela, Nalini, and Dileep Raj. 2005. "Rathi vangamo?" (Can sex be bought?). *Mathrubhumi Weekly*, December 18–24, 2005, 21–23.

Jayasree, A. K. 2004. "Searching for Justice for Body and Self in a Coercive Environment: Sex Work in Kerala, India." *Reproductive Health Matters* 12 (23): 58–67.

———. 2012. "Veritta jeevitham dushkaramaanu" (A different life is arduous). *Malayalam Weekly*, June 1, 2012, 104–5.

Jeffrey, Robin. 1975. *The Decline of Nair Dominance: Society and Politics in Travancore 1847–1908*. New Delhi: Manohar.

———. 1992. *Politics, Women And Well-Being: How Kerala Became "A Model."* New York: Oxford University Press.

———. 2000. *India's Newspaper Revolution: Capitalism, Politics and the Indian-Language Press, 1977–97*. New Delhi: Oxford University Press.

John, Mary E. 1996. *Discrepant Dislocations: Feminism, Theory, and Postcolonial Histories*. Berkeley: University of California Press.

John, Mary E., and Janaki Nair. 1998. "A Question of Silence? An Introduction." In *A Question of Silence? The Sexual Economies of Modern India*, edited by Mary E. John and Janaki Nair, 1–51. Delhi: Kali for Women.

John, Mary E., and Tejaswini Niranjana. 1999. "Mirror politics: *Fire*, Hindutva and Indian Culture." *Economic and Political Weekly* 34 (10/11): 581–84.

Joseph, Jenson. 2012. "Industrial Aesthetics, Spectatorial Subjectivities: A Study of Malayalam Cinema in the 1950s." PhD Dissertation, University of Hyderabad.

———. 2013. "Revisiting *Neelakkuyil*: On the Left's Cultural Vision, Malayali Nationalism and the Questions of 'Regional Cinema.'" *Tapasam: A Quarterly Journal for Kerala Studies* 8 (1–4): 114–44.

———. 2016. "Satellite Television and Technological Modernity in Kerala: On Asianet's Early Years." Unpublished manuscript.

Kang, Laura Hyun Yi. 2002. *Compositional Subjects: Enfiguring Asian/American Women*. Durham, NC: Duke University Press.

Kankol, Sivakumar, ed. 1998. *Visudha Smithakku* (For Saint Smitha). Payannur: Break Books.

Kapikkad, Sunny M. 2011. "Beyond Just a Home and a Name." Translated by J. Devika. In Satyanarayana and Tharu, 474–85.

Kapur, Geeta. 2000. *When Was Modernism: Essays on Contemporary Cultural Practice in India.* New Delhi: Tulika Books.

Kapur, Ratna. 2005. *Erotic Justice: Law and the New Politics of Postcolonialism.* London: Glass House Press.

———. 2012. "Hecklers to Power: The Waning of Liberal Rights and Challenges to Feminism in India." In *South Asian Feminisms,* edited by Ania Loomba and Ritty A. Lukose, 333–55. Durham, NC: Duke University Press.

Katyal, Akhil. 2016. *The Doubleness of Sexuality: Idioms of Same-Sex Desire in Modern India.* New Delhi: New Text.

Kerala Kaumudi. 2001. "Orumichu jeevikkan kazhiyathadinaal randu streekal athmahathya cheythu" (Two women commit suicide because they were unable to live together). August 26, 2001.

Kerala State AIDS Control Society (KSACS) and HLFPPT Partners for Better Health. n.d. *Anandinte thirodhanam* (Anand's disappearance). CID Arjun Investigates Series. Thiruvananthapuram.

Keshavamurthy, Kiran. 2016. *Beyond Desire: Sexuality in Modern Tamil Literature.* New Delhi: Oxford University Press.

Khanna, Akshay. 2016. *Sexualness.* New Delhi: New Text.

Kincaid, Jamaica. 1988. *A Small Place.* New York: Farrar, Straus, Giroux.

Kipnis, Laura. 2006. "How to Look at Pornography." In *Pornography: Film and Culture,* edited by Peter Lehman, 118–32. New Brunswick: Rutgers University Press.

Kishwar, Madhu, and Ruth Vanita. 1983. "An Irrepressible Spirit: An Interview with Ismat Chugtai." *Manushi* 19:2–7.

Kodoth, Praveena. 1998. "Women and Property Rights: A Study of Land-Tenure Structure and Personal Laws in Malabar." PhD diss., University of Hyderabad.

———. 2001. "Courting Legitimacy or Delegitimizing Custom? Sexuality, Sambandham, and Marriage Reform in Late Nineteenth-Century Malabar." *Modern Asian Studies* 35 (2): 349–84.

Kodoth, Praveena, and Mridula Eapen. 2005. "Looking beyond Gender Parity: Gender Inequities of Some Dimensions of Well-being in Kerala." *Economic and Political Weekly* 40 (30): 3278–86.

Kotiswaran, Prabha. 2011a. *Dangerous Sex, Invisible Labor: Sex Work and Law in India.* Princeton: Princeton University Press.

———, ed. 2011b. *Sex Work.* New Delhi: Women Unlimited.

Kumar, Udaya. 2002. "Two Figures of Desire: Discourses of the Body in Malayalam Literature." In *Translating Desire,* edited by Brinda Bose, 132–44. New Delhi: Katha.

———. 2007. "The Public, the State and New Domains of Writing: On Ramakrishna Pillai's Conception of Literary and Political Expression." *Tapasam: Journal of Kerala Studies* 3/4:413–41.

————. 2010. "The Strange Homeliness of the Night: Spectral Speech and the Dalit Present in C. Ayyappan's Stories." *Studies in Humanities and Social Sciences* 17 (1–2): 177–91.

————. 2016. *Writing the First Person: Literature, History, and Autobiography in Modern Kerala*. Ranikhet: Permanent Black.

Kumarankandath, Rajeev. 2013. "The Discursive Formation of Sexual Subjects: Sexual Morality and Homosexuality in Keralam." PhD diss., Manipal University.

Kunjabdulla, Punathil. 2002. "Paadatha painkili mattoru shakunthalam" (*Paadatha painkili* is another *Sakunthalam*). *Samskarika Vikaaram: Sahithya Masika: Muttathu Varkey Issue* 1 (6): 49–54.

Kuzniar, A. Alice. 2005. *The Queer German Cinema*. Stanford: Stanford University Press.

Levine, Philippa. 2003. *Prostitution, Race, and Politics: Policing Venereal Disease in the British Empire*. New York: Routledge.

Liang, Lawrence. 2005. "Cinematic Citizenship and the Illegal City." *Inter-Asia Cultural Studies* 6 (3): 366–85.

Lindberg, Anna. 2005. *Modernization and Effeminization in India: Kerala Cashew Workers since 1930*. Copenhagen: Nordic Institute of Asian Studies.

Love, Heather. 2007. *Feeling Backward: Loss and the Politics of Queer History*. Cambridge, MA: Harvard University Press.

Lukose, Ritty A. 2009. *Liberalization's Children: Gender, Youth, and Consumer Citizenship in Globalizing India*. Durham, NC: Duke University Press.

Madhyamam. 1987. "Lock-up Muriyil Stree Marichu: Kabaradakkam Vivaad-amayi" (Woman dies in the lock-up room: Controversy over the burial). September 12, 1987.

Mahmood, Saba. 2005. *Politics of Piety: The Islamic Revival and the Feminist Subject*. Princeton: Princeton University Press.

Mahmood, Saba, and Charles Hirschkind. 2002. "Feminism, the Taliban and the Politics of Counterinsurgency." *Anthropological Quarterly* 75 (2): 339–54.

Maitra, Ani. 2017. "In the Shadow of the Homoglobal: Queer Cosmopolitanism in Tsai Ming-liang's *I Don't Want to Sleep Alone*." In Sircar and Jain 2017, 317–51.

Majumdar, Neepa. 2009. *Wanted Cultured Ladies Only: Female Stardom and Cinema in India 1930s–1950s*. Champaign: University of Illinois Press.

Manayath, Nithin. 2015. "The Shameless Marriage: Thinking through Same-Sex Erotics and the Question of 'Gay Marriage' in India." In Basu and Ramberg 2015, 251–80.

Mangalam. 2003. "Vivaada lock-up maranathinde thelivumaayi Choyikutty" (Choyikutty with evidence of the controversial lock-up death). July 15, 2003.

Mani, Lata. 2014. "Sex and the Signal-Free Corridor: Towards a New Feminist Imaginary." *Economic and Political Weekly* 49 (6): 26–29.

Mannarkat, Mathew. 1981. "Malayala Cinemekendini Dushperu?" (Why does Malayalam cinema have such a bad name?). *Malayala Manorama* (December Annual Issue): 281–91.

Massad, Joseph Andoni. 2002. "Re-orienting Desire: The Gay International and the Arab World." *Public Culture* 14 (2): 361–85.

Mathrubhumi. 2001. "Orumichu jeevikkan agrahicha penkuttikal athmahathya cheythu" (Girls who longed to live together end their lives). August 26, 2001.

MA Visual Art Students. 2014. *None the Less Art*. Exhibition catalog. School of Culture and Creative Expressions. Ambedbar University Delhi.

Mazzarella, William. 2013. *Censorium: Cinema and the Open Edge of Mass Publicity*. Durham, NC: Duke University Press.

Menon, Bindu. 2005. "Identification, Desire, Otherness: *Susanna* and Its Public." *Deep Focus* (Jan–May): 61–70.

———. 2008. "Many Faces of Eve: Malayalam Cinema and the Category of Woman." In *Women in Malayalam Cinema: Naturalizing Gender Hierarchies*, edited by Meena T Pillai. Hyderabad: Orient Blackswan.

———. 2013. "The Blazon Call of Hip Hop: Lyrical Storms in Kerala's Musical Cultures." *Journal of Creative Communications* 8 (2–3): 231–50.

———. 2014. "Re-framing Vision: Malayalam Cinema and the Invention of Modern Life in Keralam." PhD diss., Jawaharlal Nehru University.

Menon, Dilip. 1994. *Caste, Nationalism and Communism in South India: Malabar, 1900–1948*. Cambridge: Cambridge University Press.

———. 2006. *The Blindness of Insight: Essays on Caste in Modern India*. New Delhi: Navayana.

———. 2010. "A Local Cosmopolitan: Kesari Balakrishna Pillai and the Invention of Europe for Kerala." In *Cosmopolitan Thought Zones*, edited by Sugata Bose and Kris Manjapra, 131–58. London: Palgrave Macmillan.

Menon, Nivedita. 2007. "Introduction." In *Sexualities*, edited by Nivedita Menon, xiii–lx. New Delhi: Women Unlimited.

Merchant, Hoshang. 1999. *Yaraana: Gay Writing from South Asia*. New Delhi: Penguin Books.

Mini, Darshana Sreedhar. 2016. "The Spectral Duration of Malayalam Soft-Porn: Disappearance, Desire, and Haunting." *BioScope* 7 (2): 127–50.

Misri, Deepti. 2014. *Beyond Partition: Gender, Violence and Representation in Postcolonial India*. Urbana: University of Illinois Press.

Mitchell, W. J. T. 2004. *What Do Pictures Want? The Lives and Loves of Images*. Chicago: University of Chicago Press.

Mohan, Sanal. 2015. *Modernity of Slavery: Struggles against Caste Inequality in Colonial Kerala*. Oxford: Oxford University Press.

———. 2016. "Creation of Social Space through Prayers among Dalits in Kerala, India." *Journal of Religious and Political Practice* 2 (1): 40–57.

Mohan, Sunil (assisted by Rumi Harish). 2013. *Towards Gender Inclusivity: A Study on Contemporary Concerns Around Gender*. Bangalore: LesBiT and Alternate Law Forum.

Mokkil, Navaneetha. 2003. "*Susanna* as Entry-Point to Reproblematize the Sexuality Debates in Contemporary Kerala." In *Space, Sexuality and Postcolonial Cultures*, edited by Manas Ray, 121–34. ENRECA Occasional Paper Series 6. Calcutta: Centre for the Studies in Social Sciences.

———. 2018a. "Modernity's Nightmares: Narrating Sexuality in Kerala." In *Exploring India Modernities: Ideas and Practices*, edited by Leila Choukrone and Parul Bhandari, 231–52. Singapore: Springer Nature.

———. 2018b. "Visual Practices, Affect, and the Body: The Story of a Night-Vigil in Kerala, India." *Women's Studies Quarterly* 46 (3–4): 158–74.

Mukhopadhyay, Maitrayee. 2007. "Mainstreaming Gender or 'Streaming' Gender Away: Feminists Marooned in the Development Business." In *Feminisms in Development: Contradictions, Contestations and Challenges*, edited by Andrea Cornwall, Elizabeth Harrison, and Ann Whitehead, 135–49. London: Zed Books.

———, ed. 2016. *Feminist Subversion and Complicity: Governmentalities and Gender Knowledge in South Asia*. New Delhi: Zubaan Books.

Muñoz, José Esteban. 1996. "Ephemera as Evidence: Introductory Notes to Queer Acts." *Women and Performance: A Journal of Feminist Theory* 8 (2): 5–16.

———. 2009. *Cruising Utopia: The Then and There of Queer Futurity*. New York: New York University Press.

Muraleedharan, T. 2002. "Queer Bonds: Male Friendships in Contemporary Malayalam Cinema." In Vanita 2002, 181–92.

———. 2005. "Crisis in Desire: A Queer Reading of Cinema and Desire in Kerala." In Bhan and Narrain, 70–88.

———. 2010. "Women's Friendships in Malayalam Cinema." In *Women in Malayalam Cinema: Naturalizing Gender Hierarchies*, edited by Meena T. Pillai, 154–77. Hyderabad: Orient Blackswan.

Nair, Guptan. 1947/1994. *Vyakthiyum Niroopakanum* (The Individual and the critic). Kottayam: D. C. Books.

Nair, Janaki. 1994. "The Devadasi, Dharma and the State." *Economic and Political Weekly* 29 (50): 3157–59, 3161–67.

———. 1996. *Women and Law in Colonial India: A Social History*. Delhi: Kali for Women.

Nair, Sridevi. 2011. "'A Record of Our Lives': Anthologizing the Lesbian in India." *Amerasia Journal* 37 (2): 57–71.

Nakshathrashala. 1978. "*Avalude Ravukal* Review." 1 (4): 27.

Nandakumar, V. T. 1974. *Randu penkuttikal* (Two girls). Ernakulam: CICC Book House.

———. 2000. *Two Girls* (*Randu penkuttikal*). Translated by T. Muraleedharan. In Vanita and Kidwai 2000, 311–17.

Narayan, Kirin. 1993. "How Native Is a 'Native' Anthropologist?" *American Anthropologist* 95 (3): 671–86.

Naregal, Veena. 2001. *Language Politics, Elites, and the Public Sphere: Western India under Colonialism*. New Delhi: Permanent Black.

Nguyen, Mimi Thi. 2011. "The Biopower of Beauty: Humanitarian Imperialisms and Global Feminisms in an Age of Terror." *Signs* 36 (2): 359–83.

Niranjana, Tejaswini. 1998. "Feminism and Translation in India: Contexts, Politics, Futures." *Cultural Dynamics* 10 (2): 133–46.

Nossiter, T. J. 1982. *Communism in Kerala: A Study in Political Adaptation.* Berkeley: University of California Press.

Oomji, John et al. 2005. *Laingikarogya Padhathi Chilla Vyathiriktha Mukhangal.* (Sexual Health Project: Some Different Faces). Ernakulam: SMA (Social Development Division) and Kerala State AIDS Control Society (KSACS).

Orsini, Francesca. 2002. *The Hindi Public Sphere 1920–1940: Language and Literature in the Age of Nationalism.* New Delhi: Oxford University Press.

———, ed. 2006. *Love in South Asia.* Cambridge: Cambridge University Press.

Osella, Filippo, and Caroline Osella. 2000. *Social Mobility in Kerala: Modernity and Identity in Conflict.* London: Pluto Press.

Pandey, Gyanendra. 1992. "In Defense of the Fragment: Writing about Hindu-Muslim Riots in India Today." *Representations* 37:27–55.

Parameswaran, Ameet. 2017. *Performance and the Political: Power and Pleasure in Contemporary Kerala.* New Delhi: Orient Black Swan.

Patel, Geeta. 2002. *Lyrical Movements, Historical Hauntings: On Gender, Colonialism, and Desire in Miraji's Urdu Poetry.* Stanford: Stanford University Press.

———. 2004. "Homely Housewives Run Amok: Lesbians in Marital Fixes." *Public Culture* 16 (1): 131–57.

———. 2014. "The Queer Subject of Urdu Modernism: Miraji and Gender." *Dawn,* April 13, 2014.

———. 2016. *Risky Bodies and Techno-intimacy: Reflections on Sexuality, Media, Science, Finance.* Delhi: Women Unlimited.

Patil, M. Smita. 2014. "Reading Caste, Gender and Sexuality in Dalit Writing." *Intersections: Gender and Sexuality in Asia and the Pacific* 34.

Patton, Cindy. 2002a. *Globalizing AIDS.* Minneapolis: University of Minnesota Press.

———. 2002b. "Stealth Bombers of Desire: The Globalization of 'Alterity' in Emerging Democracies." In Cruz-Malavé and Manalansan, 195–218.

Paul, M. P. 1944/2008. "Preface to 'Baalyakalasakhi.'" In *Basheer sampoorna kritikal,* vol. 2 (Basheer complete works, vol. 2), 2605–7. Kottayam: D. C. Books.

Phadke, Shilpa, Sameera Khan, and Shilpa Ranade. 2011. *Why Loiter: Women and Risk on Mumbai Streets.* Delhi: Penguin.

Pigg, Stacy Leigh, and Vincanne Adams. 2005. "Introduction: The Moral Object of Sex." In *Sex in Development: Science, Sexuality, and Morality in Global Perspective,* edited by Stacy Leigh Pigg and Vincanne Adams, 1–38. Durham, NC: Duke University Press.

Pillai, Kesari Balakrishna. 1947/2007. "Introduction." In Basheer 1947/2007.

Pillai, Thakazhi Sivasankara. 1947/2007. *Thotiyude makan* (The son of a scavenger). Kottayam: D. C. Books.

Poovey, Mary. 1995. *Making a Social Body: British Cultural Formation, 1830–1864.* Chicago: University of Chicago Press.

Pottekkad, S. K. 1971/2015. *Oru deshathinte katha* (The tale of a *desham*). Kottayam: D. C. Books.

Prasad, M. Madhava. 1998. *Ideology of the Hindi Film: A Historical Construction.* Delhi: Oxford University Press.

———. 2001. "Melodramatic Polities?" *Inter-Asia Cultural Studies* 2 (3): 459–66.

Premchand. 2004. "Cinimayile thottukuudayma" (Untouchability in cinema). In *Avalude ravukal* (Her nights), by Alleppey Shereef, 2nd ed., 9–12. Kozhikode: Mathrubhumi Books.

Premkumar, E. M. 2009. "Oru lesbian kadhayude charithram" (The history of a lesbian story). *Bhashaposhini* (July):32–33.

Priya A. S. 2003. *Ozhukkil oru ila* (A leaf in the water current). Kottayam: D. C. Books.

Puar, Jasbir. 2007. *Terrorist Assemblages: Homonationalism in Queer Times.* Durham, NC: Duke University Press.

Puar, Jasbir, and Ann Pellegrini. 2009. "Affect." *Social Text* 27 (3): 35–38.

Puri, Jyoti. 2016. *Sexual States: Governance and the Decriminalization of Sodomy in India's Present.* Durham, NC: Duke University Press.

Radhakrishnan, Ratheesh. 2010. "Soft Porn and the Anxieties of the Family." In *Women in Malayalam Cinema: Naturalizing Gender Hierarchies*, ed. Meena T. Pillai, 194–220. Hyderabad: Orient Blackswan.

———. 2016. "The 'Worlds' of the Region." *Positions: East Asia Cultures Critique* 24 (3): 693–719.

Rahim, Y. M. 1999. "Publisher's Note." In Shereef 1999.

Raj, Dileep. 2005. "Veshyavrithi feminist prashnam enna nilayil" (Sex work as a feminist issue). *Mathrubhumi Weekly*, December 18–24, 2005, 19–20.

Raj, Rekha. 2005. "Dalitsthreekalum rashtreeyadhikaravum" (Dalit women and political power). *Pachakuthira* 2 (3): 28–30.

———. 2013. "Dalit Women as Political Agents: A Kerala Experience." *Economic and Political Weekly* 48 (18): 56–63.

———. 2016. *Dalit stree: Edapedalukal* (Dalit woman: Interventions). Kottayam: D. C. Books.

Rajadhyaksha, Ashish. 2009. *Indian Cinema in the Time of Celluloid: From Bollywood to the Emergency.* Bloomington: Indiana University Press.

Rajadhyaksha, Ashish, and Paul Willemen. 1994/1999. *Encyclopedia of Indian Cinema.* London: British Film Institute.

Ramakrishnan, E. V. 2011. *Locating Indian Literature: Texts, Traditions, Translations.* Hyderabad: Orient Blackswan.

———. 2012. *Anubhavangale aarkannu pedi* (Who is afraid of experiences). Kottayam: D. C. Books.

Ramakrishnan, Malayattoor. 1967/1995. *Yakshi.* Kottayam: D. C. Books.

Ramberg, Lucinda. 2016. "Backward Futures and Pasts Forward: Queer Time, Sexual Politics, and Dalit Religiosity in South India." *GLQ: A Journal of Lesbian and Gay Studies* 22 (2): 223–48.

Rankin, Katharine N. 2001. "Governing Development: Neoliberalism, Micro-credit, and Rational Economic Woman." *Economy and Society* 30 (1): 18–37.

Rao, Anupama. 2009. *The Caste Question: Dalits and the Politics of Modern India.* Berkeley: University of California Press.

Ratti, Rakesh. 1993. *A Lotus of Another Color: An Unfolding of the South Asian Gay and Lesbian Experience.* Boston: Alyson Publications.

Raveendran. 1986. "Khandhasha sahithyam srishtikunna prashnangal" (The problems that serialized literature creates). *Mathrubhumi Weekly*, December 14–20, 1986, 157–62.

Rawat, Ramnarayan S., and K. Satyanarayana. 2016. "Introduction." In *Dalit Studies*, edited by Ramnarayan S. Rawat and K. Satyanarayana, 1–30. Durham, NC: Duke University Press.

Rege, Sharmila. 1995. "The Hegemonic Appropriation of Sexuality: The Case of the Lavani Performers of Maharashtra." *Contributions to Indian Sociology* 29 (1–2): 23–37.

Rowena, Jenny. 2005a. "Sthree savarnayakumbol" (When woman becomes upper caste). *Pachakuthira* 2 (3): 23–27.

———. 2005b. "Vayana arude jeevitham thanne?" (Reading is life—for whom?). *Pachakuthira* 1 (8): 58–60.

Rowena, Jenny, and Carmel Christy K. J. 2006. *Caste and Gender in the Urban Space of Keralam: A Case Study Based on Experience of Chithra Lekha.* Unpublished manuscript. Sarai, New Delhi.

Roy, Nilanjana S. 2010. "Giving a Voice to the Voiceless in India." *New York Times*, July 6, 2010.

Roy, Srila. 2014. "New Activist Subjects: The Changing Feminist Field of Kolkata, India." *Feminist Studies* 40 (3): 628–56.

Sahayatrika, comp. 2002. "Fact Finding Report." February and May, 2002. Unpublished.

———. 2004. "Keralathile lesbian athmahathyagal: Vasthuthanveshanangalil ninnumoredu" (Lesbian suicides in Kerala: A page from the fact-finding report). In *Mithyakalkappuram: Swawarga laingikata keralathil* (Beyond myths: Homosexuality in Kerala), edited by Reshma Bharadwaj, 58–117. Kottayam: D. C. Books.

Sahni, Rohini, Kalyan Shankar, and Hemant Apte, eds. 2008. *Prostitution and Beyond: An Analysis of Sex Work in India.* New Delhi: Sage Publications.

Sangari, Kumkum, and Sudesh Vaid. 1990. *Recasting Women: Essays in Indian Colonial History.* New Brunswick: Rutgers University Press.

Sanjeev, S. 1995. *Manichithrathazhu* (The ornate lock). *Kerala padhanangal* 5:65–69.

———. 2002. "Palunku sadacharangal: Charithrathil ninnu chila (a)shleela edukal" (Brittle moralities: Some "obscene" pages from history). *Drishyathalam* 2:65–77.

Sarkar, Tanika. 2001. *Hindu Wife, Hindu Nation: Community, Religion, and Cultural Nationalism*. Bloomington: Indiana University Press.

Satapathy, Samidha. 2006. "Rupturing the Heteronormative: Queer Possibilities in Reading Popular Indian Cinema." M.Phil diss., Central Institute of English and Foreign Languages.

Satyanarayana, K., and Susie Tharu, eds. 2011. *No Alphabet in Sight: New Dalit Writing from South India—Dossier 1, Tamil and Malayalam*. New Delhi: Penguin India.

Sebastian, K. C. 1999. "Lesbian athmahathyagal thudarunnu" (Lesbian suicides continue). *Sameeksha*, June 1–15, 1999, 15.

———. 2003. *Parasparam pranayikkunna sthreekal* (Women who love each other). Kochi: Pranatha Books.

Sen, Meheli. 2013. Introduction. In *Figurations in Indian Film*, edited by Meheli Sen and Anustup Basu, 1–20. Hampshire, UK: Palgrave Macmillan.

Shah, Chayanika. 2005. "The Roads that E/Merged: Feminist Activism and Queer Understanding." In Bhan and Narrain, 143–54.

Shah, Chayanika, Raj Merchant, Shals Mahajan, and Smriti Nevatia. 2013. *Breaking the Binary*. Mumbai: LABIA.

Shah, Svati. 2014. *Street Corner Secrets: Sex, Work and Migration in the City of Mumbai*. Durham, NC: Duke University Press.

Shailaja, K. K. 2008. "'Idangal' thedumbol vazhi thettunnavar" (Those who lose their way as they search for "space"). *Mathrubhumi Weekly*, May 4–10, 2008, 27–31.

Shandilya, Krupa. 2017. *Intimate Relations: Social Reform and the Late Nineteenth-Century South Asian Novel*. Evanston: Northwestern University Press.

Sharma, Maya. 2006. *Loving Women: Being Lesbian in Unprivileged India*. New Delhi: Yoda Press.

Shatamanyu. 2008. "Avarude ravukal" (Their nights). *Deshabhimani*, March 10, 2008.

Shereef, Alleppey. 1999. *Avalude ravukal* (Her nights). Kozhikode: Mathrubhumi Books.

Sircar, Oishik, and Dipika Jain, eds. 2017. *New Intimacies, Old Desires: Law, Culture and Queer Politics in Neoliberal Times*. New Delhi: Zubaan Books.

S. L. 1999/2000. "Fire! Fire! It's the Lesbians!: A Personal Account." In CALERI 1999. Reprinted in *Inter-Asia Cultural Studies* 1 (3): 519–26.

Slaughter, Joseph. 2007. *Human Rights, Inc.: The World Novel, Narrative Form, and International Law*. New York: Fordham University Press.

Sontag, Susan. 2003. *Regarding the Pain of Others*. New York: Farrar, Straus and Giroux.

Spivak, Gayatri Chakravorty. 1999. *A Critique of Postcolonial Reason: Toward a History of the Vanishing Present*. Cambridge, MA: Harvard University Press.

———. 2004. "Righting Wrongs." *South Atlantic Quarterly* 103 (2/3): 523–81.

Sreedharan, E. V. 1999. "Khedapurvam sandoshapurvam" (Regretfully, joyfully). Introduction to Shereef 1999, 1–6.

Sreekumar, P. K. 2012. "Kolapaathaka varthayude gender" (Gender of homicide news). *Mathrubhumi Weekly*, June 10, 2012, 98.

Sreekumar, Sharmila. 2009. *Scripting Lives: Narratives of "Dominant Women" in Kerala*. Hyderabad: Orient Blackswan.

———. 2017. "Equivocations of Gender: Feminist Storytelling and Women's Studies in the Contemporary." *Indian Journal of Gender Studies* 24 (1): 47–68.

Sreekumar, T. T. 2011. "Mobile Phones and the Cultural Ecology of Fishing in Kerala." *Information Society* 27 (3): 172–80.

Sreenivasan, K. K. 2000. "*Kerala varmayile vidyarthiyude maranathinu aranuthaaravadi?*" (Who is responsible for the death of the Kerala varma student?). *Sameeksha* (Jan): 1–15.

Sreerekha, M. S. 2012. "Illegal Land, Illegal People: The Chengara Land Struggle in Kerala." *Economic and Political Weekly* 47 (30): 21–24.

Srinivas, S. V. 2003. "Hong Kong Action Film in the Indian B Circuit." *Inter-Asia Cultural Studies* 4 (1): 40–62.

Srinivasan, Amrit. 1985. "Reform and Revival: The Devadasi and Her Dance." *Economic and Political Weekly* 20 (44): 1869–76.

Srivatsan, R. 2000. *Conditions of Visibility: Writings on Photography in Contemporary India*. Calcutta: Stree.

Stoler, Ann Laura. 1995. *Race and the Education of Desire: Foucault's History of Sexuality and the Colonial Order of Things*. Durham, NC: Duke University Press.

Sukthankar, Ashwini, ed. 1999. *Facing the Mirror: Lesbian Writing from India*. New Delhi: Penguin.

———. 2012. "Queering Approaches to Sex, Gender and Labor in India: Examining Paths to Sex Worker's Unionism." In *South Asian Feminisms*, edited by Ania Loomba and Ritty A. Lukose, 306–32. Durham, NC: Duke University Press.

Sunder Rajan, Rajeswari. 1993. *Real and Imagined Women: Gender, Culture and Postcolonialism*. London: Routledge.

———. 2003. *The Scandal of the State: Women, Law, and Citizenship in Postcolonial India*. Durham, NC: Duke University Press.

Surayya, Kamala (writing as Kamala). 1947/2009. "Stree" (Woman). *Bhashaposhini* (July):34–35.

———. (Writing as Madhavikutty). 1973. *Ente katha* (My story). Thrissur: Current Books.

———. (Writing as Kamala Das). 1976. *My Story*. Jalandhar: Sterling Publishers.

———. (Writing as Madhavikutty). 1988/2007. *Chandanamarangal* (The sandal trees). Kottayam: D. C. Books.

Tambe, Ashwini. 2009. *Codes of Misconduct: Regulating Prostitution in Late Colonial Bombay*. Minneapolis: University of Minnesota Press.

Tellis, Ashley. 2003. "Ways of Becoming." *Seminar* 524 (54).

———. 2008. "Valueless Sex and Valuable Respectability: Tracking Sex-Work in Nalini Jameela's *Njan Laingika thozhilali* and Kishore Shantabai Kale's *Kolhatyache Por.*" Paper presented at the Seventh International Conference of Labour History, March 27–29, Noida.

Tellis, Ashley, and Sruti Bala, eds. 2015. *The Global Trajectories of Queerness: Re-thinking Same-Sex Politics in the Global South.* Leiden: Brill/Rodopi.

Thampi, Anitha. 2010. "Kazhinju" (After). In *Azhakillathavayellam* (All that is not beautiful), 53. Thrissur: Current Books.

Tharu, Susie. 1999. "The Impossible Subject: Caste and Desire in the Scene of the Family." In *Signposts: Gender Issues in Post-Independence India*, edited by Rajeswari Sunder Rajan, 188–205. New Delhi: Kali for Women.

———. 2007. "This Is Not an Inventory: Norm and Performance in Everyday Femininity." In *Native Women of South India, Manners and Customs*, edited by N. Pushpamala and Clare Arni, 11–25. New York: Nature Morte, Gallery Chemould, and Bose Pacia.

———. 2008. "Binodini Dasi: An Actress in the Drama of Public Modernity in India." In *Women's Studies in India: A Reader*, edited by Mary E. John, 592–96. New Delhi: Penguin Books.

Tharu, Susie, and K. Lalita. 1993. "Empire, Nation and the Literary Text." In *Interrogating Modernity: Culture and Colonialism in India*, edited by Tejaswini Niranjana, P. Sudhir, and Vivek Dhareshwar, 199–219. Kolkata: Seagull Books.

Tharu, Susie, and Tejaswini Niranjana. 1996. "Problems for a Contemporary Theory of Gender." In *Writings on South Asian History and Society*, edited by Shahid Amin and Dipesh Chakrabarthy, 232–60. Subaltern Studies 9. New Delhi: Oxford University Press.

Ugra (Pandey Bechan Sharma). 1927/1953. *Chaklet* (Chocolate). Calcutta: Tondon Brothers.

UNAIDS. 1999. *Peer Education and HIV AIDS: Concepts, Uses and Challenges.* Geneva: Joint United Nations Programme on HIV/AIDS.

United Nations. 1975. *Poverty, Unemployment, and Development Policy: A Case Study of Selected Issues with Reference to Kerala.* New York: United Nations.

Vanita, Ruth. ed. 2002. *Queering India: Same-Sex Love and Eroticism in Indian Culture and Society.* New York: Routledge.

———. 2005a. *Gandhi's Tiger and Sita's Smile: Essays on Gender, Sexuality, and Culture.* New Delhi: Yoda Press.

———. 2005b. *Love's Rite: Same-Sex Marriages in India and the West.* New Delhi: Penguin Books.

Vanita, Ruth, and Saleem Kidwai, eds. 2000. *Same-Sex Love in India: Readings from Literature and History.* New York: St. Martin's Press.

Varkey, Muttathu. 1955. *Paadatha painkili* (The beautiful bird that does not sing). Kottayam: India Press.

Varkey, Punkunnam. 1946/1996. "Preface." In *Anju cheetha kadhakal* (Five bad stories) 1946/1996, 8–9.

Vasudevan, Nitya. 2015. "Navigating a Field of Opposition: A Rereading of Debates on 'Caste and Gender.'" *Economic and Political Weekly* 50 (17): 48–55.

Vasudevan, Ravi. 1989. "The Melodramatic Mode and the Commercial Hindi Cinema: Notes on Film History, Narrative and Performance in the 1950s." *Screen* 30 (3): 29–50.

———. 2010. *The Melodramatic Public: Film Form and Spectatorship in India.* Delhi: Permanent Black.

Venkiteswaran, C. S. 2010. "Film, Female and the New Wave in Kerala." In *Women in Malayalam Cinema: Naturalizing Gender Hierarchies*, edited by Meena T. Pillai, 41–56. Hyderabad: Orient Blackswan.

Vijayakrishnan. 2004. *Malayalacinemayude katha* (The story of Malayalam cinema). Kozhikode: Mathrubhumi Books.

Waheed, Sarah. 2014. "Women of 'Ill Repute': Ethics and Urdu Literature in Colonial India." *Modern Asian Studies* 48 (4): 986–1023.

Wald, Erica. 2009. "From Begums and Bibis to Abandoned Females and Idle Women: Sexual Relationships, Venereal Disease and the Redefinition of Prostitution in Early Nineteenth-Century India." *Indian Economic and Social History Review* 46 (1): 5–25.

Waning, Brenda, Ellen Diedrichsen, and Suerie Moon. 2010. "A Lifeline to Treatment: The Role of Indian Generic Manufacturers in Supplying Antiretroviral Medicines to Developing Countries." *Journal of International AIDS Society* 13 (35): 1–9.

Warner, Michael. 2002. "Publics and Counterpublics." *Public Culture* 14 (1): 49–90.

Weston, Kath. 1993. "Lesbian/Gay Studies in the House of Anthropology." *Annual Review of Anthropology* 22 (1): 339–67.

Wexler, Laura. 2000. *Tender Violence: Domestic Visions in an Age of U.S. Imperialism.* Chapel Hill: University of North Carolina Press.

Williams, Linda. 1991. "Film Bodies: Gender, Genre, and Excess." *Film Quarterly* 44 (4): 2–13.

Williams, Raymond. 1977. *Marxism and Literature.* Oxford: Oxford University Press.

Zaheer, Sajjad, ed. 1932/1990. *Angarey* (Live coals). Delhi: Parimal Prakashan.

Zapperi, Giovanna. 2013. "Woman's Reappearance: Rethinking the Archive in Contemporary Art—Feminist Perspectives." *Feminist Review* 105:21–47.

Films

Aniyathi pravu (Adorable sister). 1997. Directed by Fazil. Malayalam/color.

Avalude ravukal (Her nights). 1978. Directed by I. V. Sasi. Malayalam/black and white.

Chemmeen (Shrimp). 1965. Directed by Ramu Kariat. Malayalam/color.

Chuvanna vithukal (Red seeds, or Seeds of a revolution). 1977. Directed by P. A. Bakkar. Malayalam/ black and white.

Deshadanakkili karayarilla (The wandering bird does not cry). 1986. Directed by P. Padmarajan. Malayalam/Color.

The Dirty Picture. 2011. Directed by Milan Luthria. Hindi/color.

Ebang bewarish (And the unclaimed). 2013. Directed by Debalina Majumdar, Bengali/color.

Fire. 1996. Directed by Deepa Mehta. English/color.

Guruvayur kesavan. 1977. Directed by Bharathan. Malayalam/color.

Hemanda rathri (A sweet-scented night). 1978. Directed by Balthasar. Malayalam/color.

Jwalamukhikal (A day in the life of a sex worker). 2002. Directed by Nalini Jameela. Malayalam/color.

Ka Bodyscapes. 2016. Directed by Jayan Cherian. Malayalam/color.

Kalvettukal (Sculptures). 2012. Directed by Gee Imaan Semmalar. Malayalam/color.

Mumbai Police. 2013. Directed by Rosshan Andrrews. Malayalam/color.

My Life Partner. 2014. Directed by Padmakumar. Malayalam/color.

Namukku parkkan munthirithoppukal (Vineyards for us to dwell). 1986. Directed by P. Padmarajan. Malayalam/color.

Nanmakkayi (For your well-being). 2006. Directed by Invis Multimedia. Malayalam/color.

Neelakuyil (The blue cuckoo). 1954. Directed by P. Bhaskaran and Ramu Kariat. Malayalam/black and white.

Nishabdaraakapettavarilekoru ethinottam (A peep into the silenced). 2003. Directed by Nalini Jameela. Malayalam/color.

Odayil ninu (From the gutter). 1965. Directed by K. S. Sethumadhavan. Malayalam/black and white.

Odum raja aadum rani (Running king and the dancing queen). 2014. Directed by Viju Varma. Malayalam/color.

Randu Penkuttikal (Two girls). 1978. Directed by Mohan. Malayalam/color.

Sancharram (The journey). 2004. Directed by Ligy Pullappally. Malayalam/color.

Sathrathil oru rathri (A night in the inn). 1978. Directed by N. Sankaran Nair. Malayalam/color.

Susanna. 2000. Directed by T.V. Chandran. Malayalam/color.

Thiricharivinte koottaymakkayi (For a collective through realization). 2006. Directed by Invis Multimedia. Malayalam/color.

Thoovanathumbikal (Dragon flies in the sprays of rain). 1987. Directed by P. Padmarajan. Malayalam/color.

Urakkam varatha rathrikal (Sleepless nights). 1978. Directed by M. Krishnan Nair. Malayalam/color.

Velutha nizhalukal (White shadows). 2006. Directed by Santha Kumar and Naveen Raj. Malayalam/color.

Index

Bharadwaj, Reshma, 92, 94, 167,
231n11
bhootham, 164
Biswas, Moinak, 225n14
Bodhana, 54, 78
bodies: baring of, 31, 69; celebration
of, 158; commodification of, 119;
Dalit women's, 35–36, 97, 201;
disciplining of, 29; performances,
190, 194–98; prostitutes', 58, 68;
queer, 39, 125, 190; and secretion
of tears, 163; women's, 31,
67–68, 87
Bora, Papori, 202
Bose, Brinda, 212n45
Bose, Satheese Chandra, 15
British Official Development
Assistance, 102
Brown, Wendy, 117, 212n38
Butler, Judith, 17–18, 49, 120, 203,
210n25, 234n26; on assertion of
"queer," 133; on enactment of
resistance, 177; and radical
inclusivity, 23

C

Cadava, Eduardo, 83, 163, 168, 180
camera (covert), 33
Campaign for Lesbian Rights
(CALERI), 152, 224n2, 228n36
caste: dominant, 24; hierarchies of,
25, 216n17; as social authority, 35;
structure of, 210n26
Centre of Indian Trade Unions
(CITU), 31
Chaklet (Ugra), 129, 224n5
Chandra, Shefali, 8
Chatterjee, Partha, 100, 189, 208n10,
214n57, 222n27
Chatterjee, Piya, 46
Cheerath-Rajagopalan, Bhawani,
127, 153
Chemmeen (T. S. Pillai), 229n39

Chithrabhumi, 7
Chopin, Kate, 140
Choyikutty, C., 80–81, 84, 218n26
Christy, Carmel, 13, 41, 97, 115, 220n8
Chua, Jocelyn Lim, 230n6
Chughtai, Ismat, 37, 56, 74, 129–30,
224n6
Chuvanna vithukal (P. A. Bakkar), 58
cinema, 7, 20, 43, 58, 215n5, 228n38;
art house, 9, 63, 66; censor board,
59; criticism, 63; cut-pieces, 20–21,
61; documentaries, 104–8, 118;
and the film industry, 8–9, 53,
208n6; Hollywood, 68; Malayalam,
71, 102, 214n3, 225n10; reception,
57; soft porn, 61, 66–67, 70, 76,
196; South Indian, 123
Cohen, Lawrence, 128
Comaroff, Jean, 218n29f
Communist Party of India (Marxist),
29, 208n8
condoms: safe-sex practices, 98, 100,
104–8
Coppola, Carlo, 214n4, 216n16,
217n19
Couser, Thomas G., 189
Cruz-Malavé, Arnaldo, 39

D

Dalit, 28, 35; Chengara land struggle,
211n30; feminism, 41;
mobilization, 210n26; studies, 41;
women, 13, 35–36, 41–42, 143
Dalit Panthers' movement, 208n14
Das, Kamala, 130
Dave, Naisargi, 39, 166, 174, 212n46,
234n32
De Certeau, Michel, 143, 147
Deepa, V. N., 141, 151, 166, 168,
227n24, 230n7, 231n8
De Mel, Neloufer, 96, 114–15, 232n17
Desai, Manisha, 106
Deshabhimani, 29, 31, 36

Deshadanakkili karayarilla
(P. Padmarajan), 22, 43, 51, 126–28,
131–34, 147, 199, 228n31; audience,
154–58; reception of, 136–40; and
spaces, 149–50; and travel, 143–44
deshadanam, 19, 51, 134, 143–44, 149,
187, 205
desire: heterosexual, 24, 71, 73,
136–37, 157; lesbian, 39, 126, 128,
132, 136–37, 150; representation of,
22, 174; transgressive, 24, 38, 154,
156, 162, 217n18
devadasi, 56
Devika, J., 11–12, 15, 30–32, 92,
94–95, 99, 121–23; on dignity of
labor, 109; on print culture, 8
Ding, Naifei, 212n46
Doordarshan Malayalam, 207n5
Dreze, Jean, 10
Dutta, Aniruddha, 40, 232n20

E

Eapen, Mridula, 12
Ebang bewarish (Debalina Majumdar),
235n37
Encyclopedia of Indian Cinema, 59
Eng, David, 133
Ente katha (Kamala Surayya), 37,
219n4
Eyben, Rosalind, 102

F

family: heterosexual, 203;
matrilineal, 11; patrifocal, 12;
structure of, 108–9
Federation for Integrated Research
on Mental Health (FIRM), 79, 118,
219n7
femininity, 14, 195–96
feminist mobilization, 26, 54, 119,
217n22; in academia, 38, 46, 48,
167; in Kerala, 77, 92, 95

figures (concept), 16–19; of abjection,
234n31; in cinema, 223n34; of the
courtesan, 111; cultural, 58; of the
domestic woman, 108; and
figuration, 17–18, 24, 26, 69, 75, 78,
83, 111, 185, 205; heroic, 154; as
images, 134, 143; of the lesbian,
40, 125, 161–63; and movement,
195; mythical, 160, 229n2; of
the prostitute, 27, 50, 54–57,
62–63, 69, 75, 77, 85, 203, 215n11;
representative, 120, 143, 202;
sexual, 4, 14, 24, 26, 42, 75, 86, 131,
166, 203; of the sex worker, 40, 80,
83, 91, 161, 166, 220n8; social, 164;
spectral, 141; subaltern, 35;
subject and, 44, 57; unruly, 87, 187,
199, 205; unstable, 76, 178, 180;
visual, 18, 86
Filmfare, 59
Fire (Deepa Mehta), 7, 125, 130, 151,
153, 228n34
Foucault, Michel, 15, 21, 27, 80, 99,
112–13, 209n19, 217n25
Frosh, Stephen, 185

G

Gadihoke, Sabeena, 84
Gandhi, Indira, 217n20, 222n29
Gargi, 32
gaze, the, 32–33, 124; "pornographic,"
35; rational, 34; sexualized, 36,
53, 69
Geedha, 68
George, Rosemary Marangoly, 130,
229n1
Ghosh, Shohini, 97, 152–53, 216n12,
226n17, 228n35
Global Alliance against Traffic in
Women (GAATW), 113
globalization, 4–6, 39, 128
Gopal, Priyamvada, 56, 74, 119
Gopalakrishnan, Adoor, 9

Gopinath, Gayatri, 24, 37, 130, 169, 212n42, 227n25

Gopinath, I., 93, 94–95, 210n22

Gordon, Avery, 164, 177–78, 185

Grihalakshmi, 7

Guha-Thakurta, Tapati, 229n2

Gupta, Charu, 8, 55

Guru, Gopal, 25

Guruvayur kesavan (Bharathan), 237n18

H

Halberstam, J. Jack, 37, 133, 163, 212n44

Hall, Stuart, 48

Haraway, Donna, 213n54

Hareesh, V. C., 84–86

Harish, Rumi, 190, 236n10

Hasan, 32

Hayes, Patricia, 152

Hemanda rathri (Balthasar), 66

hijra: livelihood, 139

Hirschkind, Charles, 168

HIV/AIDS awareness/prevention, 22, 40, 49–50, 92, 97–100, 116, 219n5; board game, 102–4, 108; campaigns, 112, 44; discourse, 96–97, 101–2, 108, 113, 175, 192; funding, 128; and lesbians, 166; and public health, 4; and the sex worker, 78, 89–90

Hoek, Lotte, 21, 61, 215n10

homosexuality: decriminalization of, 192; matrimonial ad, 210n27; representations of, 44, 74

human rights, 159, 167; documents, 54; violations, 81

humiliation/stigmatization, 25

I

Idam (Space), 161

India: economic liberalization of, 5, 11, 39; emergency, 115; Immoral Traffic Prevention Act (ITPA), 55, 222n31; National Family Health Survey, 207n4; postcolonial, 68, 100; railway platforms of, 7; State Crime Record Bureau, 208n13; States Reorganization Act, 207n1; war with China, 208n8

Indian People's Theater Association (IPTA), 214n4

International Film Festival of Kerala (IFFK), 7

Ionescu, Vlad, 210n23

J

Jagose, Annamarie, 230n4

Jain, Dipika, 128

Jameela, Nalini, 17, 80, 88–98, 109–25, 210n22, 218n3; dual autobiographies, 26, 36, 43, 50–51, 219n4, 220n8, 223n33; meeting with, 45; reception of autobiographies, 203–4; and stuttered autobiographical practice, 195, 199

Janaki, S., 215n6

Jayakumar, Babu, 70, 215n8

Jayasree, A. K., 92, 97, 99, 188, 190, 194, 222n31, 231n11, 232n16

Jeffrey, Robin, 8, 12, 208n11

John, Mary, 48, 152, 217n23, 228n36

Joseph, Jenson, 9, 61, 207n5

Jwalamukhi, 92, 223n34

Jwalamukhikal (Nalini Jameela), 92

K

Ka Bodyscapes (Jayan Cherian), 226n16

Kairali People's Channel, 28–29, 31

Kang, Laura Hyun Yi, 34, 121

Kapikkad, Sunny, 28

Kapur, Ratna, 201

Lukose, Ritty, 11, 45, 138
Lyotard, Jean-François, 210n23

M

Madhyamam, 84
Maharashtra: dance bars, 119
Mahmood, Saba, 168
Maitra, Ani, 162
Majumdar, Neepa, 56, 212n42
Malayalam, 3, 207n1; fiction, 7; films, 8–9, 132–33; language archive, 5
Malhotra, Namita, 33, 211n36
Manalansan, Martin F, 39
Manayath, Nithin, 128, 138, 232n20
Mangalam, 84
Mani, Lata, 238n24
Manichithrathazhu (Fazil), 229n2
Manipur, 202
Mannarkat, Mathew, 59
Manorama Weekly, 182
Manto, Sa'adat Hasan, 56, 74, 129
Margaret, Swathy, 35, 212n40
Márquez, Gabríel Garcia, 7
Martina Navaratilova Club, 165
Marxist movement, 31
Mathrubhumi, 7, 231n9, 236n4
Mazzarella, William, 9, 28, 62, 69
Mehta, Deepa, 125, 130, 151, 153
Menon, Bindu, 9, 89, 229n38
Menon, Dilip, 8, 15, 24
Menon, Nivedita, 56, 212n45, 231n11
Miller, Ben, 163, 180
Minh-ha, Trinh, 46
Miraji, 74
Misri, Deepti, 202
Mitchell, W. J. T., 40
Mithyakalkappuram: Swawarga laingikata keralathil (Reshma Bharadwaj ed.), 165, 170
Mohan, Sanal, 210n26, 233n25
Mohanlal, 154
Mohanty, Chandra, 46
Muddupalani, 37

Mumbai Police (Rosshan Andrrews), 226n16
Muñoz, José Esteban, 133, 162, 190, 200, 236n12
My Life Partner (Padmakumar), 226n16

N

Nair, Guptan, 15, 56, 74, 208n11
Nair, Sridevi, 231n10
Nair, Yasmin, 212n48
Nakshathrashala, 59
Namukku parkkan munthirithoppukal (P. Padmarajan), 155
Nana, 7
Nandakumar, V. T., 173, 225n10, 233n25
Nanmakkayi (Invis Multimedia), 105, 109–10
Narayan, Kirin, 46
Naregal, Veena, 7
Narrain, Arvind, 225n13, 231n11
National AIDS Control Organization, 108
National AIDS Control Program, 100, 220n13
National Network of Sex Workers (NNSW), 209n16, 219n7
"native informant," 46
Nazeer, Prem, 59
Neelakuyil (P. Bhaskaran and Ramu Kariat), 62
NGOs, 39, 44, 100–101, 125, 167; sexuality-based, 203
Nguyen, Mimi, 168, 221n19
Niranjana, Tejaswini, 46, 152, 228n36, 238n22
Nishabdaraakapettavarilekoru ethinottam (Nalini Jameela), 92
Njan laingika thozhilali: Nalini Jameelayude aathmakatha (Nalini Jameela), 93
Nossiter, T. J., 208n8

Rajan, Rajeswari Sunder, 217n22, 222n30
Ramakrishnan, Malayattoor, 229n2
Ramberg, Lucinda, 162, 208n10, 213n50, 230n4
Ranade, Shilpa, 33
Randu penkuttikal (Mohan), 173, 225n10, 227n20, 233n25f
Rao, Anupama, 35, 201
Raveendran, 173
Rawat, Ramnarayan, 208n14
Red Ribbon Express, 108–9, 221n21
Rege, Sharmila, 97
regions, 15, 38, 50, 51, 130, 133, 158, 162, 213n55; as assemblage, 15; geographical, 143, 207n2, 227n26; Kerala as a, 5, 9–10, 13, 22, 27, 45, 57, 62, 168; and modernity, 11; and nation, 12, 15, 27, 39, 53, 55, 92, 109, 188, 207n3; regional cinema, 60, 227n25; regional contexts in India, 6, 10, 14, 17, 40, 42, 52, 63, 98, 114; regional history, 21, 87; regional identity, 4, 54, 61; regional languages, 153, 218n1; regional publics, 22, 30, 38, 43, 61, 92, 204; regional trajectories, 11, 129, 127, 192, 219n7, 221n7; in South Asia, 163
Romantic Encounters of a Sex Worker (Nalini Jameela), 110
Rowena, Jenny, 13, 35, 41, 173, 209n15, 212n39, 213n51

S

Sadanandan, Anil. *See* Sweet Maria
Sahayatrika, 26, 194, 211n29, 227n24, 230n7, 231n15, 233n21, 235n36; and hauntings, 52; interviews conducted by, 42–43, 47, 149–51; and lesbian suicides, 142, 158, 163–71; mobilizations by, 161; reports of, 174–85

Sahni, Rohini, 96
Sameeksha, 141
Sancharram (Ligy Pullapally), 43, 153–56, 158, 182, 225n12, 227n21, 228n33; birth of, 139–40; and desire, 142; locus of, 144–47; perception of, 48; plot of, 126–28; reading of, 51, 131–36, 150
Sangama, 235n36
Sangari, Kumkum, 208n10
Sanjeev, S., 63, 94, 229n2
Sanjesh, 45
Sarkar, Tanika, 208n10
Sasi, I. V., 53, 60, 214n3
Satapathy, Samidha, 143
Sathrathil oru rathri (N. Sankaran Nair), 67
Satyanarayana, K., 208n14, 209n15
Sebastian, K. C., 172–73, 232n16
Seema, 57, 214n2
Semmalar, Gee, 189–90, 236n5, 237n20
Sen, Meheli, 10, 16
sex education, 109
sexual actors, 6, 23, 202; narratives of, 17, 90, 96
sexuality: anxieties about, 27, 30, 160; constructs of, 11–12; discourse of, 39; and gender, 57; history of, 6, 47, 70, 129; in India, 4, 33, 38; policing of, 14, 217n20; politics of, 17, 23–24, 37, 39, 131, 152–53, 156, 161–63, 182, 185–86, 199; registers of, 130; representations of, 36, 53–55, 72; rewriting of, 19; theorizing, 15; vernacular politics of, 4–5, 23, 43, 134, 164; and voyeurism, 73
sexually transmitted infection (STI), 104
sexual morality, 97
sexual subjects, 4, 6, 16, 20, 161, 168, 200; CSW, 40; disciplining in public, 29; figuration, 17–18, 24,